METAL JEWELRY TECHNIQUES

BY MARCIA CHAMBERLAIN

WATSON-GUPTILL PUBLICATIONS, NEW YORK

PITMAN PUBLISHING, LONDON

First published 1976 in the United States and Canada by Watson-Guptill Publications
a division of Billboard Publications, Inc.
One Astor Plaza, New York, N.Y. 10036

Library of Congress Cataloging in Publication Data
Chamberlain, Marcia.
  Metal jewelry techniques.
  Bibliography: p.
  Includes index.
  1. Jewelry making—Amateurs' manuals. I. Title.
TT212.C45 1976   739.27   75–46626
ISBN 0–8230–3036–9

Published in Great Britain by Sir Isaac Pitman & Sons Ltd.
39 Parker Street, London WC2B 5PB
ISBN 0-273-00126-4

Manufactured in U.S.A.

First Printing, 1976

ACKNOWLEDGMENTS

The greatest pleasure in assembling any book is the renewal of old friendships and the reward of gaining new friendships. Many jewelers throughout the United States and England freely contributed photographs of their work. Many others contributed their technical knowledge just as freely, including Florence Resnikoff, Marcia Lewis, Eileen Hill, Pat Sherwood, Arlene Fisch, Gene and Sate Pijanowski, Richard Gompf, and Tom Thomason.

Institutions and their personnel were of great assistance as well, including Patricia Heilenen of the Minnesota Museum of Art, Judith Kaiser from the Milwaukee Art Center, and Carol Stiero of the Museum of International Folk Art in Santa Fe, New Mexico. Kind support and assistance was generously given by Lois Moran, Director of the Research and Education Department for the American Crafts Council.

Close associates made the reality of demonstrations as well as a coherent text possible. Ruth Stege gains my everlasting appreciation for the 'hands' that made the photography possible, and the editing of Jennifer Place and Peggy Stephenson made my words literate and understandable.

CONTENTS

Mask by Jonathan O. Parry. Silver, feathers, gold plating, forged and fabricated, 1975. Collection of the Minnesota Museum of Art. Photo by Bradford Palm.

INTRODUCTION

To decorate, to embellish, and to draw attention; to symbolize possession and wealth, to invest, to exchange, and to save for the future; to call on the Gods of fortune. All these are consummate reasons for making metal jewelry. Jewelry is made to adorn the human form. It is the rings on your fingers, the bells on your toes, and you are the jeweler who can put them there.

It is the intent of this book to present, in a practical format, the tools and materials for jewelry making, as well as selected examples and projects that will aid you in becoming immediately involved in creating your own original personal adornment. The book is limited to the metal processes that can be used quite simply in a small work area without the large equipment usually associated with starting any craft.

Jewelry is an art expression in itself, not immediately related to any other general art expression beyond the superficial and mechanical similarities. However, metals and their techniques are interchangeable with those used in making objects not related to personal adornment. The materials, tools, and techniques included here are not limiting in nature. They will also be helpful to you should you decide to expand your interests to forms of metalwork other than jewelry.

In broad terms, this book is organized into three sections. The first series of chapters—tools, materials, and designing—forms the foundation for the remaining chapters. They are reference chapters that you will return to repeatedly while working. The second section —chapters on fabrication, construction with heat, and casting— constitutes the techniques necessary to the assembling of your jewelry.

The remaining chapters— surface treatments, combining metal with other materials, findings and fastenings, and cleaning, polishing, and finishing—are concerned with auxiliary, but very necessary, techniques used in making jewelry.

Making metal jewelry is a comparatively "new" craft, even though there is evidence of a very sophisticated knowledge of metallurgy in history. For example, the Chinese made aluminum ornaments over 2,000 years ago, obtaining their aluminum from bauxite in a sophisticated chemical-electrical procedure. Middle Eastern tombs and Peruvian burial grounds yielded jewelry made of platinum, a metal that requires a melting temperature of 1800° C. Accompanying each chapter are photographs of contemporary and historical jewelry. These have been included to suggest the great wealth of variety in the continuum of jewelry production. These examples reflect an everchanging pattern, emphasizing the artists opportunity for infinite variation.

Jewelry design has been part of human social development, of mankind's need to ornament and adorn his body in a decorative and functional manner. Styles may change and vogues may prevail, but the most fascinating aspect of making metal jewelry is the opportunity for you to become part of this rich heritage.

Tool Set by Gary Noffke. Steel, wood, forged and carved, 1974. Shown in the exhibition, "The Goldsmith," presented by the Renwick Gallery of the National Collection of Fine Arts, Smithsonian Institution, Washington, D.C. and the Minnesota Museum of Art, St. Paul, Minnesota. Photo by Bradford Palm.

1
TOOLS AND MATERIALS

Timeless pieces of jewelry used to adorn the human form are created by applying time-tested ways of using tools and materials to new problems in structural design.

Very little change has taken place in the design of jewelry tools over the past 2,000 years and, while the technology of metallurgy has become more complex, the fundamental body of knowledge about it has not changed. In a sense, jewelry techniques have their foundation in the interaction between the material and the tool. Tools and materials support artistic expression; artistic expression should not be subservient to tools and materials.

Unlike past traditions when the apprentice system was either nepotistic or a direct investment in cheap child labor, most of today's education has a broad, humanistic base. We enter into the art community out of an emotional rather than a practical need.

The traditional apprentice system taught by extended experience that painstakingly built one block of learning onto another until each action with tool and material became a natural and familiar one. Today, our humanistic education teaches us to transfer learning experiences from one subject area to another. Technology has refined ready-made tools and basic materials, processed them for our immediate use, and put them easily within our grasp.

A large inventory of tools is not necessary for making beautiful jewelry, just as it is not necessary to expect precious metals to be your only choice of materials.

This chapter will give guidelines for selecting and maintaining basic tools, a brief description of their uses, and the technical information on metals available in today's market.

HAND TOOLS

While the selection of jeweler's hand tools is relatively small—fitting into the equivalent of a fishing-tackle box—it is of major importance that each be a high-quality and precision-made tool. The initial investment in finely machined tools pays many dividends in ease of work and time saved. Always buy the best quality and you will have many years of satisfied use.

Tools themselves become favored extensions of the hand. Though you may have several tools designed for a specific task, you will find that you have a favorite one. Eventually, you may even want to make your own tools.

There are guidelines for using and maintaining all small hand tools as well as larger machinery. Here are a few of these guidelines:

1. Choose the correct tool for the job to be done; practice creativity with the design, not in the use of the tool. More often than not, the "creative" use of a tool leads to its abuse and diminishes its effectiveness in the job it was designed to do.

2. Choose the tool that works fastest for the job to be done. For example: do large cutting with a saw or metal snips, then use a large file if space permits, and complete the refining of the form with a small file. Work in descending order of coarseness. That is, do large cuts first, followed by detail work.

3. Hand tools for working metals should be made of steel. The metal of the tools must be harder than the metals you are working. This is true of all cutting, bending, forming, and hammering tools with a few mallet exceptions.

4. Metal tools should be stored in such a way that they are protected from moisture. Store saw blades and other sharp tools so they cannot be banged against each other. If possible, hang them in a protected area. This will help maintain their cutting edges, increase their life, and ease your work. Contamination from dirt, oils, and moisture (causing rust) should be avoided since it reduces tool effectiveness. Wipe your tools thoroughly with a clean, dry cloth before storing them.

5. All tools have a potential danger when misused or mishandled. Keeping cutting edges sharp is

safe; using dull tools is not. Storing your tools properly and using them correctly preserves their sharpness.

Be sure handles are on securely, especially on files and hammers. The tang (the projection used for attaching the handle) of a file should always have a firm-fitting handle. If you use a file without the handle and it bumps something or jams to a sudden stop, the tang may be driven into your hand. Hammer and mallet handles should be securely fastened into the eye of the head to prevent possible injury.

6. Tools can break. Most of the metalworking tools you are using will be of tempered steel. Tempering increases the strength of steel but it also makes it more brittle. Tempered steel can chip if dropped. Also, the rapid motion in sawing and drilling builds up heat through friction. Excessive heating can affect the temper of the steel causing it to lose its strength and break. Small drill bits and fine saw blades will snap if they are overheated.

Don't force your tools to do a job or you may damage or break them. Remember, a tool should be an extension of your hand. If unusual force is required then you have the wrong tool for the job, the tool is already damaged, or you are using it improperly.

In all crafts you will find a small selection of hand tools that seem indispensable. As your sophistication in jewelry construction and tool use increases, you will quite naturally increase your tool inventory. The following text will describe a general selection of basic tools. They have been partially grouped by their use: cutting, bending, hammering, forming, decorating, heating, and measuring.

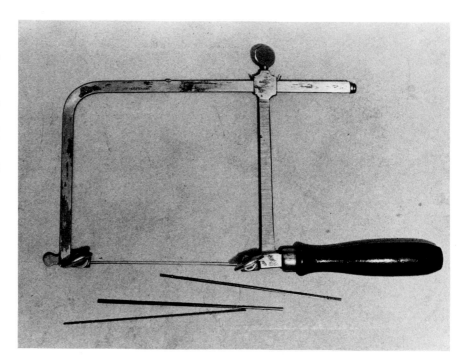

CUTTING TOOLS

In this category you will find saw frames and blades, files, drills and bits, snips and diagonal cutters, center punches, and a bench pin.

There are numerous variations to choose from in cutting tools, especially size variations. All tools will seem quite small at first, but remember jewelry is really diminutive compared to other types of metalwork and the tools are reduced in size accordingly. Remember also that the numbering systems used to denote coarseness or fineness in saw blades or drill bits may vary from the standard sizes.

A STANDARD SAW FRAME comes in varying depths from 2¼" to 8". It should have serrated clamps to hold the saw blade firmly and it should be adjustable. This helps draw the blade taut and also makes it possible to use broken blades by shortening the frame. If you buy just one frame, select one that is at least 5" deep.

Jeweler's saw blades are graded by number: fine, 8/0 to 0; and coarse, 1 to 14. The teeth are set alternately at a slight angle to the blade's body on all saw blades. This allows the saw to pass freely back and forth as it cuts and makes a cut slightly larger than the blade itself. The blades, called piercing saws, used most frequently are numbers 2/0 and 4/0 and can be purchased by the dozen.

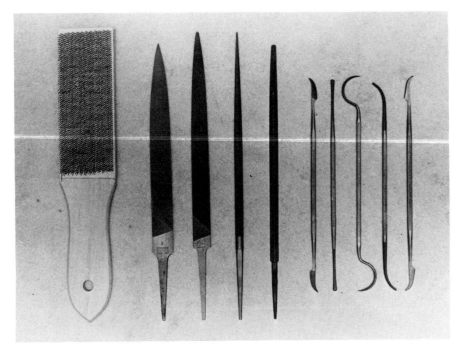

FILES come in a vast variety of sizes and cuts. Shown above are a file card half-round, barrette, round, three-square, and a variety of riffle files. For making metal jewelry you will need a selection of 6" files with handles, a set of smaller needle files, and one or two riffle files.

Files are either single-cut or double-cut. You will need double-cut files. They are graded according to the spacing and size of their teeth, sizes 00 to 6 (the finest). The length of this type of file is always understood to mean the length of the cut part only. The cut part is called the face and the smooth graduated end is called the tang. The tang should fit firmly into a wooden handle. In the beginning, you should have four differently shaped 6" files with a cut of number 2 or 3. These four basic shapes are called barrette, half-round, three-square, and round or rat-tail. To clean bits of metal (called pins) from the files, you will need a file card, which is a brush made of brass or steel wire.

NEEDLE FILES are very small, slender files that usually come in sets containing a variety of shapes. They are 5½" to 7¾" long (the cut face averages about one half of this length) and come in cuts of 1/0 to 4–6 (the finest). A beginning set of needle files with a number 4 cut is recommended.

RIFFLE FILES, while not always part of a beginning workshop, soon find their way into it. They are made especially for removing metal and smoothing in tight places. They are the same size as needle files, face-cut on both ends, and available in two size cuts, number 2 and number 4 (the finest). There are about eighteen different riffle shapes.

THE BENCH PIN is used to support your work while sawing, filing, or stone setting. Bench pins are used with two different styles of holders. One type of holder screws onto the side of your workbench permanently. The alternate is a combination of anvil and bench-pin holder that is mounted on the workbench with an adjustable clamp and can be removed when not in use. Both holders allow for the replacement of the hardwood bench pin when it becomes too worn. You will need to saw a "V"-shape in the pin as shown above before you begin working.

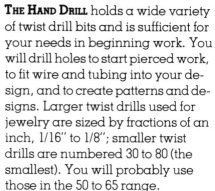

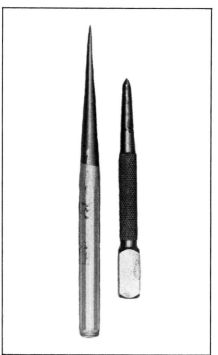

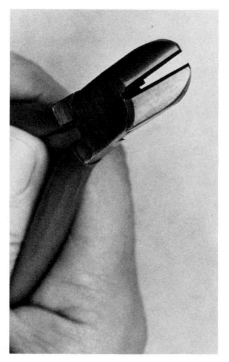

THE HAND DRILL holds a wide variety of twist drill bits and is sufficient for your needs in beginning work. You will drill holes to start pierced work, to fit wire and tubing into your design, and to create patterns and designs. Larger twist drills used for jewelry are sized by fractions of an inch, 1/16″ to 1/8″; smaller twist drills are numbered 30 to 80 (the smallest). You will probably use those in the 50 to 65 range.

THE CENTER PUNCH is used to make a small dent in your metal as a starting point for drilling. Position the point of the punch where you wish to drill and tap it with a small hammer. Two types of center punches are shown here, a 45° center punch (right) and a metal workers' prick punch (left). The prick punch can also be used for pierced work on lightweight metals because of its long, sharp, very tapered point. If struck too hard against thin-gauge metal, however, the punch will pierce a small hole through the metal.

If you try to drill a hole without first locating it with a center-punch mark, the drill will usually move around the face of your metal. This is called "wandering." When a drill wanders, you not only lose control of the exact location of the hole but also the wandering will scar some metal surfaces.

NIPPERS are for cutting a wide variety of wires. The traditional nipper, also called a "dic," most used by metalworkers has a full, parallel, simultaneous bit on all parts of the cutting edge. Nippers should have a box-joint construction that will help them to retain their precise alignment even after considerable use. Dic nippers will leave a wire peak on the cut ends. There are cutters for soft wire that have full-flush edges and will cut straight across without leaving a peak.

SNIPS are used for cutting lightweight metal sheet including solder sheet. They are available with either straight or curved blades and with or without return springs in the handle. Curved snips are used for cutting circular or curvilinear shapes.

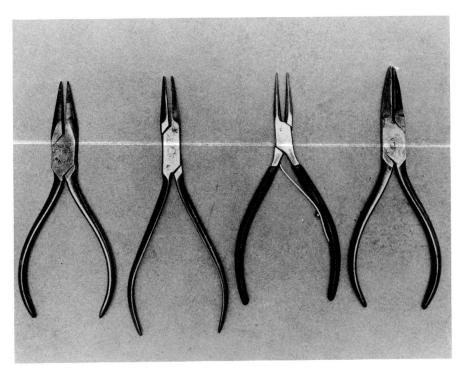

BENDING AND HOLDING TOOLS

You will need to manipulate the metal you are working in various ways, as well as to hold it more firmly than you can with your hands. There are many varieties of bending and holding tools. In the beginning you will need four types of pliers, a hand vise or a ring holder, and a small bench vise.

PLIERS are for gripping, manipulating, and pulling a variety of wires and strip metals. The four pliers shown here are, left to right, flat-nose, round-nose, half-round/flat-nose, and chain-nose, round-nose, half-round/flat-nose, and chain-nose. These are the most frequently used, and each performs its special task well.

Chain-nose pliers are used to make bends, loops, and similar forms with wire or sheet metals. Flat-nose pliers are used for gripping or holding flat or square ob-

jects securely and for making angular bends. Round-nose pliers are for making bends, loops, circles, and coils in wire or sheet metals. The combination half-round/flat-nose pliers are very useful when bending ring shanks or other curved, flat surfaces.

All pliers should have a box-joint construction for continuous accurate use. Pliers are made in several sizes and are measured by their overall length. You should buy the one that fits your hand size: 4"–4½" for smaller hands, 5" for larger hands.

Bending and holding tools can scar your metal surface. One way to avoid this is by gluing a thin pad of leather on the face of the jaws. This will allow a strong grip and can be replaced when worn.

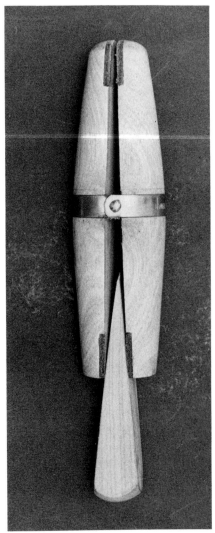

A RING HOLDER or ring clamp holds small work securely while filing, polishing, or stonesetting. It is a double-ended, wooden clamp with leather inserts in the jaws to protect small pieces from slipping and from scratches.

For holding larger, heavier work, you will need a bench vise. Any style bench vise will do. However because you will have only one, select it for its precision, strength, and versatility. It should have twin guide rods to assure parallel closing and rigidity, it should have a swivel base that permits positioning in any direction and locks into place, and the jaws should be smooth to prevent marring the metal.

DECORATING TOOLS

The term decorating may be a misnomer in that the tools are not used to apply a decorative surface but rather to create an ordered surface change in the metal itself. For example: repoussé, a low-relief forming technique, is decorative in nature because the metal surface is changed predominantly more than the form and it is traditionally worked from the back. The decorative tools discussed here are those that cut away or indent the metal surface rather than raise as in repoussé. They include tools for chasing, beading, and engraving. Etching, another decorative technique, is predominantly chemical in nature and uses acids rather than hand tools.

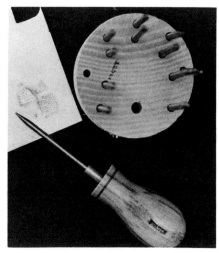

CHASING PUNCHES may be used in combination with or following repoussé. They are with the chasing hammer to indent the face of the work. Chasing punches are made in a great variety of shapes as shown above. Of the tools discussed here, they offer the first opportunity for the craftsman to make his own original and unique patterns. They are broadly categorized as tracers, curved, modeling, matting or graining, and ringing tools. Blanks may be purchased for creating your own patterns, or they may be carved of ¼" steel stock with needle files, then polished and tempered.

BEADING TOOLS purchased in sets containing a series of graduated sizes, are circle-making punches. When they are punched in an ordered and controlled series, they offer an effective counter pattern for highly polished metal surfaces that is typical of classical Japanese metalwork called *Ishime*. They may also be used on wire to create decorative gallery wire mountings or bezels for stone setting. Beading tools are used to raise beads for holding diamonds, half-pearls, and other stones. They may also be used to tighten stones that have become loose in their settings.

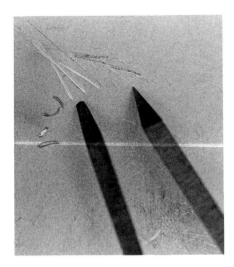

ENGRAVING TOOLS cut away the metal with very sharp, wedge-shaped points. Engraving is linear in design quality rather than textured or patterned. Shown above are two such tools and the types of marks they make on the metal surface.

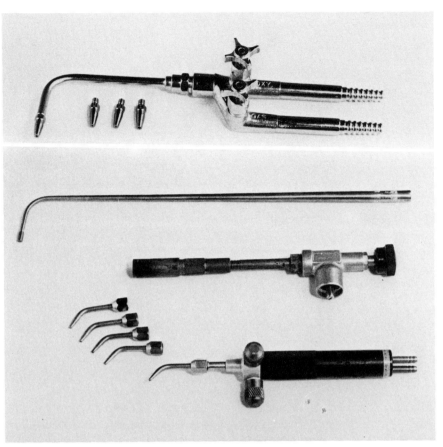

HEATING TOOLS

Heating tools, primarily torches and the auxiliary equipment used for reflecting heat and holding heated objects, constitute a small but important number of items in the jeweler's workshop. Even when you are constructing metal jewelry that does not require soldering, it may require heat to keep the metal malleable. For this reason, one of the most important investments you will make in your workshop will be your torch.

THE JEWELER'S TORCH can be fired with a variety of fuels and uses a variety of different tip sizes. The most highly recommended torch, shown above, uses natural gas and oxygen as fuel. However, torch selection may depend on which type of fuel is readily available in your area. Also shown below the jeweler's torch are a mouthpipe, a propane torch, and a mini-gas/oxygen torch.

If natural gas is not easily available (there are no portable natural gas units) the next most practical fuel is propane and oxygen. Propane burns about 100°F hotter than natural gas, is inexpensive, and puts out the clean flame necessary in making jewelry. Compressed air may be substituted for oxygen, but it reduces the effectiveness of gas and it accumulates water causing sputtering and blow-out. Acetylene heat is the hottest.

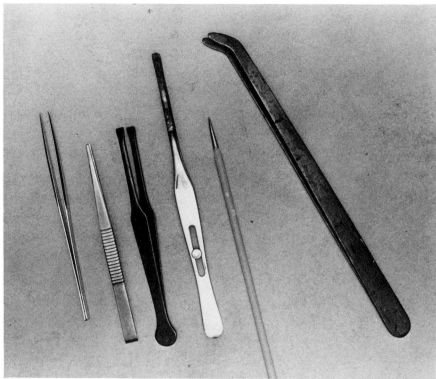

MATERIALS USED WITH HEAT, shown above, include those items that allow you to manipulate hot metal. Asbestos sheet is used to protect the workbench when soldering. The asbestos block serves a similar purpose, but has the advantage of being soft so your work or pins can be easily pressed into it.

A charcoal block is made of chemically treated hardwood so it will glow under heat and thus reflect heat back into your work. This makes the torch flame more effective. The block may also be punctured with pins to hold your metal while soldering. Iron bailing wire is used to hold pieces together when pins are not useful.

TWEEZERS, A SOLDER PIC, AND TONGS are used for manipulation when assembling, sorting, and soldering jewelry parts. You will need two types of tweezers: one with fine points and one that is self-locking with rounded points. The tips of the latter are processed to withstand heat.

The Solder Pic, shown center, has an insulated handle with a long, sharp point that has been tempered to withstand heat. It helps you place solder quickly and accurately. While soldering, the pic is used to place small metal items such as findings or to adjust metal pieces that may have moved without removing the torch.

Tongs are used to move or lift items in areas where it is not safe to put your hands. You will need a pair of copper or wooden tongs to lift articles out of pickling or acid solutions (these materials do not react with the solutions and cause chemical change). You will also need crucible tongs made of iron or steel that will not be affected by the heat and weight of the molten metals you are using.

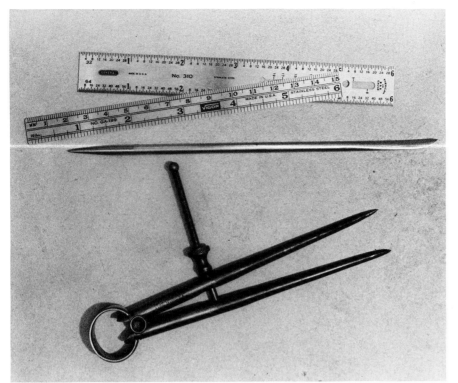

MEASURING TOOLS

Instruments for sizing, laying out your design, determining the gauge of metal stock, linear measuring, marking, and weighing are all needed in the preliminary planning and designing of metal jewelry.

A Steel Rule and Scribes are indispensible for all measuring. You should choose a flexible steel rule that has both inch and millimeter markings. The scribe is a sharp, pointed steel tool used for striking designs and marking lines on metal for sawing. Spring dividers and circle scribes measure and mark circular lines on metal for sawing.

The B & S Gauge measures metal, both wire and sheet. It is also called the American Standard Wire Gauge, and it has sizes marked on one side from 0 to 36 with the decimal equivalent markings in thousandths of an inch on the reverse side.

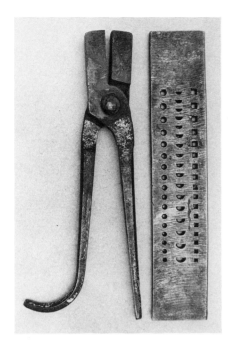 

THE DRAWPLATE is used to reduce wire thickness or change its shape, as well as in making tubing from thin metal sheets. Drawplates have a graduated series of holes, round, square, half-round, rectangular, triangular, or a combination of these. The plate is held firmly in a bench vise while in use. Draw Tongs are used with the drawplate to grip the wire firmly. They have a curved handle to keep your hand from slipping while pulling the wire through the drawplate. Beeswax or Vaseline is used to lubricate the wire while pulling.

A ROLLING MILL may be one of the larger investments you will want to make for your workshop. This one is for working sheet metal; others work wire and rod or a combination of wire, rod, and sheet. You can reduce your general investment in materials with it. For example, keep a few basic gauges of metal on hand and use the mill for any reduction you may need. Mills can also be used as forming tools, making it much faster to do many of the forming techniques discussed here.

ADDITIONAL EQUIPMENT

There are miscellaneous supplies and general auxiliary equipment that you may need when working. These supplies are expendable and need replenishing from time to time while you are working. Here is a list of these expendable supplies, chemicals, and supplementary pieces of equipment; the use of each is explained in the pertinent text and demonstrations that occur throughout the book.

Acetone
Alcohol
Beeswax
Binding wire and steel pins
Brushes
Buffing wheels and shells
Casting plaster, sand, and wax
Cuttlefish bone
Emery paper
Gum guaiacum
Pumice
Rouge
Sawdust
Scotch stone
Sealing wax
Solders
Steel wool
Tripoli
White diamond
Yellow ochre

CHEMICALS AND COLORANTS

Also used during the metalworking processes are a number of chemicals and compounds. There are four items that are most important and are a part of every beginning jeweler's workshop: flux, potassium sulphide, borax, and Sparex (nitric acid and sulphuric acid).

These next items are optional:

Ammonia
Ammonium chloride
Ammonium sulfide
Copper nitrate
Copper sulfate
Iodine
Iron perchloride
Isopropyl alcohol
Hydrochloric acid
Phosphoric acid, 75% solution
Potassium chloride
Platinum chloride
Sodium hydroxide
Zinc chloride

METALS

More than fifty metals have been discovered since the first—copper. Metals occur in the earth and in this state are called ores. The most common native ores (found in pure form) are silver, gold, copper, and platinum. Native ores are also found either with oxides or sulphides. In process ores, the oxides or sulphides are removed to bring the metals into a purer working state.

Metals are measured and sold by Troy weight. It should be noted that the molecular weights of metals vary. This means that two pieces of different metals the same size will have different weights. Gold is almost twice the weight of silver, for example. The molecular weight of each metal is indicated in the text by the number following the metal's chemical symbol.

Another individual quality of native metal is its melting point. If the native metal is alloyed (combining one metal with one or two others to form a third) the melting point of the alloyed metal may become either higher or lower. The melting point of metal, its molecular weight, and its physical and mechanical properties all will influence your jewelry design.

PHYSICAL AND MECHANICAL PROPERTIES

All metals have an internal orderly arrangement of atoms, as does all matter. In metals these atoms form crystalline grains that haphazardly join together to form the opaque metal surface we see with our eyes. All metals may be fused and melted, allowing the removal of impurities as well as the formation of alloys. In addition to these internal structural similarities, processed metals in either pure or alloy form have mechanical properties that appeal to the jeweler. These are luster, which is related to the individual metal's hardness, malleability, and ductility or plasticity.

There are two major classifications of metals: ferrous and nonferrous. The first group identifies all metals and alloys containing iron. The latter, metals without iron content, is divided into three subgroups: precious, base, and alloy metals. In the precious group are gold, pure or fine silver, and platinum. Base metals are copper, aluminum, lead, tin, nickel, and zinc. Base and precious metals are used to make alloys such as brass, bronze, pewter, nickel silver, sterling silver, karat gold, and solders. Throughout history since the onset of the Iron Age, ferrous metals have played a minor part in jewelry production, possibly because they lack the appealing visual and working qualities of nonferrous metals. Iron jewelry became very popular in Germany, for a short period during the nineteenth century, and technical advances since World War II have created some interest in jewelry made from stainless steel.

Luster is the natural result of a continuously refined surface treatment called polishing. Variations of polishing are sheen and satin-sheen. A high polish, mirrorlike in character, is possible on silver and copper but gold polishes less well and platinum even less. The hardness of the metal determines the degree of luster or polish possible. Satin-sheen and sheen are terms applying to less reflective surfaces and are produced by miniscule scratches left or deliberately placed on the surface that reflect and diffuse light.

Malleability in metals allows them to be bent, compressed, formed, and twisted. The internal structural grains "roll" against each other, rearranging themselves as you work. The metal hardens on the surface or "skin" as this rearrangement takes place.

Ductility is the property in metals that allows them to be drawn or stretched. A ductile metal can be pulled into wire or rolled into sheets. Drawing and rolling will rearrange the metal's grains and compress its surface much in the same way as hammering or bending. Heating the metal returns any metal granular distortion to its original structural form. This heating, which relieves the hardening and returns the metal to its natural quality, is called *annealing*.

PRECIOUS METALS

Jewelers enjoy working with precious metals, not just for the "precious" quality of the material, but also for the ease with which they can be worked. All precious metals—gold, silver, and platinum—rate ver high in ductility and malleability and can be given a variety of polished surfaces.

GOLD (Au 79, its chemical symbol and molecular weight) is designated as 24K (karat) gold in its pure state. It is not affected by chemicals in the air, a process called oxidation, which accounts for the excellent state of preservation of gold

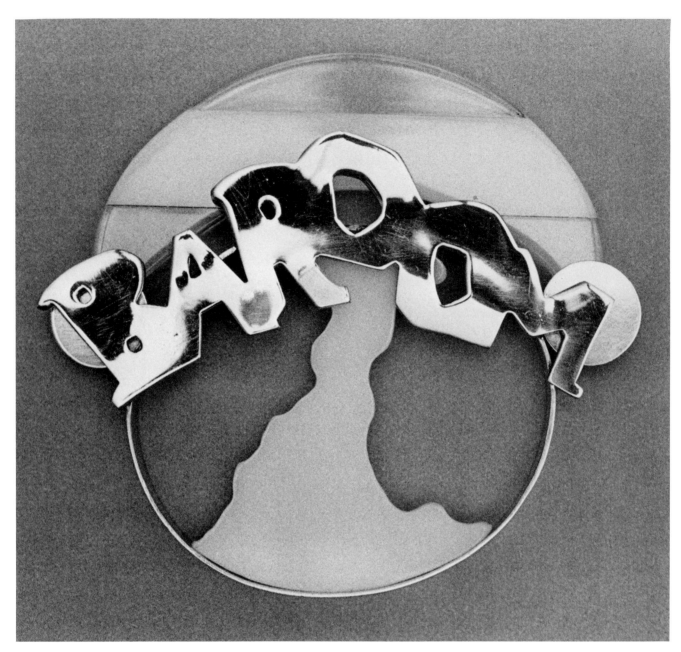

Pin by Rick Guido. Silver and acrylic, 1974.

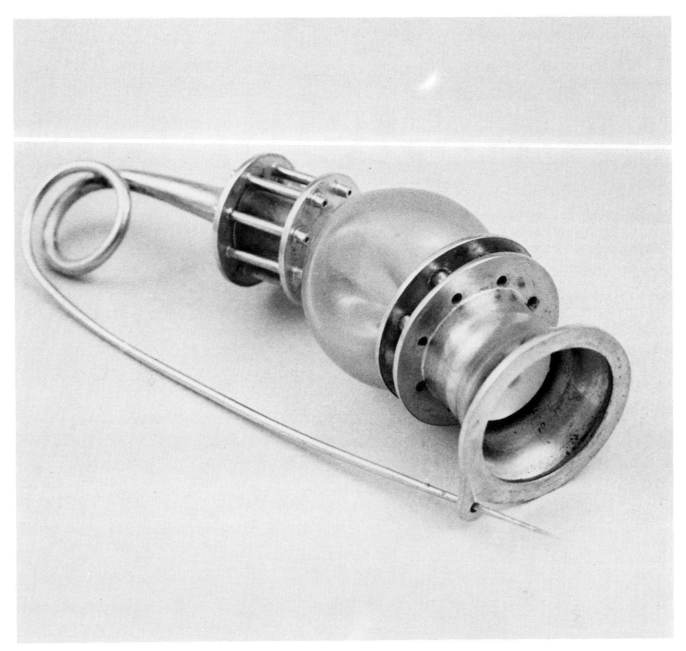

Squeek Fibula by Gerry Evans. Gilt brass, rubber, 1975. From the Exhibition "The Goldsmith," presented by the Renwick Gallery of the National Collection of Fine Arts, Smithsonian Institution, Washington, D.C., and the Minnesota Museum of Art, Saint Paul, Minnesota. Photo by Bradford Palm.

jewelry found in the ancient tombs of Asia, Africa, and the Americas. Gold is very soft in its native form, but can be strengthened by alloying. Gold is usually alloyed with copper, silver, nickel, or zinc and is designated by the degree of gold purity in terms of karats. For example, 18K gold is 75% gold and 25% alloy metal.

SILVER (Ag 47) is called fine silver in its pure form. It comes closest to gold in malleability and ductility and can be polished to a high luster. Its one drawback is its susceptibility to sulphurs that are always present in our air. These sulphurs tarnish silver. Silver is soft in its pure form, as is gold, and is also generally alloyed. In its alloyed form it is called sterling silver and it has a content of 925 parts silver and 75 parts copper. Any article with less than 90 parts silver content, including the solder content, may not be marked as silver according to U.S. law.

PLATINUM (Pt 78) is the best known metal from a group of related metals including rhodium, ruthenium, palladium, osmium, and iridium. Its reputation is a result of its fine working characteristics. It resists corrosion and is harder than the other precious metals, which makes it particularly attractive to the jeweler. However, it is considerably more expensive than either silver or gold.

BASE METALS

Base metals used in jewelry production include copper, lead, tin, zinc, aluminum, nickel, and mercury. When these are combined with each other or with precious metals, they form alloys.

COPPER (Cu 29) was the first metal known to man. Its first use dates from about 8,000 B. C. and predates the Bronze Age by roughly 4,000 years. Some of the first mirrors in Egypt were of polished copper.

Copper is easily fabricated, has good soldering or joining characteristics, and polishes to a fine luster. It may be formed either hot or cold and annealed if it hardens to enable you to continue forming. Copper may be colored through heat or chemical action. It is susceptible to oxidation by the air. Jewelry made from copper is usually lacquered, plated, or used for jewelry that does not come in direct contact with your skin (both the metal and your skin will discolor).

ALUMINUM (Al 13) is the lightest base metal by weight. This is perhaps one of the reasons it is limited in use for making jewelry since there is a certain psychological resistance in attributing a quality of preciousness to a material that lacks heft. Actually, because it was relatively unusual before the development of commercial electrical power, aluminum was considered one of the rare or precious metals and was used to make jewelry. Aluminum is taken from bauxite by an electrical process. It is malleable, resists corrosion, and polishes to a high luster. It may be highly colored by a process called *anodizing*. As with all coating techniques, anodizing affects only the surface and it may be scratched or cut away to expose the base metal again. Aluminum works best with casting techniques since soldering it requires special techniques.

TIN (Sn 50), because it is very resistant to organic acids, is traditionally used for plating food containers made of copper, bronze, or steel. Because it is soft, low in tensile strength, and not very strong in itself, it is used mainly for alloying with copper for bronze and with lead for pewter and soft solders.

ZINC (Zn 30) is another base metal used mainly for alloying, especially with silver. It is also used as a plating metal to prevent corrosion because it naturally resists oxidation. Neither tin nor zinc are appropriate for jewelry except in alloys.

LEAD (Pb 82) is usually found in combination with gold and silver in a mineral ore called *galena* or sulphide of lead. The mineral is processed by adding a small amount of zinc to attract the precious metals, which float away from the lead because they are lighter. The most common use of lead in jewelry is in the form of alloys, especially in soft solders. It may be used for casting but its softness and heavy weight, as well as its lack of luster after exposure to air, reduces its appeal.

NICKEL (Ni 28) is primarily used to alloy with other metals where it increases hardness. Pure nickel is not used for handcrafted jewelry production because of this very hard quality. However, nickel silver and Monel metal, both alloys, are used.

MERCURY (Hg 80) is the only metal that is liquid at normal temperatures. It is obtained by collecting the condensation of vapors from heated cinnabar and is sometimes known as quicksilver. It is used in metalwork by alloying it with gold or silver to form what is termed an *amalgam*. In using an amalgam, the mercury is worked off either by vaporizing or by compression that in turn leaves a deposit of the precious metal. These amalgams are used mainly for plating in jewelry or for dental fillings.

ALLOYS

When two or more metals are combined, the new metal is termed an alloy. Many alloys—such as brass, bronze, and pewter—have names that are familiar to you. These, as well as Britannia or white metal, nickel and sterling silvers, and karat golds work well for jewelrymaking. Jewelry solders are also alloys.

Copper alloys include brass, bronze, nickel silver, and Monel metal. Brass is an alloy of copper and zinc. Depending on the percentage of zinc, brass is subdivided into two groups: Alpha brass for cold working and Beta brass for hot working. The percentage of copper

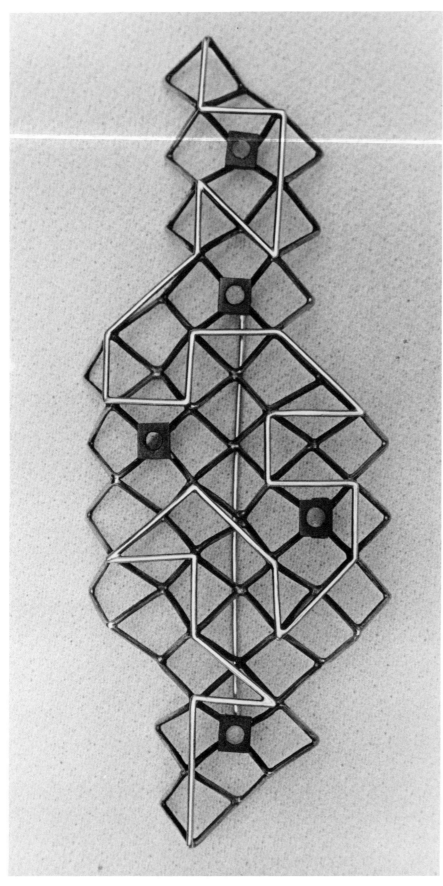

to zinc determines the grouping and the color variation. Bronze metals are generally alloys of copper and tin with melting points slightly above those for brass. Bronze may become brittle when soldered beyond a red heat, while brass may split with brittleness if hammered cold.

Nickel silver and Monel metal are two of several jewelry metals containing no silver but that are silver in color. Nickel silver has copper, nickel, and a small percentage of zinc. It is sometimes called German silver and may be formed and soldered much the same as sterling silver. Monel metal includes copper but is predominantly nickel with small amounts of several other metals and minerals. Because its melting point is well above the other metals discussed here (2460°F.), it is best used for fabrication. It can be soft-soldered and silver-soldered very well.

Pewter and Britannia, or white metal, are alloys with low melting points. Pewter, the older form of white metal, is a lead alloy that is soft in character and lackluster in appearance. The white metal that was developed as a substitute for pewter is called Britannia metal because it was developed in the mid 19th Century in Sheffield, England. Britannia metal contains no lead; it is an alloy of tin, antimony, and copper. White metal sustains its sheen or luster and has increased hardness and ductility. Both pewter and Britannia metal are used primarily for casting since they lack the strength of other metals. White metal is particularly good because it sustains fine detail from the mold and is lighter weight than pewter. Both may be soldered with soft solder.

All of the alloys mentioned above are suitable for jewelry production, although some work better in casting while others are best for fabrication. You will find demonstrations using many of them in the following chapters.

Pin by Margaret De Patta. White gold wire with gem inlays in onyx. Collection of the Oakland Museum. Lent by Eugene Bielawski.

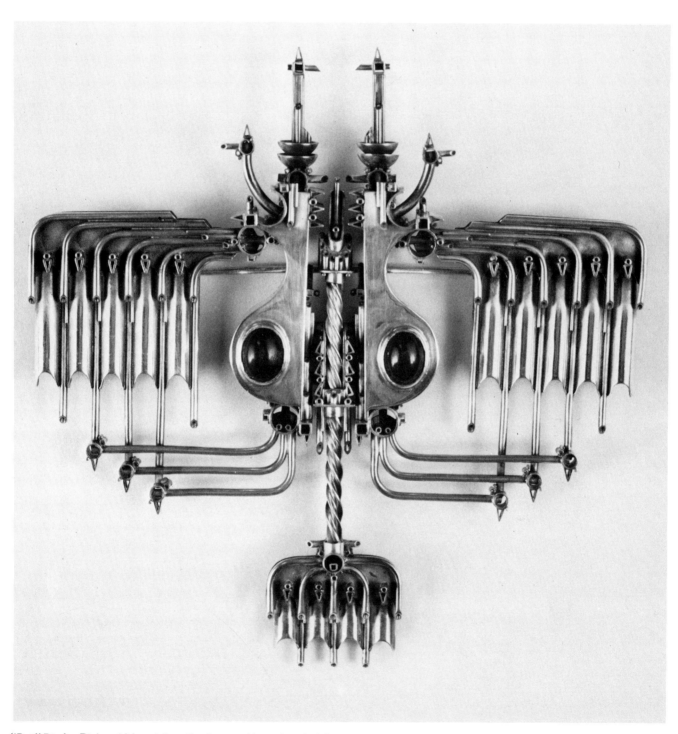

"Bat" Pin by Richard Mawdsley. Sterling and lapis lazuli, fabricated, 1974.

2
DESIGNING

Until the Industrial Revolution in the late 1700's, most art imagery was limited to what one saw or believed he saw rather than that from the supernatural, or not seen. Designs were abstracted from the visual in a number of ways. First, the image was made from a different material than that of the original object. Second, the major reason for making the object was emphasized. The artist distorted from reality to draw the observer's attention. It can be said that painting portrayed a three-dimensional subject on a two-dimensional surface.

The Industrial Revolution brought technical advances that allowed us to see much not seen before, for example, the microscope and telescope as well as the camera. These inventions did not remove our dependency on nature for visual forms, but they did open an infinite new world of visual stimulation.

NINETEENTH CENTURY JEWELRY

Two very diverse practices in jewelrymaking resulted from the extensive industrial and technical changes of the mid-nineteenth century. For the first time, shabby imitations of historical designs were mass produced using new alloys. On the other hand, finely crafted, costly, jewelry was exemplified by the work of the Russian, Carl Fabergé. His elaborate, unique pieces still followed the concepts of design that emanated from the Renaissance.

At this same time came the intellectual challenges of the impressionist and post-impressionnist painters, especially Manet, Cézanne, Monet, Renoir, and Degas. These painters were to have a great influence on architecture and sculpture as well as crafts. Even more important, however, was the development of art nouveau toward the end of century.

Art nouveau was largely decorative, emphasizing formal elements rather than subject matter. Color, line, and texture all became necessary considerations. The artist also became knowledgable in the techniques of more than one media. Gaudi, the Barcelonian architect, was just as attentive to pottery, mosaics, wrought iron, and woodworking as he was to his main concern of architecture.

Because of its flat, decorative quality and its emphasis on flowing line and flat areas of color, art nouveau stimulated a revival in enameling and the introduction of semi-precious stones in jewelry. Both were used more for their color and intrinsic beauty rather than as an encrustation or for brilliance.

TWENTIETH CENTURY JEWELRY

In designing jewelry you will find yourself with some of the same concerns and problems as contemporary jewelers. Every artist has a prime need for individual expressiveness, and craftsmanship often takes second place to this concern.

Margaret de Patta, who made her first piece of jewelry in 1929, trained as a painter and sculptor. She had the expressive intent but lacked the skills to make her own wedding band, so she went out to learn the techniques needed to make what she already had in mind.

In the decade before World War II, most artistic expression was understood to mean painting, architecture, and sculpture. Crafts were private, intimate objects produced for personal consumption or admiration. There were, however, a few organizations in America that banded craftsmen working in different media together to show and sell their work. They resulted from mutual interest and economic need, and they were the first stirring of the crafts toward becoming public. It was yet another step toward closer bonds in attitude and artistic expression between all of the visual art forms.

MAJOR TRADITIONAL CHANGES . We find two additional influences on contemporary jewelry following World War II. Sophisticated skills developed partly due to the technology of war. A not so incidental side effect of this time was the change in traditional boundaries between sexes. Up to this point in our history, men made the jewelry and women wore it. It was used, of course, as a symbolic sign of wealth and possession. During the war years, however, women took on many of the tasks that were traditionally

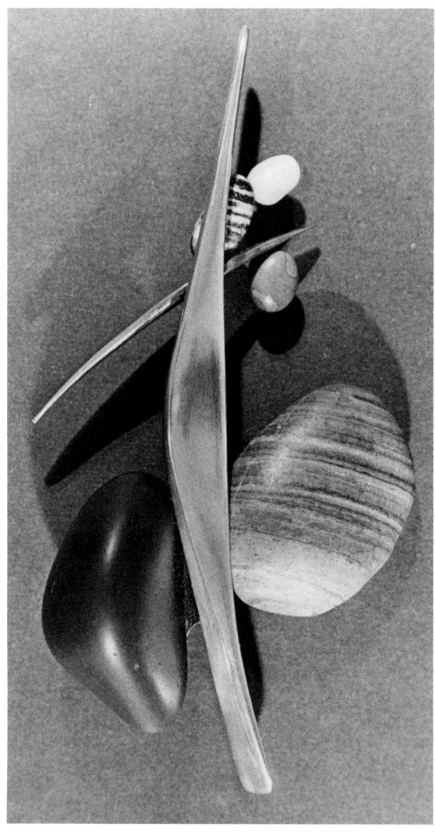

Pin by Margaret De Patta. Sterling with polished natural pebbles. Collection of the Oakland Museum. Lent by Eugene Bielawski.

men's in working with metals and all the accompanying industrial equipment.

Even more important, perhaps, our technology allowed us to see more of both the new and the ancient. We saw, for example, the work of the ancient Orient and of Africa. The work fascinated us because we saw technically good and beautifully designed pieces of jewelry. We saw jewelry in museums and we saw it in the marketplace. We saw it as part of people's living culture and as their heritage.

The phenomenon of the 1960's was to find a wider participation base both from these new skills and newly discovered images than we have had in America since Colonial times.

Young and old started making craft objects in great quantities. Communes and communities devoted their collective energies to the production of both woven and tiedyed fabrics. Production potteries emerged. Knotted wire, cords, and leather thongs became wall hangings or jewelry. In many cases, the individual's need for expression has been paramount and this has contributed to diminishing his craftsmanship.

Thus, we find several welltraveled paths for the practicing jeweler today. You will find your own path, whether as a professional artist or as an individual who wishes to make jewelry as a fascinating hobby. Here are some general thoughts and perceptions on design that may be helpful regardless of which path you choose.

DESIGN CONCERNS

Designing jewelry includes the complete series of processes to be followed from start to finish. It is deciding the intent of the jewelry: will it fit your finger, go around your neck, or button your coat? It is deciding if the piece will be functional or purely decorative. It is knowing how to get through the technical processes of manufacturing as well as knowing which process will best assist you in expressing your ideas. It is understanding which material will best suit your needs. Most of all, it is selection. You must select from the wealth of available visual and intellectual stimuli. In designing your jewelry you will be totally involved from its inception to its completion. This is design.

JEWELRY AS NON-OBJECTIVE ART

Jewelry adorns the body. It is sometimes, but not always, functional. It always rests on the body and depends on it for display. Jewelry is a decorative, enriching object; it is also an intimate object. In contemporary fabricated jewelry, the basic form of the materials—sheet, wire, and rod—is very conducive to non-objective expression.

Non-objective art does not take its image from nature as does abstract art. Rather, it takes its imagery from the mind. The image can be devised in the mind from basic materials as they occur in bulk form. For example, non-objective shapes can be cut from sheet metal or bent from wire. Non-objective jewelry need not look like anything; it need only look like jewelry. Designing in this way becomes an original expression of the artist, and it therefore

offers great freedom and possibilities.

There are numerous philosophies of non-objective design with many descriptive words and terms that are used to give order to intellectual thought and emotional expression. For purposes of this book, you will find the words *shape*, *form*, *surface*, and *color* used as follows: shape refers to a flat, defined area of metal, as in "the shape of a square." Form is used when developing dimensionality, as in "the form of a cube." Surface and color are characteristics that contribute significantly to the artistic form and final impression of a piece of jewelry.

Other terms often used when discussing design relate as conditions to, on, or about these four. They are *line*, *texture*, *pattern*, *mass*, and *scale*. When texture is ordered or formalized, you will find the term pattern used, especially in the chapter on surface treatments. Mass and scale are words often referring to the relative size of shape and form, one to another as well as their total effect.

ABSTRACT JEWELRY DESIGN

Jewelry designs using abstract motifs sometimes result in a less

satisfying experience than designing non-objective jewelry. This is often due to a desire to be overly specific in details. Beware of the poodle dog, the Shasta daisy, and the goldfish. Images like these lead to a superficiality in expression that betrays artistic shallowness. Other dangerous qualities inherent in abstracting designs into jewelry forms are triteness, repetitiveness, and, a major visual giveaway, eclecticism. These subjects have been abstracted from one to another to another until there is no vitality or understanding to express about the subject.

This does not negate using natural forms as a design resource. Georges Rouault said, "In truth, I have painted by opening my eyes day and night on the perceptible world, and also by closing them from time to time that I might better see the vision blossom and submit itself to orderly arrangement."

Study nature to understand its infinite variety and vigorous, ingenious solutions to structural problems. Or look and analyze proportions between one shape and another; analyze subtle relationships and transitions between textures, line, and mass.

Simple casting techniques lend

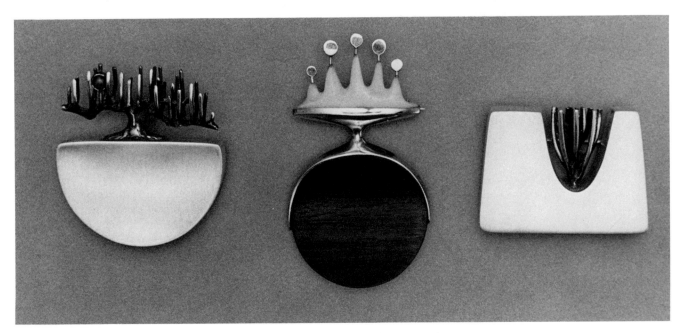

Pins by John Leary. Sterling, 18k yellow gold, coral, shark's tooth, and iron wood.

BEGINNING THE PIECE. After you have made a preliminary series of sketches, select the most satisfying one among them. Select the appropriate size and type of metal for the design (see Table 1). Then, as shown above, lay-out and then transfer the component parts of your design to the metal. This may be done in several ways. You will need a metal scribe, a steel rule, and spring dividers or circle scribe. You may also need a pencil, carbon paper, and a whiting-alcohol solution. The latter is quick drying when painted on metal and allows scribe and pencil lines to show up better on the reflective metal surface for sawing or cutting.

You can mark the shapes directly on the metal by measuring from your drawn design or from the paper pattern. They may also be traced by using a sharp pencil with carbon paper. Remember that there is no direction to metal as there is with fabric or wood. The shapes may be layed out in any direction and can even be reversed on the metal. This greatly reduces waste. Start at an edge rather than the middle of the sheet metal.

Use the straight rule and scribe or the circle scribe for all geometric lines. Lightly mark the metal surface. If you press too hard you may lose control of the line and scratch the surface. You may use the circle scribe for striking a straight strip—providing the sheet metal has a flat edge—by running one point along the edge as a guide and scribing with the other.

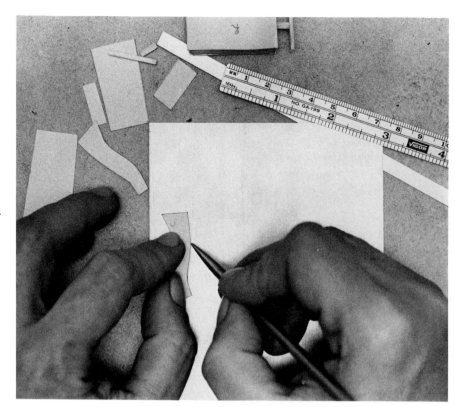

If you use carbon paper and a hard lead pencil to trace your design on the metal, go over the carbon lines immediately with the scribe or they may rub off. Non-geometric lines should be done this way or by tracing around the templet with the scribe. In laying out the shapes, remember to have at least the width of a saw blade between each piece. You will be sawing on the outside of the scribe line in all instances except one: you should saw on the line when you use a templet and you have scribed around it. In the beginning, it is best to lay out and cut all of your shapes first. There probably will not be too·

many and, with care, they will fit together very nicely. As you become more sophisticated, complex, and secure in your designs, you may want to lay-out and cut the larger pieces, assemble them, and then return to cut out the smaller or more intricate pieces.

Generally, too, you should work with the harder metals and then the softer ones if you are combining them into one piece. The softer metal is more likely to be scratched or damaged, thereby diminishing the fresh quality needed in fine craftsmanship.

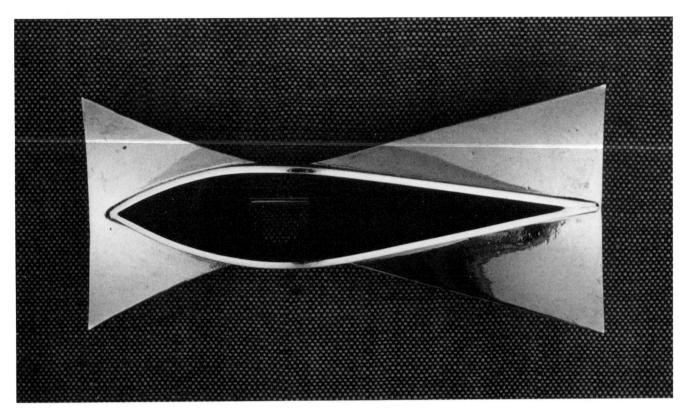

Pin (Above) by M. Chamberlain. Sterling, fabricated, 1954. Photograph by Warren Carter.

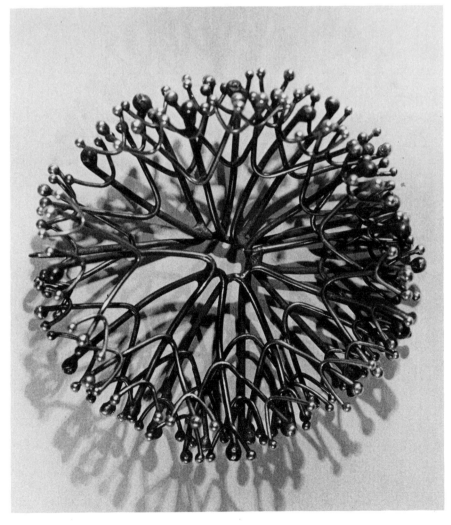

Pendant (Left) by Merry Renk. Sterling and 14k yellow gold. Here Merry Renk has carefully developed a feeling of spatial tension and volume by selection of materials and linear progressions.

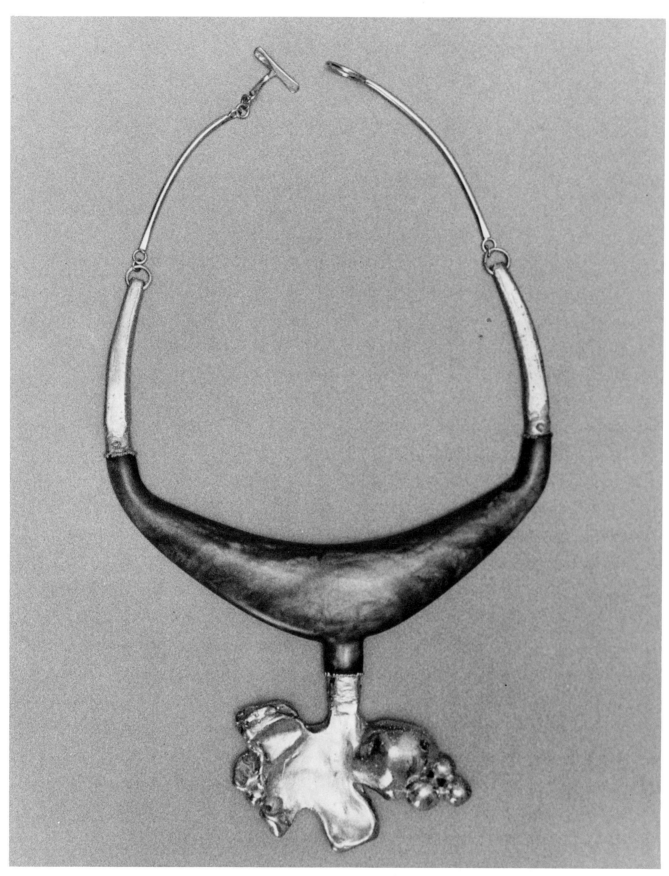

Neckpiece (Above) by Florence Resnikoff. Silver-gilt with cast polyester resen, electroformed and fabricated, 1975.

Ring (Right) by Arlene Fisch. Sterling silver, 14k gold, pearl, forged and fabricated. Collection of Mrs. Robert E. Lee.

DESIGN CHECKLIST

Be selective—in fact, in the beginning be very selective. Choose a design that only deals with one problem, such as line.

Before you start making the piece of jewelry, check yourself on the progress of its design. What is the purpose of this special and individual piece of jewelry? Where will it be worn on the body? Will it touch the skin or is there a separating fabric between it and the body? Are there parts of it which must really "work," like a size to fit or a clasp to fasten securely? These are the very practical concerns in your design.

Question yourself on the relationships between each shape and the total form. Is there a variety of shapes making up the form; is this variety too diverse? Having too many different shapes detracts from the total form. Many times it is better to change the scale between two pieces of the same shape; have two squares of differing sizes rather than a triangle and a square. This offers variety as well as repetition, yet maintains stability. Ask the same question about the surface variations. Question the relationships between all the visual elements in your preliminary jewelry design including the use of line, texture, pattern, mass, and the scale between individual elements.

Another review of your preliminary design should reinforce your emotional intent, the concept of the jewelry. Does it look as if the jewelry, when worn, is at rest? Within the piece, are there parts that look as if they will fly off at any minute? Are the shapes active or passive within the piece of jewelry? The emotional attitude of your design should be one that points attention to the body, not away from it, and for this reason, most jewelry has contained form.

Finally, select the material and the means of constructing your preliminary design. Many lovely designs may be fabricated without the use of heat or permanently joining shapes together. A number of possibilities are demonstrated in the following chapter. These are followed by another chapter with information on processes using heat.

Always remember to ask, at the end of each decision, "Have I been selective enough?"

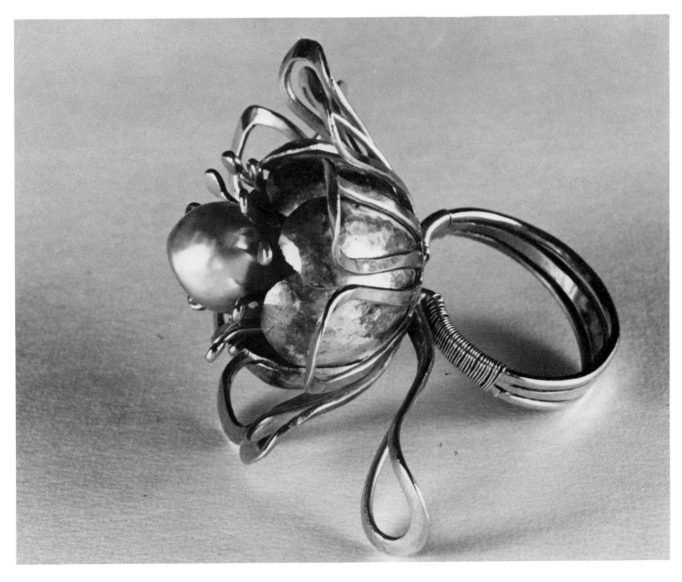

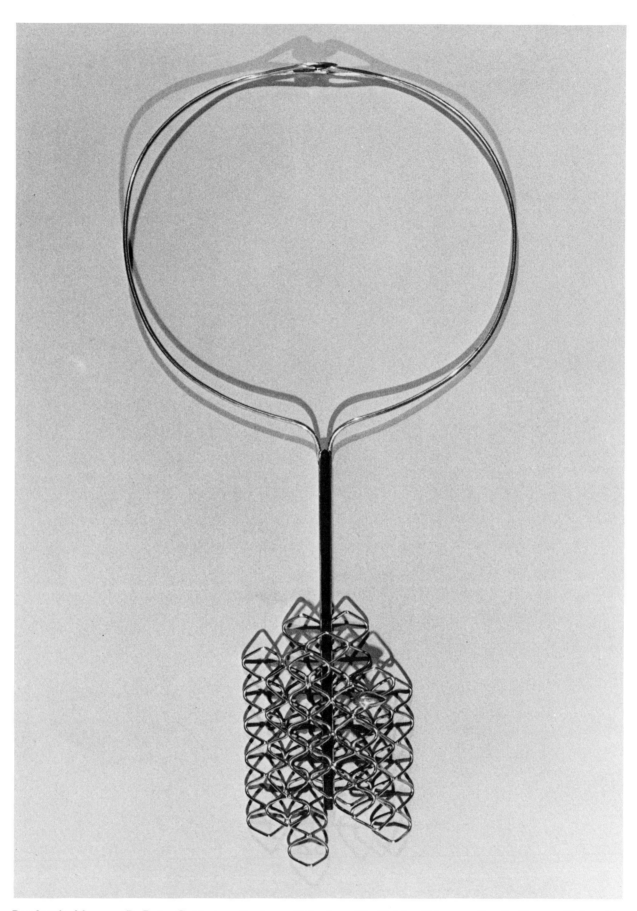

Pendant by Margaret De Patta. Gold wire with ebony. Collection of the Oakland Museum. Lent by Eugene Bielawski.

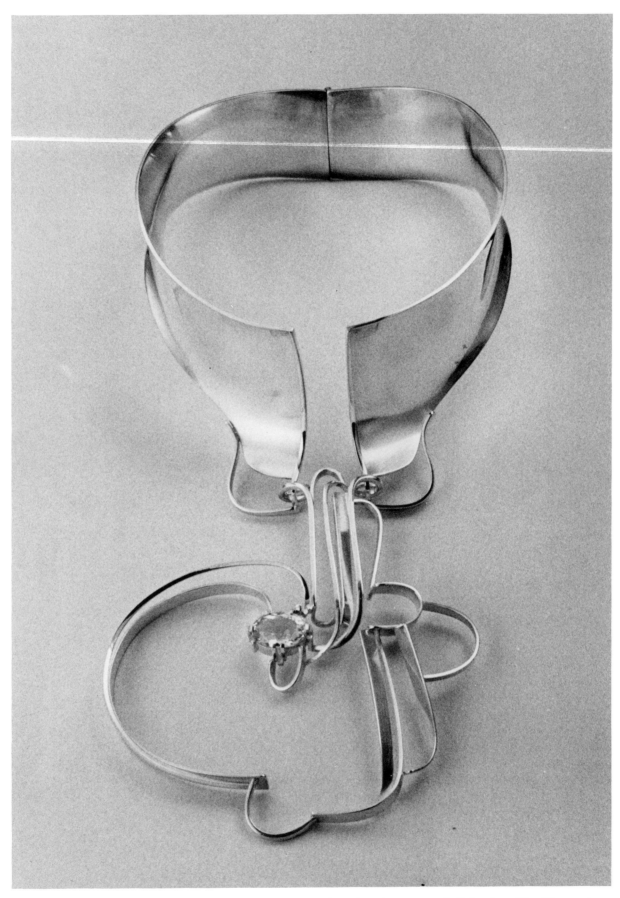

Collar with Pendant by Helen Shirk. Silver with morganite, forged and constructed. Collection of the Minnesota Museum of Art. Photo by Bradford Palm.

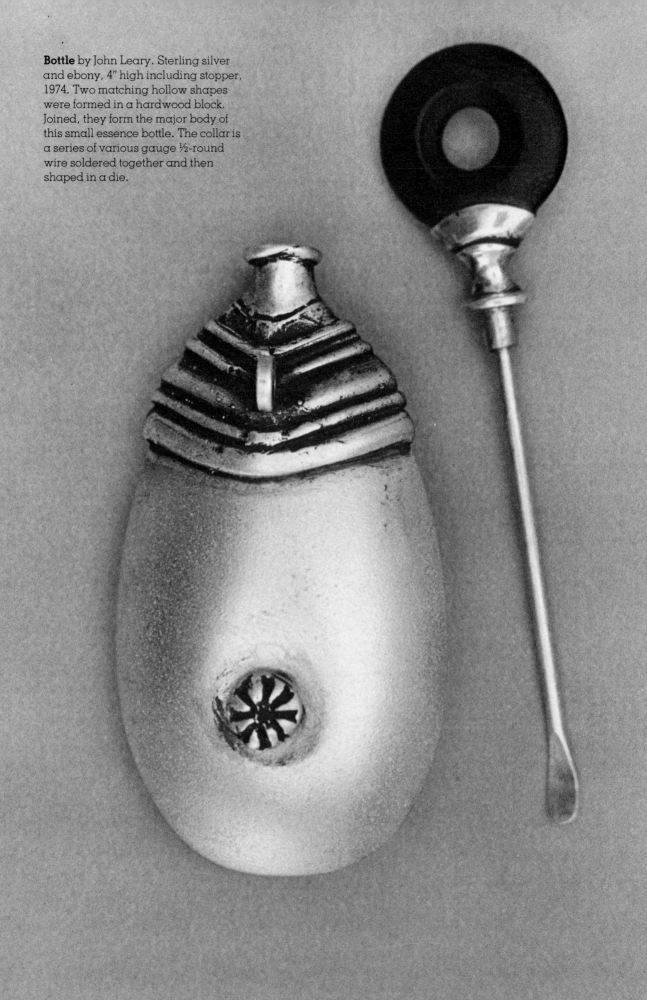

Bottle by John Leary. Sterling silver and ebony, 4″ high including stopper, 1974. Two matching hollow shapes were formed in a hardwood block. Joined, they form the major body of this small essence bottle. The collar is a series of various gauge ½-round wire soldered together and then shaped in a die.

There are several basic ways to manipulate metal: cutting, sawing, bending, filing, and forging. You will be using these methods throughout all your jewelry production, and these, therefore, are the first techniques in which you must become accomplished. In both the bending and forging processes, you will need to anneal the metal if it becomes too hard to bend or too brittle to work without cracking. While annealing is a heat process, it is included at the end of this chapter because of its general application throughout all jewelry fabrication.

3

METAL FABRICATION

Round Box by John Leary.
Sterling silver with amethyst,
3″ high, 1975.

TOOLS FOR CUTTING

The general assortment of cutting tools is shown in Chapter 1. They include saws, metal snips, drills, files and a supporting bench pin. Use the saw frame with appropriate blades to cut heavier metals, 22-gauge or thicker. Use the metal snips for cutting lighter weights, 24-gauge or thinner. All snips and shears will depress the edge of the metal when cutting, so you should cut slightly outside the scribed line. The thinner the metal you are sawing, the smaller the saw blade (04–1); the heavier the metal, the coarser the blade (1—6).

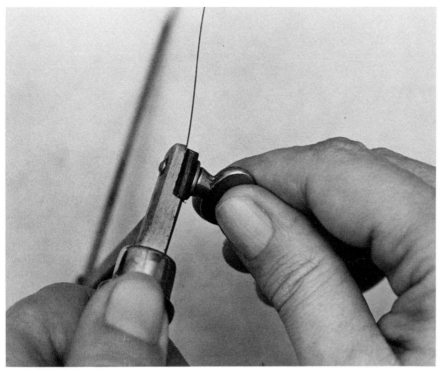

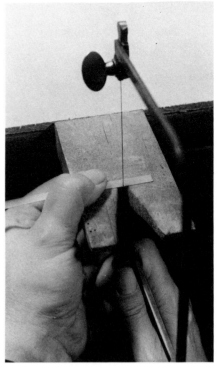

SETTING THE SAW BLADE. To set the blade into the saw frame, first loosen the set-thumb screw on the back of the frame and generally adjust the frame length to the length of the blade. Tighten the screw. Loosen the other two set-thumb screws—one at the top of the frame, the other near the handle. Place the saw frame against the edge of your workbench with the handle toward your stomach and the frame opening facing up. Suspend the blade between each of the two loosened set screws. The teeth should face up (not toward the inside of the frame) and should point toward the handle of the frame. It is sometimes difficult to see the direction of the teeth in smaller blades. Run your finger gently over the blade to determine this. Push the end of the blade into the top screw opening as far as possible and tighten the screw. Now, push forward on the saw handle with your body until the other end of the blade is pushed fully into the screw opening (it should start to bow to the side). Tighten the screw on the blade.

A well-set blade will "sing" when plucked. The higher the tone, the better the blade is set. One reason why blades break is that they are not set tightly enough in the beginning.

STARTING TO SAW. Lay the sheet of metal flat on the bench pin with the marked (design) side up. Determine where you will begin sawing and place this point at the center of the V of the bench pin. To start the cut, place the blade against the edge of the metal (at the mark), holding the frame handle down. Pull down once or twice to make a small starting groove for the rest of the saw cut. All saw cuts should be made by holding the saw frame at a vertical right angle to the metal or you will not have a true right-angle cut. All cutting action takes place on the downward stroke of the blade. Press forward with the frame only when doing the downward stroke. Do not press forward for a cut when you raise the saw for the next stroke.

Guide the cut on the outside of your scored design to give you a small material allowance for filing and finishing. The only time you should cut on the scribed line is if you have traced around a pattern. If there are interior lines or holes (called pierced work) in the design, it is usually best to cut these first before cutting out the larger metal shape. This is especially true if the pierced shape is too small to hold firmly while sawing.

STEP 1. At the edge of the desired hole or at the end of the line you are cutting, tap a starting point for the drill with the center punch. Select the appropriate drill size to match the saw blade size you will be using. You should drill a slightly larger than blade-size hole if you are cutting out an area; you should drill a corresponding size hole if you are cutting a line design. Table 2 shows the size comparisons between saw blades and drills.

STEP 2. Tighten the drill firmly and drill a hole at the center-punch mark. You will have to hold the metal sheet in a bench vise so it does not move or revolve during your drilling. Back the metal with a scrap piece of wooden block as shown. This supports and keeps lighter-gauge metals from bending under pressure. For heavier-gauge metals it aids in making a clean hole free of metal burs.

STEP 3. Remove the metal from the vise after drilling the hole. Thread your blade through the drilled hole and set it into the saw frame. Be sure that the scribed design faces up so you can follow it when sawing. Cut the line or around the hole as described earlier. To remove the metal from the saw frame, reverse this process after completing the cut.

Successful, rapid cutting with a saw needs only a few tries before you get the feel of it. Remember to always have the blade taut in the frame, to hold the saw at a vertical right-angle to the sheet metal, and to press forward to cut only on the downward stroke. Rapid sawing motion is not important for speed. In fact, very rapid, jerky sawing can heat the blade and cause it to break as well as give you an irregular edge.

FILING METALS

You are continually refining in jewelry makimg—working from large to small or coarse to fine. Sawing is a coarse cutting technique that gives you basic shapes; filing is the next step in the refining sequence. The third stage in cutting and refining, polishing, will be discussed in a later chapter.

Files come in a vast variety of sizes and cuts. Those you will be most concerned with are the basic larger metal files: barrette, half-round, three-square, and round. In addition, you will need a set of smaller needle files in assorted shapes. When choosing the correct file to use you should take several things into consideration. Is the metal edge a long, flat one? A short one? Curved? How tight is the curve? How thick is the metal? Use files that correspond to the shapes being filed—larger files for larger surface edges and smaller files for finer, refined edges.

Just as in sawing, cutting with a file takes place in only one direction. Cutting occurs from the file tip to the handle. In other words, cutting is done as you push the file, not as you bring it back from the stroke. Dragging the file on the metal on the return stroke can mar the metal and, just as important, dull the file. Push down and forward firmly with the file and release the pressure on the return.

When filing your metal should be firmly set either on the bench pin, in the bench vise, or in the ring holder. If you are filing a long, flat, straight edge, set the file flat on the workbench and move the metal edge against it, holding the metal with your fingers. The longest sweep possible with the file is the best and results in a smooth, flowing, finished edge. Short, choppy filing strokes result in an irregular edge.

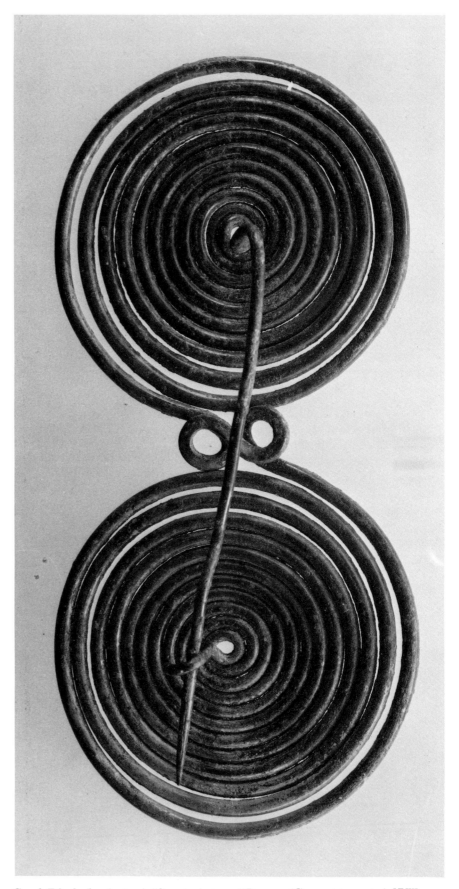

Greek Fibula (back view). "Spectacle type," Bronze, (Geometric period, XVIII century B.C. From the Metropolitan Museum of Art, Fletcher Fund, 1937.

Necklet by Arlene Fisch. Fine silver wire, sterling silver and amber clasp, spool knit construction, tube 1½″ diameter, 1974. The artist has used a larger spool and more pegs than the usual in spool knitting. She used fine silver wire because of its malleability and because its surface is less prone to oxidation.

FORMING WIRE AND SHEET

Bending shapes and forms from metal sheet and wire is one of the basic forming processes. The best tools for this are the fingers because they do not put unnecessary nicks and kinks in the metal. When sharper angles are needed or if the work is too small to control in this manner, use one of the several jeweler's pliers. Other forming tools include the bench vise, blocks, hammers and mallets, drawplate and tongs, and the burnisher.

Always remember that one surface will stretch and the counter-surface will compress when metal is curved. The slipping of the metal crystals is greater in some metals than in others, but there is a limited tolerance to this stretching-compressing action in all metals. The more often bending is repeated, the more this tolerance is tested until the piece of metal will crack or break. Annealing, discussed at the end of this chapter, helps prevent this.

REMOVING KINKS. Most of the wire you purchase is in a softened or annealed state and therefore is susceptible to kinking. There will be a few slight kinks as the wire comes off the spool and it may develop more serious ones as you work. Wire must be free of kinks at all times for well finished work. A good method of removing the kinks from wire as you work is shown above. Lay your wire on a large piece of soft wood, and holding a smaller piece of wood in one hand, press down hard on the wire. Hold the wire with pliers and gently pull the wire through the two pieces of wood. This method can be used for copper, gold, and silver wire.

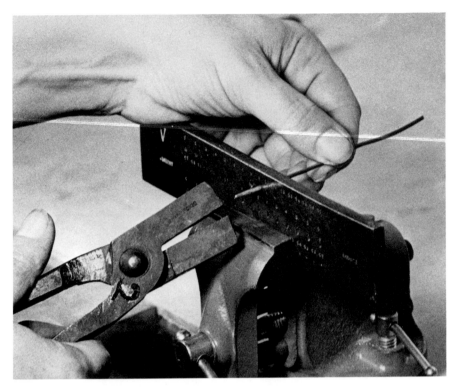

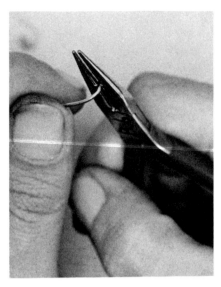

DRAWING WIRE. Kinks may be removed from wire before you begin work by pulling it through a drawplate with draw tongs. Wire can also be reduced in size by pulling it through successively smaller holes in the drawplate. Its shape and profile may be altered this way. For example, round wire can be made square; square wire can be made round.

Besides the drawplate and tongs, you will need a bench vise that is firmly attached to a heavy surface or workbench, and Vaseline or beeswax. There is a very heavy pull during this process and the bench vise must be immovable.

To insert the wire in the drawplate, gradually taper the wire with a metal file or grinding wheel for about 1″ to 1½″ from one end. This allows enough wire to go through the drawplate hole, and also gives a firm grip with the draw tongs. Clamp the drawplate firmly in the bench vise. Lubricate the wire with either beeswax or Vaseline. Stick the pointed wire end through the first hole in the drawplate that it will not fit through easily.

Grip the tapered wire end with the draw tongs and pull the wire

through the hole with a steady but rapid pull. Be sure that the wire is at right angles to the face of the drawplate at all times or it will develop a curl. Repeat the drawing process, progressing hole by hole until the desired metal gauge is reached.

To pull half-round wire, solder the ends of two round wires together, taper the end, and draw them together through the appropriate round hole in the drawplate. At the same time, hold your burnisher firmly between the wires and against the back of the drawplate. This prevents the wires from twisting in the drawing process. Drawing these wire pairs through a square-hole drawplate in the same manner will make triangular wire.

Drawing wire will lengthen it because the metal crystals are being pushed along the wire length. The crystals also become somewhat compressed and distorted on the surface. The wire will therefore become more rigid, brittle, and springy in character, and harder to pull through the plate. Annealing the wire will return it to a more malleable condition.

BENDING WIRE. Select the desired gauge wire and remove all kinks and anneal if necessary. In doing scrollwork it is best to use a 6″ to 10″ length of wire to avoid excessive kinking. Grip the wire with the nose of the pliers so the wire tip is in the center line of the jaws. Do not let the tip end extend past the jaws or you will not get a perfect, flowing circular line. Holding the wire length between your thumb and forefinger, guide the wire as you rotate the pliers—using a wrist motion—with the other hand. Keep the wire snugly against the jaws as you guide it. There is little or no motion with the hand holding the wire; the hand holding the pliers rotates at the wrist. The pliers do not change their grip on the wire at any time.

Once you have formed a perfect wire circle, a number of scroll variations are possible. Shift the plier position from the tip end to near the closing of the circle, about three-quarters of the way around it. Grip the wire at this point. Guiding the wire with one hand, rotate the other hand about a quarter turn until it becomes awkward to continue. Release the pressure of your hand on the pliers but do not move them. Keep the pliers at the same position on the center circle. Comfortably regrip the pliers and continue to twist and curve the wire again. Note that the thumb holds the wire while the forefinger forms the slight open curve of the wire.

BENDING SHEETS OF METAL. Bending sheets or wide strips of metal, especially heavier gauges, may require the use of additional, heavier tools such as the bench vise and mallets.

First, lightly scribe a straight line at the bend point on the back of the sheet, then clamp the sheet into your vise. Make sure that the scribed line is level with the top surface of the vise jaw. Place the edge of a smooth, hardwood block along the scribed line on top of one vise jaw. Press the metal over the other vise jaw. Pound the block with a mallet to set a tight bend. You will never be able to get a very sharp outer edge when bending either wire or sheet strips. The metal will not stretch or compress enough to achieve this look. Very sharp edges can only be constructed by soldering separate pieces of metal together.

BENDING METAL STRIPS. Bending sheets and strips of metal is similar to bending wire, although you will generally be doing individual bends rather than continuous ones.

Bending heavy-gauge wire or metal strip in its widest dimension can be done without the use of pliers as shown above. Set a piece of hardwood firmly into your bench vise. Cut a groove, as wide and deep as the metal strip you wish to bend, into the hardwood block. File one edge of this groove to the radial arc desired. Fit the metal strip into the groove and pull it against the arc. Continue closing the arc by moving the strip along in the groove and pulling the end around. If the metal begins to buckle, lay it on a steel block and hammer it flat with a rawhide mallet.

Flat-nose or combination-nose pliers are used most often when bending strips in their smallest dimension. However, chain-nose pliers can be used when bending either small curved or flat bends. Essentially the same wrist and guiding motions described for bending wire are required for bending strips. Always work the metal firmly against the plier jaw. Always select the plier jaw to fit the contour of the bend. This means using flat-jaw pliers for making angular bends and the combination pliers with one curved jaw to make open bends. A specific example is bending a metal strip to form a simple ring. Use the curved jaw on the inside curve and the flat jaw on the outside of the bend.

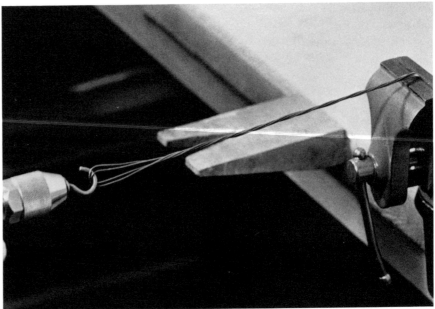

GALLERY WIRE. Several wires and/or thin metal strips in various combinations can be twisted together to form a heavy-gauge, decorative wire called gallery wire. The photo shows only a few possible variations. You can experiment in making many more by using various combinations of different gauges and shapes of wire and strips, using several metals together, twisting tightly or loosely, or by reversing the twist at designated intervals. The twisted wire can be hammered after forming to change the surface appearance. Several wires can be twisted together and one wire removed for a corkscrew effect. Twisted wire can also be pulled through a drawplate, thus compressing and flattening the surface.

TWISTING WIRE. The easiest way to form a consistent twist in wire is to use a hand drill with a hook firmly set in the chuck. Set one end of a doubled group of wires in a vise and loop the other end around the hook in the hand drill. Twist by turning the drill handle. All wire must be the same length and must be kept taut while twisting. Twisting a single wire in this manner will harden it—a desirable quality when making pin stems. Annealing will return the twisted wire to its more flexible state.

FORMING A TUBE

Tubing is made from thinner-gauge (22 to 28g) sheet metal. The walls of the tube will become thicker after forming because the metal is being compressed in the process. Tubing is made with the drawplate and tongs and follows similar procedures as those for drawing wire. The preparation for drawing tubing, however, is somewhat different because you are using a flat sheet stock.

In addition to the tools necessary for drawing wire, you will need a wooden or lead block with a long, narrow channel in it, a steel rod slightly smaller in diameter than the channel, a hammer and steel block, a burnisher, and metal snips.

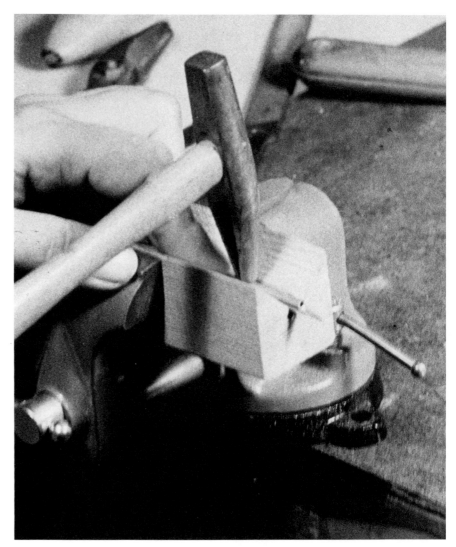

DRAWING TUBING. Cut a strip from a sheet of thin metal. The strip should be at least 4″ but not more than 6″ long. Its width should be slightly less than three times the diameter of the largest hole in your drawplate. The strip may be narrower but never wider. The pull required for tubing is heavier than with wire, so it is better to make several short tubes rather than one long one. With metal snips, taper the end of the metal strip by cutting back each side about 1½″ to form a point.

Place the strip of metal over the narrow groove formed in the wood or lead block and bend it into the slot. Use the length of steel rod and a hammer. Bend the taper as well as the entire length of the strip. Using a small hammer and a steel block, close the taper so the two sides meet. Now lubricate the length of metal strip with beeswax or Vaseline. Place the point of your straight burnisher tightly into the tapered cone and insert the taper through the largest hole of the drawplate. Grip the taper firmly with the tongs and pull straight through the drawplate. The edges of the strip will start to close with this first draw. Repeat, going through successively smaller holes until the tube is completely closed. Anneal the metal occasionally so it maintains its malleability. Tubing can be drawn smaller after it is closed. It can also be soldered closed and drawn again or it can be drawn closed, soldered, and drawn again.

FORGING

The broad definition of forging includes the techniques of making both small and large-scale dimensional objects by hammering while the metal is either hot or cold. Forging and silversmithing are very similar and are often interchangeable in practice. Rather than constructing or fabricating a form, the form is achieved by forcing the metal crystals of a single piece of metal to "move." It is as if you pinched or flattened the metal at one place and thereby shifted part of its mass somewhere else within the same piece of material. When there is compression in one area, there is always stretching or expansion in another.

The craft of forging can require a whole supplementary set of tools in addition to those discussed in Chapter 1. These include specialized raising hammers, stakes of various shapes to fit numerous forms achieved by forging or raising, and a large anvil. All these tools are of steel, and all have very carefully polished faces that are free of pits, rust spots, and blemishes.

For the silversmithing projects in this book, the special forging hammers you need are a raising or cross-peen hammer and a planishing hammer. They may be purchased in varying weights from 3/4 to 6 pounds. Choose the size you feel most comfortable with. Some types of hammering, on punches for example, may put dents on the face of your hammer. You should therefore have separate hammers for forging and silversmithing. They should not be used for any other purpose. Any blemish on the face of the hammer will transfer on to the metal surface and mar it.

Forging in this book has been limited to using the following forming tools: mandrels; hammers and mallets; steel, wood, tempered Masonite, and lead blocks; and a dapping die with punches. Limiting the tools, however, does not imply limiting expression or forging possibilities. Heavier metals, 4- to 14-gauge wire and 8- to 14-gauge sheet, are used when forging.

Stretching, cupping, and drawing-in are basic forging techniques. Planishing is a polishing technique used on forged metal, not a primary forming technique. Repoussé is sometimes associated with forging but it changes only the surface and not the fundamental form of the metal so will be discussed under surface techniques.

STRETCHING METALS. Stretching is a technique in which a piece of metal is made thinner and either longer or wider. Specifically, this is done with a cross-peen hammer on an anvil or a flat stake. You may achieve a similar action in the metal by using the edge of the flat face of a ball-peen hammer and a steel block.

Successful stretching as well as all other forging techniques depend on your developing an even, controlled hammering rhythm. Let the weight of the hammer assist you in your work. Grip the hammer toward the end of the handle and let the head weight add to the force of the blow. The metal will move in the same direction as the hammer stroke. Be sure that all surface areas —the steel block, the metal your are working, and the hammer face— are clean, smooth, and unblemished. Change the force of your blow to coincide with the amount of movement you need in the metal to achieve the desired form.

STRETCHING

This demonstration uses oil clay rather than metal because it acts in an identical way.

STEP 1. Hold the metal firmly on a steel support. Strike the metal with a slight forward blow of the hammer, starting at the edge of the metal. Work into the body with repeated hammer strokes. The repeated hammering will "move" the metal in the direction of the angle of the hammer face, thus stretching it. Moving the metal in this manner will push it outward, making it thinner and either wider or longer. As the stretching progresses to the desired form and thinness, reduce the strength of the blows. You can also rotate the material to assure an even and straight stretch.

STEP 2. Stretching metal so it is either thinner or wider is done in the same manner as lengthening it. Strike harder blows at first, hammering toward the center. Lighten your blows as the desired shape or form is approached. Planishing will stretch the metal a little more.

By alternating the angle of the blow or by using the round face of the ball-peen hammer, wire can be stretched or forged into a flat curve. Instead of striking the blows at the end of the wire, aim along the lateral edge. The metal will stretch and flatten where the blows fall, making the parallel sides uneven in length and curving the wire away from the blow.

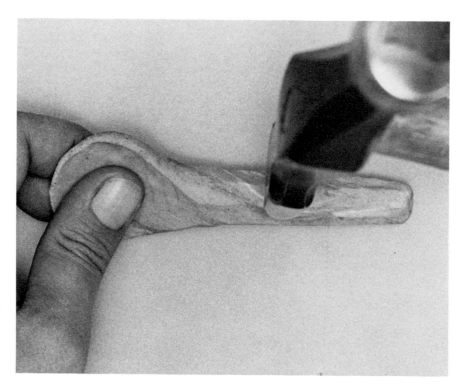

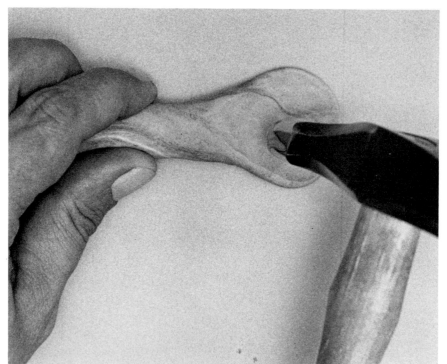

CUPPING METALS

As the term implies, cupping is a forging process used to make concave or convex forms. A very simple example of cupping can be seen when you strike a single blow into a soft wood or oil clay with the spherical end of the ball-peen hammer. This leaves a concave dent or small cup shape.

Because the ball end of the hammer is spherical, the metal will stretch in all directions away from the center of the blow. Not only will the stretched metal become wider and longer and the curve deeper, but the cupped metal will also become thinner. The untouched edges, however, will remain their original thickness.

You will use a ball-peen hammer and a flat steel block for cupping. Remember that the metal used should be a heavy gauge to allow for the metal's bulging and stretching.

STEP 1. Hold the metal sheet firmly with one hand and lay it on the steel block. Using the spherical end of a ball-peen hammer, strike the metal at the center of the space you want to cup. Hammer carefully, using repeated blows toward the center of the sheet. The metal will bulge downward.

STEP 2. Continue hammering, directing the repeated blows outward from the center of the cup. Be careful not to stretch the metal too thin or to break through it. You can make circular or oval shapes as well as asymmetrical ones in this manner. Again, the metal may become brittle as it is hammered and may need annealing before you continue forming.

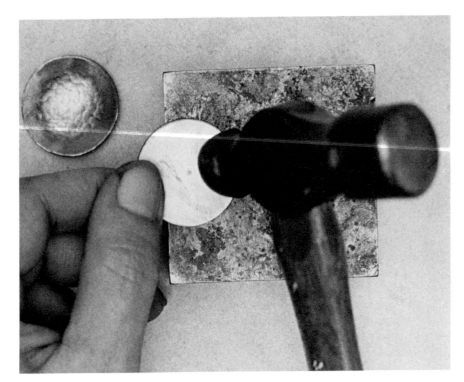

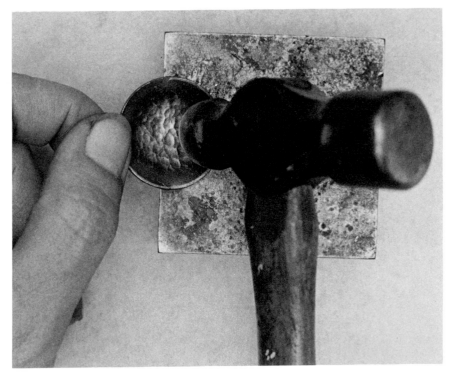

THE DAPPING DIE AND PUNCHES. The dapping die (or block) and punches are used to make small, round dome shapes in a manner similar to the cupping process. You should start with a circular metal blank cut slightly larger than the desired dome. There is not much stretching in this process so the gauge of the metal used should be close to the finished thickness desired.

Choose the hollow in the dapping block that most closely fits your metal circle without having the metal hang over the edge of the depression. The metal circle must fit *inside* the opening. Select a punch that has a slightly smaller head than the hollow. Place the punch over the metal circle, and tap the punch with a rawhide mallet. This forces the metal circle into the die hollow. To make the dome deeper, move the metal into the next smaller hollow. Repeat the doming with a smaller punch. Any depth of dome up to a half-sphere can be made by this process.

The steel dapping block is used for repeating the identical dome form many times.

Carve a hollow shape to the desired depth in a hardwood block with a wood gouge. For a very deep dome, carve several hollows of decreasing widths and increasing depths. These hollows will eventually become scarred by the sharp metal edges, but you will be able to get a limited number of repeated cut shapes using the same hardwood die. Use the same punches as you do with the steel block. The shapes may be varied; they are not limited to circles.

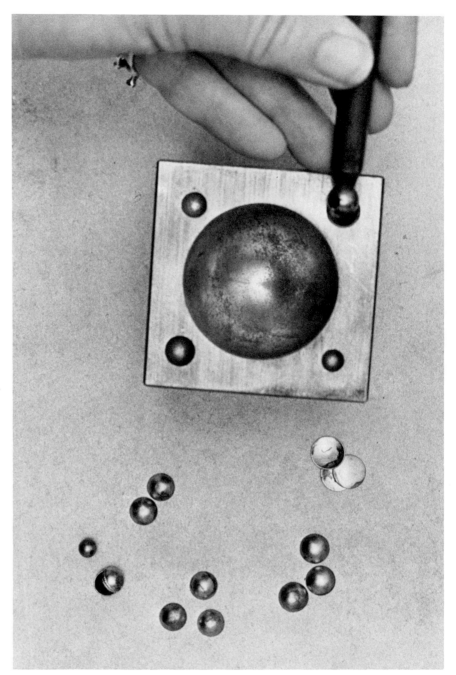

If you need only one dome shape, hammer a hollow into a lead block and use it as a die. The lead die will deform as you hammer into it, so its use is limited to a one-of-a-kind dome shape. Be very cautious using the lead block because lead can contaminate the surface of silver and cause pitting. Clean all your metals with fine emery paper after using the lead block and before going on to the next construction step.

Any dome shape can be formed in hardwood or lead blocks except those with sharp angles, which can only be achieved by using tempered Masonite as a die base.

DRAWING-IN AND UPSETTING

Drawing-in is the forging process that makes a sheet of metal narrower and, at the same time, thicker. Basically, you are hammering on the narrower edge of a metal strip rather than on its wider dimension. This compresses and thickens the metal. It also lengthens the strip. Drawing-in is a squeezing-stretching action of the metal.

The metal strip should be quite thick—a heavy gauge—in relationship to its width. Otherwise, the strip will have a tendency to fold or bend instead of compress. This means no more than a 4:1 or 5:1 ratio of width to thickness. Drawing-in is traditionally done with a forging hammer or a modified short-handled sledge hammer.

To draw-in metal, hold the metal strip on its edge on the steel block. Strike the edge of the metal with the flat face of your hammer. Begin with heavier blows, but take care to distribute the blows evenly along each edge and throughout the width of the piece. The edges can "mushroom" over if this is not done. If mushrooming occurs, turn the metal strip flat and hammer the curled edges down.

As with all hammering processes, the metal will eventually become rigid and brittle. After annealing, begin again with heavier blows. This shifts the metal crystals toward the center of the strip and causes a greater amount of compression.

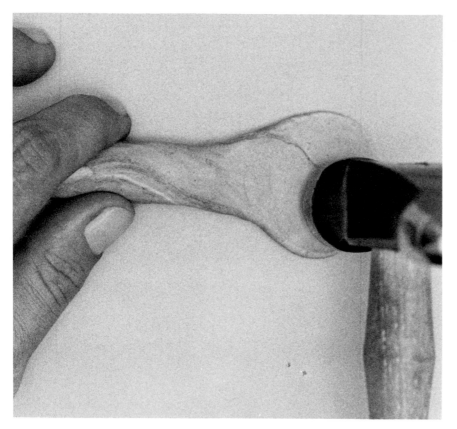

PLANISHING. Planishing, more a polishing process than a forging one, smooths the metal surface. The wide, flat plane of the planishing hammer head beats down the bumps and hills developed during stretching, cupping, or drawing-in. Planishing also stretches the metal somewhat as it reduces the bumps.

When planishing, support the metal piece with a corresponding profile of formed metal. Otherwise, the curve or shape of the metal will flatten and distort or destroy your design. If you do not have the tradi-tionally shaped forging stakes designed for this purpose, use the polished spherical end of your ball-peen hammer or the ball-shaped punches from the punch and die set. Remember, all steel surfaces must be very smooth, clean, and free of blemishes. You should occasionally polish these faces with polishing buffs and compounds just as you do your jewelry.

Clamp the support in your bench vise while you use the planishing hammer. Hold the metal piece firmly over the support, and using the large, flat face of the hammer, strike the blow in a light manner with a slight forward push.

ANNEALING

Annealing is the softening by heat of nonferrous metals that have been hardened by various working processes such as bending, hammering, twisting, drawing, forging, or polishing. Annealing is fundamental to all the metal processes discussed in this chapter as well as those that will follow. You will need to anneal metal throughout the construction process, especially if you bend, hammer, or twist the metal. Annealing takes place naturally when you solder.

Forming processes distort or flatten the metal's surface crystals; reheating restores them to their original form and placement. The distortion is called hardening. It is useful when you are making forms, such as clips, that need natural spring. Polishing also hardens the surface, a desirable quality in the finished work.

When making metal jewelry and especially when you are developing dimensional forms, you will generally need the metal to be as malleable as possible. Otherwise the metal may crystallize, crack, or break into pieces. Periodic annealing prevents this.

Annealing sheet metal—such as gold, silver, or copper—means heating it with a torch flame to a low, dull red color, between 1100°–1200°F. Many metals should be immediately quenched or cooled by dropping them into cold water or directly into a cleaning solution called pickle. Gold does not have to be quenched; it should air cool naturally. Table 3 shows various metals, their annealing temperatures, and if they should be quenched or air-cooled.

Annealing will discolor the surface of most metals; this is called *oxidation*. You should clean the metal by dropping it in a pickle solution before you continue working. Leaving the oxidation on the metal will result in a blemished surface. Cleaning and pickling procedures are outlined in the following chapters as they are essential to all processes involving the use of heat.

To anneal metals, you will need a torch, a charcoal block, and a pair of fire tweezers. If the metal is one that needs quenching, you will need a wide-necked jar or Pyrex dish filled with water. You should always use a flat sheet of asbestos on your workbench surface under the charcoal block when you use a torch.

Place your metal on the charcoal block, then heat the metal by moving your torch back and forth across the entire surface. The flame should be soft (the interior blue cone should not be too sharp in appearance). Check Table 3 for the annealing temperatures of various metals.

When the metal is annealed, pick it up immediately with fire tweezers and quench it by dropping it into a jar of water or pickle. If the metal is to be air-cooled, move it off the charcoal block and on to the asbestos using the tweezers.

ANNEALING WIRE. Wire must be annealed in a different manner because it is so thin compared to pieces of sheet metal. Its length makes wire awkward to handle and heat will not distribute evenly along its length, which is a necessity in annealing. Wind your wire into a compact coil and bind it tightly with a length of silver wire. The coil should be solid with no loose loops. Paint the bound wire with liquid flux (see Chapter 4 on types of flux available) and let it dry.

Small coils of wire may be annealed on a charcoal block. Turn the coil from side to side with fire tweezers to assure an even distribution of heat throughout the coil. Larger coils of wire should be placed on a wire grid that is sup-

ported by a tripod stand. Play the torch flame back and forth both on the top and on the bottom of the coil through the grid. It is essential that the heat evenly penetrates the whole coil including its interior.

Quench the coil if the type of metal requires it. Wash the coil under tap water, dry it completely, then gently unwind it. Wire should always be in an annealed stage when doing any of the bending processes.

Annealing is the most general heat process you will use throughout your jewelry fabrication. It is the one single process that keeps metals malleable throughout each, and all, of the forming processes.

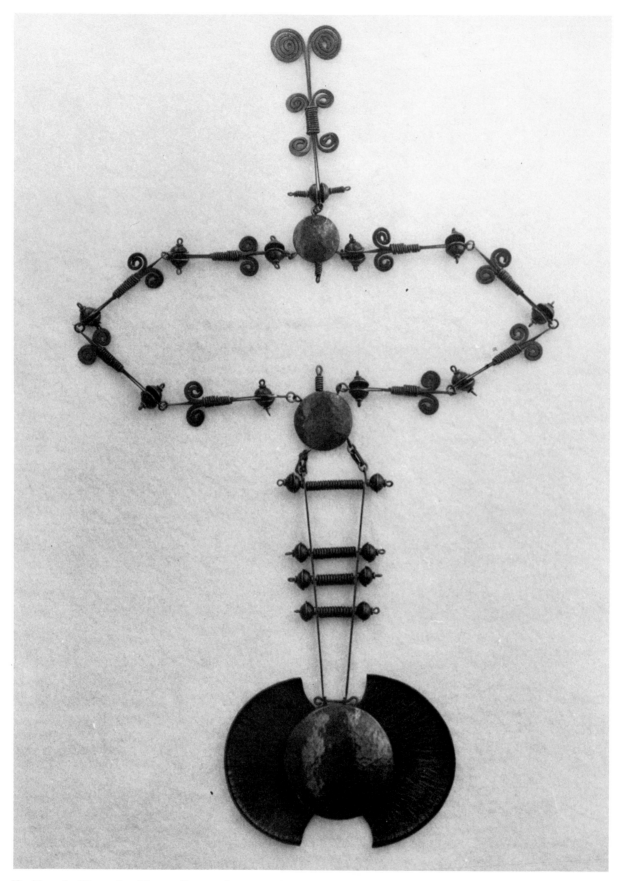

Necklace by Nancy Loo Bjorge. Copper, hammered and linked, 1974.

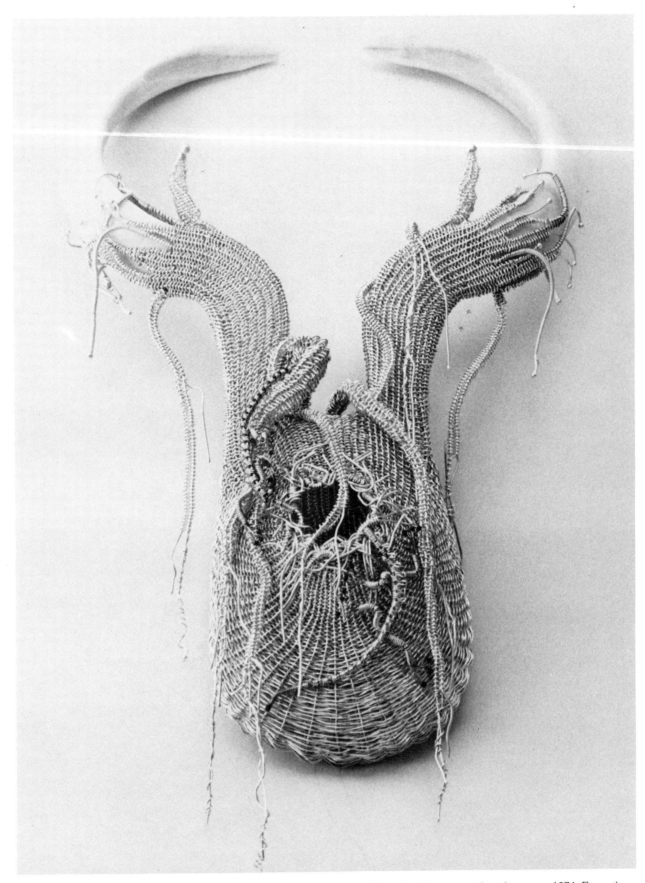

Neckpiece #8 by Mary Lee Hu. Sterling silver, gold-filled brass and boar's tusk, wrapped and woven, 1974. From the exhibition "The Goldsmith," presented by the Renwick Gallery of the National Collection of Fine Arts, Smithsonian Institution, Washington, D.C., and the Minnesota Museum of Art, Saint Paul, Minnesota. Photo by Bradford Palm.

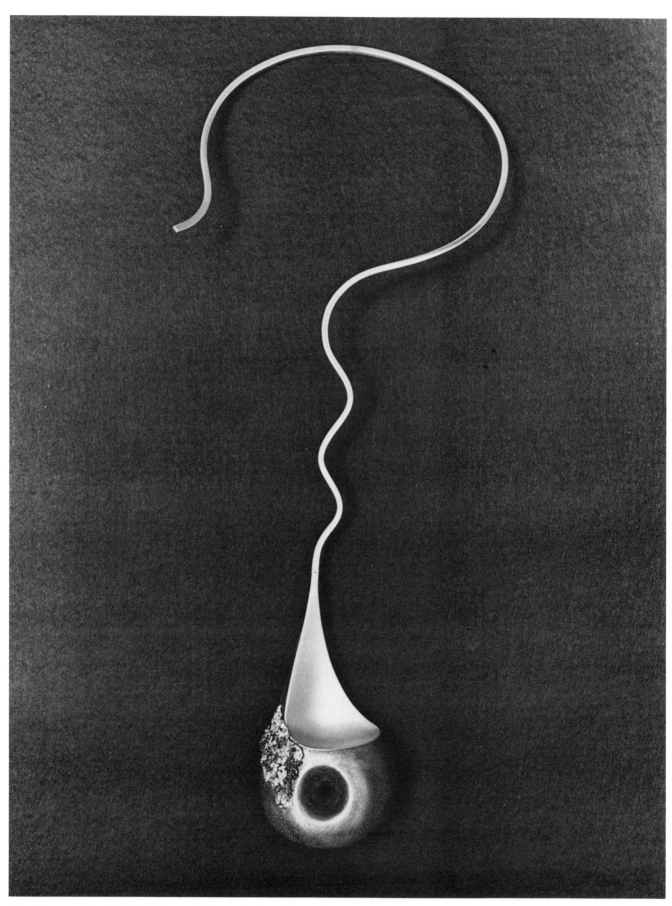

"Continuous Form" by Ruth Laug. Silver, raised and forged.

4
CONTRUCTION USING HEAT

Learning to use heat in jewelry construction is as essential as learning to use heat in the preparation of food.

This chapter will discuss the different uses of heat and how to control it for successful jewelry fabrication. First, heat is used to keep the metal malleable for continued ease in working. This process is called annealing, and it was discussed in detail in Chapter 3. You also use heat to permanently join sections of metal together for both strength and dimensionality. This is called soldering. Heat used in combination with chemicals to keep the metals clean is called pickling. These processes—annealing, pickling, and soldering—are dependent on one another in jewelry fabrication.

TOOLS AND MATERIALS

The tools and materials used in heat construction are deceptively simple. Many are familiar to you. The major concern in their use is safety because you are working with heat and chemicals.

For working tools you will need a charcoal block, an asbestos sheet and block, a hand torch, a hotplate (preferably with a gas burner), steel pins and iron binding wire, jeweler's snips, soldering tweezers, a scribe or poker, small sable brushes, a small covered jar, a small Pyrex dish or chemical crucible, and a large uncovered glass container.

Materials you will need, other than the metal, include water, acids for cleaning (or a commercial mix called Sparex), solder of various hardnesses, fluxes, yellow ocher, and fine emery cloth or paper.

CLEANING METAL SURFACES

When heat is applied to a metal alloy, the alloy percentages of the metal surface change so the "skin" differs from the rest of the body of metal. For example, sterling silver is an alloy of pure silver and copper. Copper crystals accumulate on the skin when heat is applied. Copper is affected by oxygen and this is evidenced by its change of color when it is exposed to air. The gold content in both karat gold and gold alloys is changed by heating, and this also affects the surface skin of the metal. The term used to identify this change is firescale. Firescale of cupric oxides is the oxidation of the metal surface and will be particularly evident to you when you start the final polishing. It is always present, and it continues to build during all the heat processes. It is therefore very important to continually attempt to restrain or retard its accumulation, especially during annealing and soldering.

There are several other metal surface conditions that must be controlled when you use heat: natural metal oxides or firescale, oils from your skin, natural dirt and dust, and flux-glass continually coat the metal surfaces. It is very important that areas are freed of these substances because surface contamination prevents the flow of solder.

Two chemical solutions are used to clean and control surface contaminations. These are pickle, a liquid solution of sulphuric acid, and flux, which is either a liquid, paste, or powdered solution of fluoride or borax.

PICKLING

Pickling, a cleaning process, is done continuously throughout your work using heat. Pickling is accomplished by using warm solutions of acid and water. The most common pickling solution is sulphuric acid.

For convenience, the pickling solution is made up in large quantities and stored. You will draw on it continuously, using small amounts and returning the surplus to its original storage crock. You can make up your own solution or use a commercial pickle called Sparex. It is purchased in dry form and can be used with any non-ferrous metal. In both bases, you are working with an acid solution and it can be dangerous unless handled properly.

Pendant by Aimée Johnson.
Fused silver.

MIXING A PICKLE SOLUTION. A cardinal rule of chemistry when mixing an acid solution is that you *always add the acid to the water*. Adding water to an acid can result in an explosion and noxious gases. Acids are meant to attack metals, so mixing, storage, and heating are always done in glass or ceramic containers.

Add one part sulphuric acid to ten parts water in a half-gallon ceramic crock. These proportions are equivalent to a quart of water to four tablespoons of acid, or a 10% solution.

Trickle the acid *very slowly* into the water. Stir gently with a wooden spoon or glass rod to mix the solution. (Be sure to mark the outside of the crock with its contents, and cover the acid solution for storage.)

From this reserve, pour enough pickle into a Pyrex container or chemistry crucible to cover your work. Letting the metal stand in this cool solution for 15 to 20 minutes will do the job but, if you are short of time, heat the solution to a low boil on a gas burner before removing the work. Remove your jewelry from the acid pickle with copper or wooden tongs and wash it under running tap water to remove the pickle solution. The pickle solution can be reused throughout your work session and returned to your reserve stock at the end of the day. Wash the pickle dish and tongs. It is a very good idea to have two separate, identifiable (different in shape, for example) acid containers. You will be working with a second acid later when finishing and polishing your work and the two acids should never be mixed or confused with each other. Marking each container for its individual use and content is essential.

Metal surfaces can be cleaned mechanically as well as chemically. Filing, sanding, or scraping will also remove surface contamination.

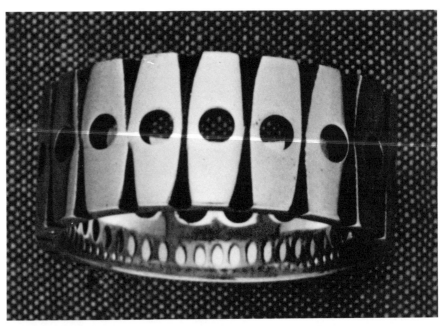

Ring by M. Chamberlain. Sterling, 1954. Photo by Warren Carter.

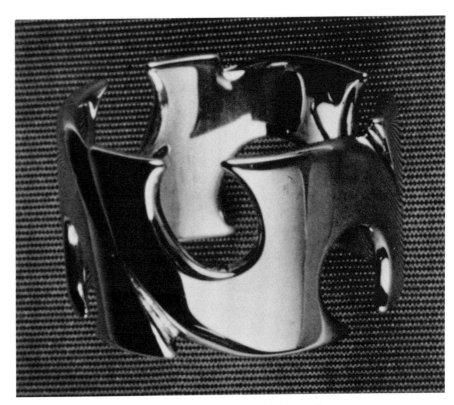

Ring by Donna Cressey. Sterling, 1954. Photo by Warren Carter.

FLUXING

Flux is a chemical that assists the flow of solder during the soldering process by dissolving, inhibiting, or preventing contamination of the metal surface. It can be purchased in liquid, paste, or powder form and is either a borax or fluoride flux.

Battern's Self-pickling Flux, a liquid, is a fluoride and is very convenient for the studio jeweler. Store your reserve stock in a covered bottle and keep it at the workbench in a small covered glass container to reduce evaporation. It is applied with a small sable brush used only for fluxing. As the name implies, this liquid flux is a self-pickling or self-cleaning flux. It primarily cleans skin oils and dirt from the metal surface and assists the solder to flow.

Handy Flux is a paste flux and can be used in the same way as the liquid. It is especially good for use with copper or alloys containing copper, which oxidize and form firescale rapidly. Paste flux usually has a borax base. The soldering demonstrations in this chapter give an example of the surface changes as the heat both dries and melts the Handy Flux. The excess melted flux is called flux-glass or borax-glass when cooled. This flux glass must be removed by pickling before you continue.

Powdered flux, available at the grocery as borax powder, is in a convenient form to use with solder filings. Filings are generally used in select soldering processes where larger, flat shapes of metal are joined face-to-face—a process called sweat soldering. In this type of soldering, flux-glass is a problem if you use paste flux, and the bubbling or drying action of the liquid flux can move the metal out of place. Mix the borax powder and solder filings with a very small amount of alcohol (not water) before brushing it on the metal.

There are other flux compounds for use with specific metals. These come in liquid, paste, and powdered form and are most commonly used with gold, silvers, copper, tin, zinc, nickel, and their alloys. Metals with lower temperatures, such as aluminum, demand a different flux and solder that can be purchased at the same supply source as the metals.

SOLDERING

Solder is used to permanently join pieces of metal together. It is a metal alloy that melts and flows at a lower temperature than the metal to be joined. Solder will join the ends of wire together, either to make the wire longer or to close the wire ends into a loop. It will join the edges of two flat forms together or it will join the forms at an angle to form a dimensional design. It can also be used to join flat sheets placed one on top of the other in a process called sweat soldering.

There are many types of solder available, each individually alloyed to suit the metal to be soldered as well as the soldering sequence.

Solder is available in several hardnesses: hard, medium, soft, and ready-flo (or easy). It can be purchased as wire, flat sheets, strips, rods, pellets, and in filed or powdered forms.

Hard solder melts at a temperature slightly less than the melting point of silver. Therefore, it will flow without affecting or melting the silver if used carefully. Medium solder melts and flows at a lower temperature than hard; soft solder flows at a still lower temperature, and ready-flo flows at the lowest temperature. Hard solder contains the most silver and is visually closest in appearance to sterling silver. As the solder alloy is changed to lower its flow temperature, its appearance will change in your work. For example, solder seams will show more in finished work with a lower temperature solder (soft) than with hard solder. This is primarily due to the natural oxidation of the copper or other metals added to the silver. For this reason, the fourth solder, called ready-flo, should be used for soldering findings, the last soldering step before polishing. The following table indicates the melting point and flow point of the relative solders discussed below.

Use solder in decreasing hardness (melting temperature) for successive soldering steps. For example, if you plan three separate solderings, the first will be done with hard which has the highest flow point. The second will be done with medium and the third with soft solder. With successful planning and a little practice you can solder several seams at once to reduce the number of separate soldering steps. Remember that the more often you apply heat to your metal, the more firescale will build up and the harder it will be to do successive solderings.

SOLDER	MELTING POINT	FLOW POINT
Hard	1435° F.	1435° F.
Medium	1335° F.	1390° F.
Soft	1260° F.	1325° F.
Ready-flo	1165° F.	1200° F.

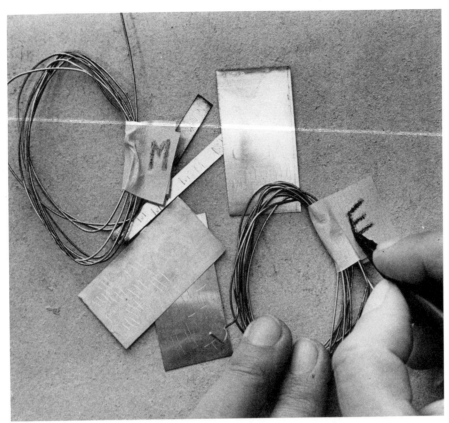

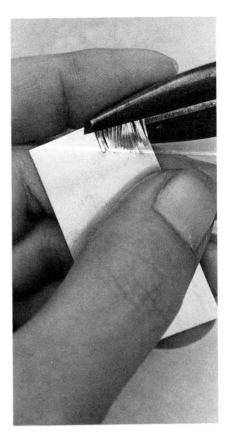

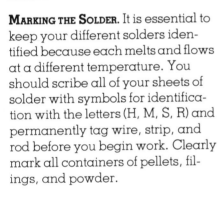

MARKING THE SOLDER. It is essential to keep your different solders identified because each melts and flows at a different temperature. You should scribe all of your sheets of solder with symbols for identification with the letters (H, M, S, R) and permanently tag wire, strip, and rod before you begin work. Clearly mark all containers of pellets, filings, and powder.

PREPARING THE SOLDER. You should cut only as much solder from sheets, rod, or strips as you will need. Polish the solder area you are cutting into snippets on both sides with fine emery cloth. This assures a clean, dirt and grease-free solder. Snip 1/16" or smaller, rectangles. Temporarily drop the snippets into your liquid flux. These may be used in this flat form or they may be balled separately before placing them on your work for soldering.

Balling the squares has definite advantages. Because the process makes the piece of solder smaller, it makes a snugger contact at the solder point. Also, combining solder with flux increases its flow when it is reheated so reduces the amount of time the metal is under heat during the soldering process. Snippets cut from wire solder have the first advantage but not the second. By reducing the number of times you reheat your metal, you also reduce the probability of firescale buildup as well as the possibility of pitting or blemishing the metal surface. This is especially true when working with sterling silver where zinc burnout can happen.

To ball the solder, take snippets, called *paillon*, from the flux with tweezers and place them on a charcoal block. Heat the snippets with a gentle flame until the solder "balls" but does not flow. Use the balls of solder as you would the flat snippets. Both can be kept free of contamination by temporarily leaving them submerged in the flux solution or water.

COMMON SOLDERING PROBLEMS

Sweat soldering, butt joints, angle seams, and soldering wire to sheet present four of the most common problems you will encounter during the soldering processes. During any of these you will need to rely a great deal on your ingenuity plus gravity and jigs. Jigs temporarily hold or support your metal pieces while you solder. These can include your heat tweezers, steel pins used with fine iron binding wire, broken pieces of refractory brick, improvised hoods of heavy binding wire, Nichrome wire or steel cotter pins, or pieces from a broken charcoal block.

Any surface receiving solder must be completely clean and each piece must be tangent to the other. Solder does not fill cracks or spaces left between two pieces of metal. Improvised jigs help support and bind well-fitting pieces of metal, but they cannot press out imperfections in the metal edges or surfaces. The initial cutting and fitting process must be such that a perfect fit is achieved before soldering begins.

It is essential that all joining surfaces be flush. In sweat soldering, both sheets must be flat. In soldering angle seams, all edges must be flush and even with the joining edge or surface. Ends for butt soldering, whether wire or edge-to-edge sheet, must be parallel with no surface waves or irregularities. All wire must continuously contact the sheet surface when soldering wire to sheet. A dip away from one surface, no matter how small, will not solder and will show up on the finished piece of work as an incomplete solder joining. One easy way to check for a good fit is to hold the pieces up to a light. If you see light through any part, it is not properly fitted for soldering.

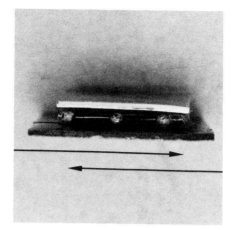

SWEAT SOLDERING. Sweat soldering means joining two pieces of metal together to increase thickness. Sweat soldering could be described as creating a sandwich of sheet metal with solder in between. It should always be done on a smooth, flat, level surface. Gravity, then, becomes your best aid when sweat soldering.

Using a small brush, paint the surface of the top of the sheet metal with flux. Place flat paillon of solder about ⅛" apart around the edge of the fluxed metal with pointed tweezers or a brush. Add additional pieces to the center if the area is large. If there are thin projections to be sweat soldered, place the paillon down the center of the projec-

tions rather than around the edge. If there is too much solder flow, it will run past the edges and make a disagreeable surface on the base sheet. The top piece may also have a tendency to slip out of place during the soldering process. It is best to let the flux dry before assembling the sandwich as that will hold the paillon in place.

The bottom sheet should be resting flat on your charcoal block. Set the top sheet in place once the solder paillon have been positioned. Play the torch heat around the metal on all sides to build up the heat evenly. When the solder paillon melt and flow, the top sheet will drop into place. Immediately remove the heat and quench the soldered unit in water or pickle with your fire tweezers.

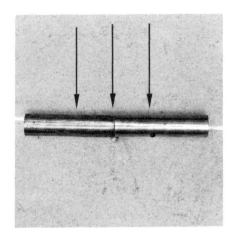

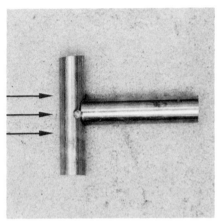

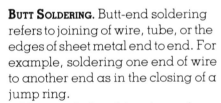

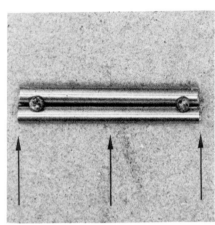

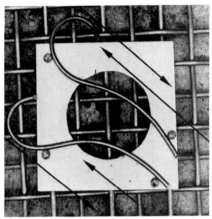

BUTT SOLDERING. Butt-end soldering refers to joining of wire, tube, or the edges of sheet metal end to end. For example, soldering one end of wire to another end as in the closing of a jump ring.

Use very little solder; the surface to be joined is very small. Place the solder ball or paillon on, or as close to, the ends to be joined as possible. Wire heats very rapidly and the solder has a tendency to flow away from the joint over the wire surface rather than into the seam.

Fit one wire end as true as possible to the surface of the other wire end or profile. If you have cut the wire with dics, the cut end will have a slight peak that must be filed flat before butt soldering. Use hard solder whenever possible. It provides a stronger joining and flows less than lower-temperature solder. Little fillets can be seen at butt joints where solder is used.

PARALLEL SOLDERING. You may wish to join several parallel lengths of wire or tubing together side by side. Parallel soldering is best achieved by placing the paillon or solder balls at each end of the wire or tube and drawing it with heat toward the center of the seam. This protects the visual cleanness of the line in the wire or tubing. Occasionally, when solder is overheated before it flows, the paillon create ghosts, a kind of collapsed image where the solder was before the flow. When ghosts appear you should carve them away with the scraper.

As with all wire or very fine soldering, use your torch heat carefully. Tubing will collapse and fuse together if it gets too hot before the solder flows.

SOLDERING WIRE TO SHEET. Both sheet metal and wire conduct heat. Actually, it is the same degree of heat if it is the same metal. However, the wire will conduct and build heat faster because it has a smaller volume and a greater surface in proportion to sheet. The wire can even melt before the solder in extreme cases. It can also slump, puddle or distort during the soldering process. It is best to play the heat over the general sheet area and then over the wire; remove the heat at times and reapply it. Watch the color changes between the wire and the sheet very carefully and be sure the color between the two remains constant. Be especially careful to avoid overheating any wire projections (unsupported wire projecting away from the sheet).

Place solder balls or paillon sparingly along the wire where it rests tangent to the sheet and on the outside of any curves. It is easier to clean excess solder or ghosts from the outside of a curve than from the inside.

  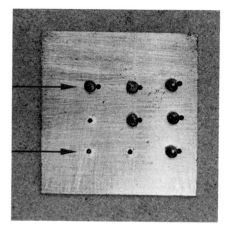

SOLDERING ANGLE SEAMS. While gravity is your primary assist in most soldering processes, soldering a straight metal strip at an angle to another metal sheet requires other forms of assistance. These can be iron binding wire, steel pins, scrap charcoal block, Nichrome wire pins bent to your own design, cross-lock tweezers, or just about any other "third hand" you can improvise. If the strip is bent in some manner it will stand alone. However, your usual construction problem will be trying to hold straight strips of metal in place and on edge. How you brace these two pieces together is really a matter of ingenuity on your part.

The strips must not move during soldering. Also, be very sure that the seam is truly fitted with no irregular edges. Remember that solder will not fill holes or spaces and it only flows evenly along tangent metal edges. It will stop flowing if there is an open space in the seam.

Flux the seam with a small brush. Capillary action should draw the flux along the seam. Do not use too much: liquid flux will boil and cause the solder paillon to move; borax flux causes flux-glass that must be cleaned before going on to the next step. Place the balled solder or paillon along the seam at about ¼" intervals, and make sure that one piece of solder is at each end of the seam.

Pass the torch heat back and forth along the seam on the reverse side from where the solder is placed. This concentrates the heat where the solder should flow and not on other parts of the metal. You can see the solder run along the seam when it flows. It will look like a kind of wet, bright, thin streak. Be sure to draw the solder along the entire length of the seam including the ends.

SOLDERING SHOT. The little beads formed by fusing silver or other metal are called shot. These "B-B" shot, carefully arranged and soldered in place on a surface, can form an interesting relief effect. But, how do you hold them in place during the soldering?

They are very small and have a tendency to melt quickly when overheated or roll around with too much pressure from the torch flame. If they are very small, the paillon of solder can drown them. The illustrated example shows one way of placing solder and shot. In this case, the shot is fluxed. A very small indentation made with the center punch will hold small shot in place. This gives a larger soldered surface in joining and keeps the shot from moving around as a result of the torch flame.

SOLDERING PARALLEL WIRES. The same problem of movement that occurs in shot soldering also occurs when soldering a series of parallel wires to a sheet if they are not tangent to each other. Because wire is usually very lightweight, straight lengths have a tendency to move together when you are soldering one after another. This is not true of bent wire as it has the same stability as bent strips in soldering.

Scribe a straight line or a series of straight lines where the wire lengths are to be soldered. Place and solder one wire at a time. Position the solder as you would when soldering one wire to a sheet, that is, at each end and only on one side of the wire. Always place your solder on the same side of every wire if you are soldering more than one. Because the heat is not as close to the first soldered wire as to the next one, the solder should not flow again on the first. But, if you feel

that there is a danger of this, use some yellow ocher on the previously soldered seam. Be very careful not to get any yellow ocher on any of the other areas to be soldered.

Yellow ocher is an iron oxide powder that is mixed with water to a paste consistency. It is painted over solder seams with a small brush used only for this purpose. Ocher reduces the probability of unsoldering previous work by dirtying the metal surface and preventing solder flow. It does not prevent the solder from melting, however. Yellow ocher should be used very sparingly because it does dirty the metal surface and there is great danger of its contaminating future soldering efforts. Second, it is very stubborn to remove if overheated. Yellow ocher should be washed off completely before continuing any further construction or soldering.

PIC SOLDERING. All soldering should be a quick, careful, and exacting process. The longer the metal is under heat, the more cupric oxides (firescale) will build up and the more difficult the following processes such as finishing will be. Fast heat on very small bits of metal, however, can unintentionally melt everything. Doing smaller soldering jobs takes equally smaller torch flames. Very small units can be successfully soldered suspended in the air.

Clamp the small pieces in your cross-lock tweezers and support this unit steadily on your bench with either a tweezer holder or a makeshift bracing arrangement of broken refractory brick. Jump rings or assembled chain link can be soldered by holding one loop at a time over a hanger made of Nichrome wire that has been anchored to an asbestos or charcoal block. Carry your solder to the seam on the end of a soldering pic when the small metal pieces are equally heated and close to soldering temperature.

Almost all soldering of small units such as findings is done with a low-flow temperature solder. This is because of the rapid heat buildup and the fact that these units are usually the last soldering jobs before finishing begins. If you have the unique situation where other soldering is to follow, you can use yellow ocher with moderation. You should never use any solder that has lead content, even for the sake of needing a low temperature flow point. Lead solder will pit and errode your precious metals.

SOLDERING PIN FINDINGS

There are unique problems with soldering units that hold and fasten such as pin assemblies, earring backs, cufflinks, and tie tacks.

A pin assembly has three parts: the hinge, the stem, and the clasp. The hinge and the clasp are soldered in place and the stem inserted and riveted securely after the pin is completely finished. Their correct placement and other design factors are discussed in the later chapter on findings. Here, we are concerned only with the problems of soldering the two units that must work as one—the clasp and the hinge.

These tiny units tend to draw heat rapidly and thus pull solder into their holes or moving parts rather than around them. The surest way of soldering these findings is to pre-melt ready-flo solder on the pin body back at the exact location for the findings and then reheat the solder with the units in place. Another method is to preheat the solder and, at the moment of flow, set the unit in place using the soldering pic or fine-pointed fire tweezers through the small holes in the hinge unit and the clasp. Be sure that you use enough solder to puddle an area equivalent to the entire base of the findings. These get heavy wear and bear the weight of the entire jewelry piece and so must be well soldered.

Locate the units slightly above the center axis of a horizontal pin design and on the central axis of a vertical pin design. Check to see that the hinge finding has the slot for the pin stem aligned along the axis. A second factor to check is the direction of the clasp. The open position should be toward the bottom of a horizontal pin and ever so slightly lower on the axis than the hinge unit. On a vertical design, the clasp is at the bottom with the opening facing left as you work.

SOLDERING EARRING AND TIE TACK FINDINGS

Use enough soft solder to fill the finding cup when soldering earring backs. As with the pin assembly, always use a small, soft torch flame or the small wire findings will melt along with the solder. A hotter flame will anneal the wire, making it pliable and destroying the spring. Soft solder cools more slowly than harder ones so check to be sure it is set before quenching it in water. All soft soldering should be well washed in soapy water to assure acid removal. The flux usually used with soft solders is a mixture of glycerine and muriatic acid, and any residual of the muriatic acid left on an earring will cause severe burning of the ear lobe.

Tie tack posts are soldered in the same manner as earring findings. Pre-melt the solder on the back of the tie tack and drop the post into place. Hold it with fire tweezers. Always remember that you can not do any further soldering after using soft solder, and always wash any jewelry that uses soft solder to remove the acids. These acids are harmful not only to skin but also to clothing fibers.

FUSING

Fusing is a method of joining metal without the use of solder. It is also the process by which metal beads can be formed, either at the ends of wire or as individual granules. The photo above shows a way of fusing beads on the ends of a group of wires. The torch is held near the end of the wire until it balls, then is moved on to the next end. To form granules, dig out small pits in your charcoal block and place equal-size snippets of metal in each pit. Heat just until the metal balls. These granules can then be soldered on to another metal surface.

To join pieces of metal by fusing, arrange small scraps or shapes of sheet or wire on a flat piece of metal sheet that is resting on a charcoal block. Carefully play the torch over the metal surface until it takes on the appearance of an orange peel with little puddles of melted but not flowing metal. Remove the heat and then put the pieces in pickle. The roughened surface can then be filed, stoned, buffed, or oxidized.

Bridal Crown and Groom's Ornament, Austrian, mid-nineteenth century. Courtesy of the International Folk Art Foundation Collection, Santa Fe, New Mexico. Photo by David Donoho.

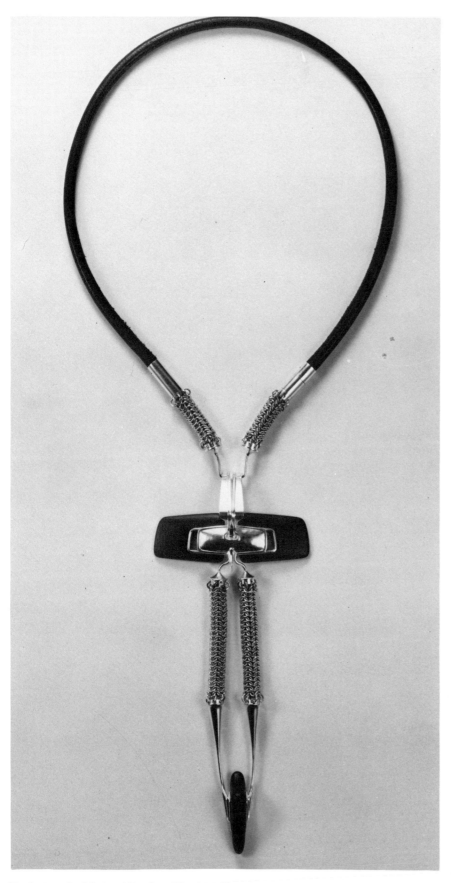

Neckpiece by Michael Pinder. Silver, palisander wood and leather, fabricated. Screw fastening is concealed in the wearer's left-hand end of the leather neckband.

SOLDERING OTHER METALS

All the previous text related to general problem solving in soldering, and it used silver as a norm because of its availability. There are specific and individual techniques that you must solve for yourself when assembling your own jewelry, and you may also find a need for more specific information on soldering specific metals.

For example, the reference to solder flow temperatures relates specifically to silver solder, both in metal content and color. It is compatible with copper in temperature but not in color. Visually this may or may not make a difference in your finished piece depending on whether or not the copper is to eventually be plated.

A guideline in successful silver soldering is the successive changes in the color of the metal as it is heated. However, this color change does not occur when soldering golds and it is not nearly as evident when soldering copper, brass, or bronze. The obvious color differences between the solders and the metals also applies here.

SOLDERING GOLD. All the procedures discussed for soldering silver apply to soldering gold, but the solder itself and some of the metal reactions vary.

In most instances, you will be using karat golds—24K, 18K, and 14K—for your jewelry, and you will need to use karat gold solders. These solders are alloyed so they are visually comparable to karat golds, but they are about 4K lower in purity. Therefore, you will be using 18K solder with 24K metal, 14K solder with 18K metal, etc. It is not essential to know this in order to work successfully with golds, but as a professional goldsmith you have the responsibility of truthfully identifying and hallmarking the specific gold content of your jewelry and this is controlled by law. Every reduction in karat content, including the karat of solder used, is relatively weighted against all other karat content and this total is the true gold

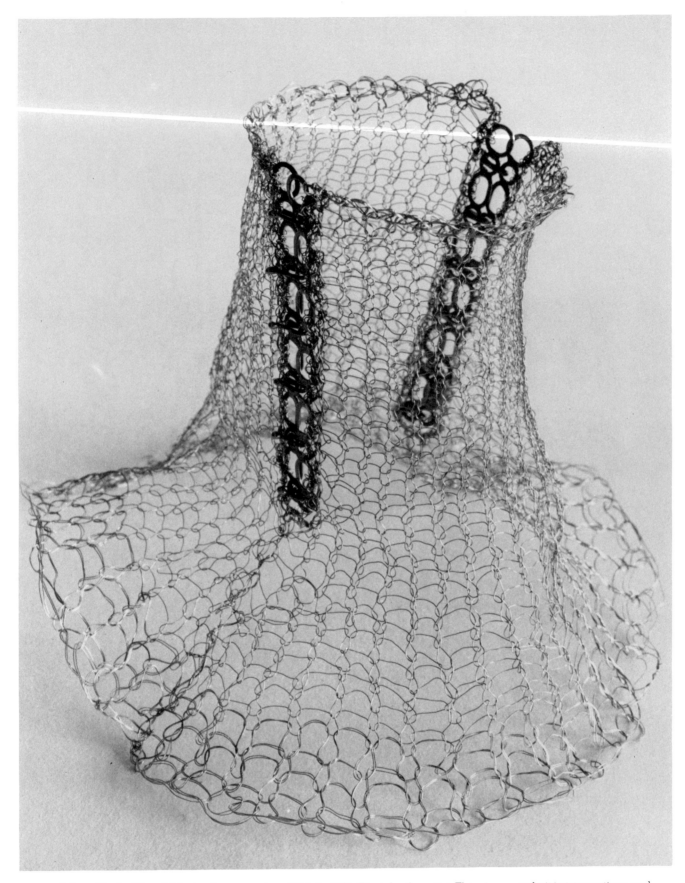

Cuff by Arlene Fisch. 18k gold, knitted construction, 6″ high, 1971. Photo by the artist. This piece was knit in two sections and then joined. Note the doubling of the gold wire at the cuff flair in order to equalize the necessary rigidity between the smaller and larger diameters.

content to be stamped on the jewelry.

The color of gold under heat is not a good indicator when soldering because gold does not change color significantly. Therefore, much greater care should be used when soldering golds. Stop applying heat immediately when solder flows or the metal pieces will collapse with little warning.

Gold solder is slow flowing. It is close to ready-flo silver solder in character, so it will not draw along a seam with the ease of the typical hard silver solders. If there is a great disparity between the sizes of the metal pieces being soldered, wire to sheet for example, a lower karat solder should be used (10K solder on 18K metals for instance).

Gold can be pickled in the same 10% sulphuric acid pickle used for silver. Gold does not develop the same cupric oxides or firescale that silver does. Jewelry made with gold can be given its finishing and polishing surfaces without the interim step of stripping or bright-polishing. Note, too, that quenching is not a necessity when using yellow, white, or green golds. However, red golds harden if air-cooled and should therefore be quenched when hot from soldering. This is important when annealing golds, also. Check the annealing table in the appendix if you have any question of annealing or soldering the various metals and the attending differences between air-cooling and quenching hot metals.

COPPER, BRASS, AND BRONZE SOLDERING. All surfaces of these metals must be clean and free of oxides and grease before soldering. The mechanical techniques of soldering are the same as for silver. The silver solders and flux can be the same, although you may want to use other solders because of the color differences between the metals and these solders. Solders made specifically for these metals are called *spelters* and are sold in rod and wire forms of varying sizes. When spelters are used, the process is called *brazing* and the borax flux, sold in powder form, has a different chemical formula to complement the metals in spelters.

You need to do the same careful fitting of seams for successful brazing as with soldering. Bind the assembly with iron binding wire, if necessary. Use a heavier binding wire than with silver or gold, no less than the gauge of an ordinary steel sewing pin. Apply the borax flux where you want the spelter to solder. Place small pieces or lengths of spelter as you did in silver soldering, holding them in place with the flux. The spelter metal will only solder where there is flux and it does not draw with heat. Spelter metals follow the flux. If you need to add more solder on an incomplete seam, for example, be sure to add flux or it will not join. You can heat the tip of a small length of wire or spelter, dip it into the powdered flux, and draw the tip of it along the seam being soldered. Be sure to remove the iron binding wire before pickling.

Overheating during copper, brass, and bronze soldering causes more problems than it does with either gold or silver. With copper, or any metal with a large copper content, overheating causes heavy and rapid oxidation. Heating must be more rapid and a heavier flux coat applied than with silver or gold. Slow, long heating will exhaust the flux and cause the solder to freeze rather than melt and flow. Overheating can also burn out the zinc content of the spelter and cause a rough, pitted surface.

When in doubt about which solder or spelter to use in soldering various metals together when there is more than one soldering sequence, refer to the comparative temperature table on the flow temperatures of metals and of solders. Do sequential soldering with consecutively lower temperature metals and solder. Do not reverse the process at any time or previous soldering may fall and the metal pieces, themselves, may collapse.

Pendant by J. Fred Woell. Copper, brass, steel, glass, silver.

FERROUS METALS. Special spelters are available for soldering ferrous metals that can be used with a borax-based flux. Brass wire can also be used, although again the color is off and the joint is weak. Do not use either the sulphuric or nitric acid baths with ferrous metals as there is a strong, toxic gaseous reaction. Wash the flux residue off with warm water.

SOLDERING ALUMINUM. Specific solders have now been developed along with a special stearin flux for use with aluminum, so this material is now becoming attractive for the studio jeweler. Presently, however these are only available at the metal supply houses selling aluminum, not at jewelry suppliers. Aluminum has a much lower melting point than any of the previously discussed metals and greater care must be used when brazing or soft soldering. There are specialized soldering irons using ultrasonic waves developed specifically for soldering and welding aluminum. The major problem with aluminum is the rapid surface oxidation that takes place under heat and prevents easy soldering. Also, you can not solder, braze, or weld aluminum to any other metal.

Using any spelter for soldering results in a crude solder seam because the solder tends to lie on the surface rather than flowing between the metal pieces. The delicate and precise work usually associated with fine jewelry construction is therefore not possible with spelter. When it is used, the design must take into consideration the brazing effect of piled solder at the seams and the artist must plan accordingly.

For all successful soldering including brazing be sure that the component parts are well fitted, that they are free of contamination, that the joints are fluxed, that the solder paillon are in place, and that the torch heat is properly adjusted.

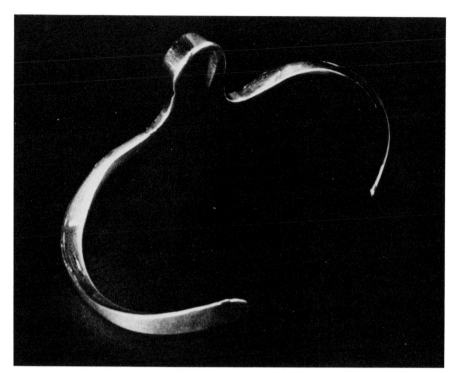

Bracelet by Tom Thomason. Sterling wire, forged. Photo by David Donoho.

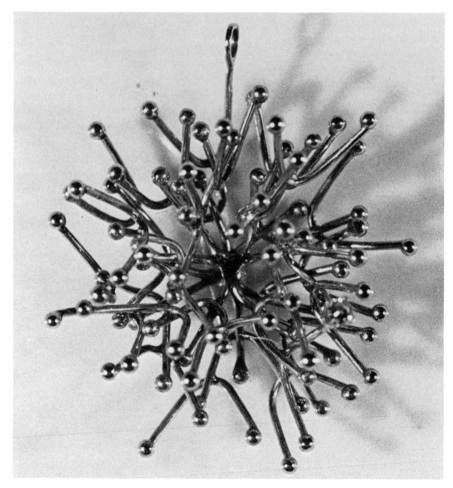

Pendant by Merry Renk. 2″ diameter, white gold and diamond, fused tips and fabricated.

Necklace by Mary Ann Scherr. Brass, copper, steel and sterling wire, tiger eye stratta stone, silver.

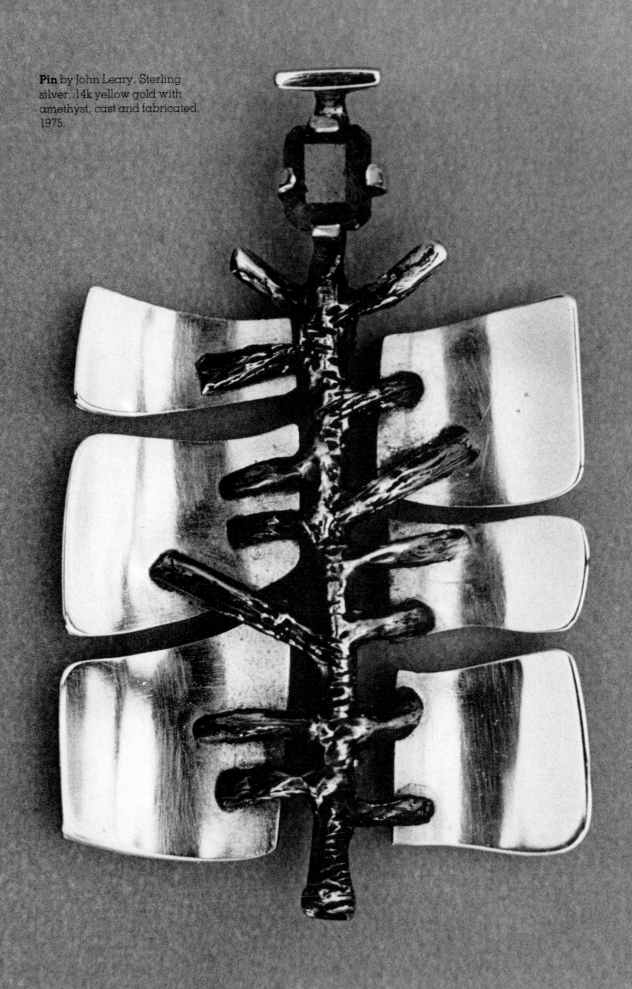

Pin by John Leary. Sterling
silver, 14k yellow gold with
amethyst, cast and fabricated,
1975.

5 CASTING

Casting in jeweler's terms means pouring molten metal into a mold. Historically, the mold material has been baked clay, porous stone, sand, or soft bone, and the metals have been numerous. Most casting prior to the twentieth century and the advent of centrifugal casting used the force of gravity to pull the metal into the mold. Now, centrifugal casting is the most basic production technique used for commercial costume jewelry. It also intrigues the studio artist.

The void in the mold material is formed in several ways: by directly carving the pattern into porous stone; by pressing a hard, previously carved or shaped pattern into a softer bone material, by packing fine sand around a hard shape and temporarily containing the sand with a rigid frame, or by making a master form from wax, surrounding it with clay, then melting the wax out of the clay which creates a void.

The master pattern in casting is usually made of a hard, smooth-surfaced material such as wood or metal. It is made of wax for the lost wax process (cire perdue). There are literally hundreds of waxes available on the market but not all are suitable for jewelry production. The pattern is always removed before the pour regardless of its material.

Three methods of casting are demonstrated in this chapter: grav-ity, steam, and centrifugal. In the gravity casting section, the artists use molds made from tufa stone, cuttlebone, and sand.

PREPARING THE MOLD

Every mold used for casting metals has certain basic components. The mold can be in one piece or have several parts that are carefully fitted together. Molds with several parts often have keys set or cut into them to assure the careful matching of sections.

The mold also has an opening depression into which the molten metal is poured. This is called a *sprue*. The sprue can be hand-carved. It can also be made by packing or pouring the mold material around a sprue former. The sprue former and pattern are removed from the matrix before casting. Sprues and sprue formers are conical in shape with the exception of the dome-shaped one used for steam casting.

On very simple, small forms the sprue distributes the metal adequately into the interior void of the mold. If the casting is complex in form, however, gates are added. These gates branch off from the interior end of the sprue, are smaller in diameter than the sprue, and are attached to the pattern in places where flowing metal might be trapped before a casting is complete. Gates are used most often in centrifugal casting and on larger gravity-cast sculpture.

When hot metal hits the mold material it releases steam and gases in the mold. If these gases cannot escape from the interior chamber the mold will crack, break, or explode from the pressure. They will also push back against the flowing metal and prevent a perfect cast. To allow for the release of these gases, you must also make vents in all casting molds.

MELTING THE METALS

Metals for casting can be melted directly in a crucible or melted separately in a furnace and then poured into a crucible before emptying into the mold. Furnace melting is generally related to rapid and repetitive mass production. In our demonstrations the metal is melted directly in the casting crucible. This technique is suitable for any metal with a melting point not exceeding 2500°F.

Ceramic crucibles are made of various materials. Fused silica and clay bond crucibles have a higher thermal shock range so there is less chance of their cracking under direct heat. These are best for melting silver, gold, bronze, and other alloys such as pewter and white metal. Crucibles with a high carbon, graphite, or silica-carbide content are best used with platinum or palladium. They have a low thermal shock resistance and are not suitable for use with metals in the lower melting range.

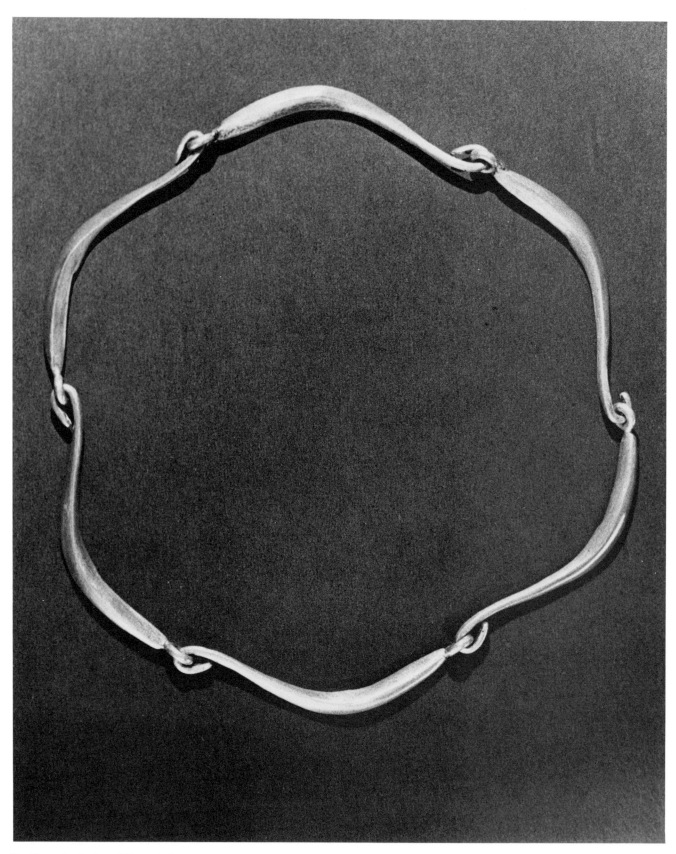

Necklace by Richard Gompf. Sand-cast sterling silver for limited production.

Adjusting the Torch. Control of the torch flame is very important when melting metals for casting. Too much oxygen in the flame will produce a porous and rough casting so the flame needs to be hot, but it should be a reducing flame. A good reducing flame from an air-gas unit has a blue-green inner cone and a bright blue outer flame. If you have an oxygen-gas unit, the reducing flame will have three distinct colors: a blue-green inner cone, a yellow-green center area, and a blue-red outer tip.

GRAVITY CASTING

Gravity casting can be done with any porous mold material. Because gravity is the only force drawing the molten metal into the mold, the design to be cast should be relatively simple with few details. Gravity casting takes a minimum of equipment. The enriched surface of the casting material gives tufa, sand, and other gravity-cast pieces their honest and direct integrity of design. Tufa channel casting is one method of gravity casting where the jewelry form is carved directly into the mold material.

TUFA CHANNEL CASTING

Tufa stone is a soft, lightweight, porous rock indigenous to the Southwest. Quarried by the American indians, tufa has served for more than a century as a readily available mold material for the Navajos. Their designs, usually cut as a "V" into the soft surface, give this type of work further designation as "channel" casting. The casting is done exclusively by pouring molten metal directly into the tufa mold with no force other than gravity to carry the metal.

Tom Thomason, who demonstrates here, started his career as a professional jeweler using tufa as a casting material. Tufa is readily available in the Southwest but may be more difficult to purchase in other geographical areas. A substitute can be mixed by using casting or investment plaster (a finely ground plaster) with a powdered refractory material, such as powdered pumice, to relieve its density. Using three parts plaster to one part refractory material and mix them with water to the consistency of heavy buttermilk. Pour it into a shoe box lid to set it in a slab. After setting it can be used in the same manner as tufa. Allow the plaster slab to dry completely (warm to the touch on your cheek) before casting or the mold will crack or explode when the hot metal hits it. This type of mixture will result in a smoother cast surface on your work than is characteristic of the natural material.

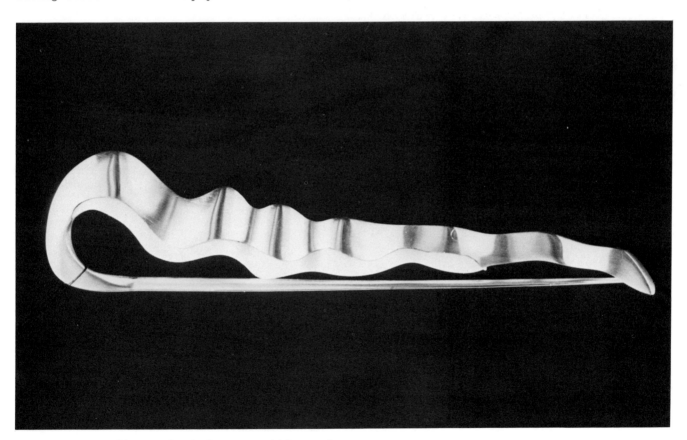

Brooch by Nadene Wegner. Cast by lost wax and fabricated.

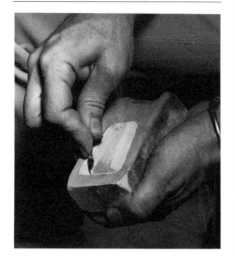

STEP 1. File the surface of two tufa slabs flat using a coarse metal file. After filing, rub the two faces together to get a close-fitting, smooth join between the two. Carve the form and design you want for the front of your jewelry piece into the smooth face of one of the blocks with a sharp knife. The back of the work is usually flat and is formed by the smoothed surface of the second block. Designs can be carved into the second block, but great care needs to be taken when putting the two mold parts together or the design will not register correctly.

STEP 2. You must always have two types of openings carved into the tufa from the design to the outside of the block. The first, called a sprue, is larger and is the opening into which you will pour the molten metal. The second type, called vents, are smaller and allow steam or gases to escape.

Carve away a funnel-shaped channel from the top of your design to the outside edge of the block. This piece of metal is usually cut away in later finishing processes. In traditional Navajo castings, however, part of the sprue is finished and drilled to form a rounded bead.

Choose the largest part of your design as the top of your casting. This is not necessarily the actual top of the finished piece. The molten metal should fall into the smaller parts of your carved design first and gradually fill the design mold with the heavier parts cast last.

Scratch or carve away a number of smaller vents. Note in the illustration that these vents lead away from the design, then join a single vent that leads to the top of the mold. Vents should not lead to either the sides or the bottom or the metal will follow them and cut off the venting process.

STEP 3. Bind the two slabs together with heavy iron binding wire, checking to see that the sprue forms cut into each side match and that all surfaces are flush. As shown above, the surface of the cut design can be smoked with your torch before binding to add a carbon surface.

STEP 4. Set the mold upright with the sprue opening facing up and easily accessible for you to pour the metal into it. Be sure the mold is steady and that it will not fall over when you do the pour. Clean and flux the metal before you start heating it. Then melt the metal in a ceramic crucible with your torch.

STEP 5. When the metal is molten, pour it slowly and carefully into the sprue opening, keeping the torch heat on it until the metal flows to the top of the sprue. Remove the heat and stop the pour.

STEP 6. In a moment or two, (timing depends on the metal used) the casting will set and you can remove it from the mold. Use tongs and asbestos gloves to handle the hot mold and casting. Cut the iron binding wire from around the mold and remove the metal casting.

STEP 7. Let the casting air-cool. Saw or snip off the vents and sprue, saving them to melt down for subsequent castings. Your casting is now ready to process further. In the photo above Tom is adding a bezel for a stone setting and catch rings for the neck wire.

STEP 8. The completed neckpiece shows the unique characteristic of tufa casting on the surface of the pendant. Tom has enhanced the intrinsic, textured surface by polishing the raised portion of his design and by adding a semi-precious stone for color. It is reminiscent of the Southwest landscape that is the origin of both the process and the designer.

CUTTLEBONE CASTING

Limited in size by both its thickness and width, cuttlebone is used as a mold only for small jewelry work. Cuttlebone is easily recognized as the white bone used for pet birds to sharpen their bills and provide them with lime. It is a soft material, so the pattern is simply pressed into the prepared cuttlebone to form the shape to be reproduced. All of the requisite and elementary casting processes are the same in cuttlebone as in tufa casting, for example, the mold is two-piece and you will need both a sprue and vents. Initial preparation of the mold material is different and the pour of metal can be different.

For cuttlebone casting you will need a piece of cuttlebone, medium sandpaper, your jeweler's saw and torch, a pattern made from a hard material (not casting wax), three small, pointed wooden pegs, a coarse file, iron binding wire, a knife, borax flux, water glass (silicate of soda) in a 50% solution, a piece of charcoal block, and fire tongs.

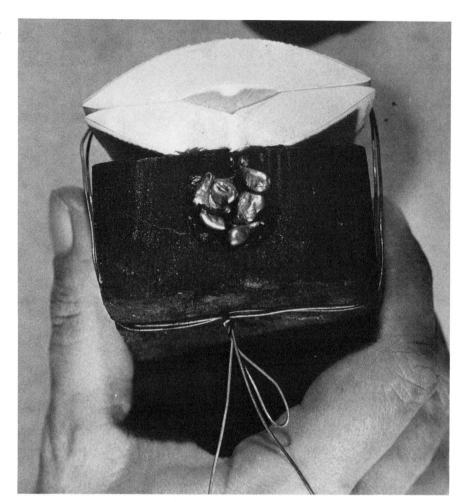

PREPARING THE MOLD. Saw your cuttlebone into two equal parts. Sand the softer side of each section until the faces are flat and flush with each other. Holding the two pieces together, sand the smaller top surface smooth. Then, flatten the outer surface of one of the halves at the thick top end with a file. Press three small, sharpened wooden pegs into one sanded face of the bone mold.

Press your pattern a little way into the second half of the mold face. Place the first mold half over the second and press them firmly together. This will force both the wooden pegs and the pattern into both surfaces of the soft bone material. The two faces should meet. With the mold closed in this manner, file the outer edges so they match. Open the mold and remove the pattern.

Carefully carve the sprue and small vents into one of the bone pieces as described in Step 2 of Tufa Channel Casting. Again, be sure that the vents do not lead all the way to the outside of the mold or the metal will run out during the cast.

Paint the interior of the mold with borax flux. Let it sink in and then paint a coat of water glass over the same surface. Use a 50% solution of half water and half silicate of soda. These two coats help toughen the mold surface. When both coats have sunk into the bone material, oil your original pattern slightly, return it carefully to the mold, and close it. Press the halves together firmly. This will assure a sharp mold surface for your casting. Remove the pattern and bind the two halves together with iron binding wire. Let the mold dry sufficiently to ensure that all moisture has evaporated before casting.

Carve a hollow into a piece of charcoal block large enough to hold the metal you are going to cast. Bind this charcoal block to the flattened outer side of the bone mold. Check that the top surface of both the mold and the block are level and flush. Cut a small channel or gate between the sprue in the mold and the hollow in the charcoal. You are now ready to cast.

Place your small metal pieces in the charcoal hollow and heat until they are molten or the brightness disappears. Hold the combined unit with fire tongs and tilt it, allowing the metal to run into the mold. As soon as the metal is set, cut the binding wires and recover the cast form from the disassembled mold.

SAND CASTING

Two major rules for successful sand casting are that there can be no undercuts in the pattern to be cast, and that the pattern should have a smooth, slippery, or polished surface.

The pattern will be embedded in packed and treated sand that is held in place with a two-piece mold or form. One side of the mold is called the *cope* and the other side is called the *drag*. These forms can be purchased or you can make your own. The drag has pegs and the cope has corresponding holes so the two halves will fit together perfectly. Generally, the pattern will be set halfway into the cope and halfway into the drag. From the parting line—the line between the cope and the drag—the pattern should taper inward, not outward. Remember, no undercuts.

The pattern will be removed from the sand before the metal is poured into the void. A pattern with a smooth, polished surface can be drawn from the sand more easily and lessens the chances of breaking the sand form and subsequent repairs.

Patterns can be made of any material that can be given a smooth, hard surface. Wood coated with shellac or smoothed plaster both work well. Be sure to steel wool them before packing in the sand. In the demonstration that follows, artist Richard Gompf uses sculptor's wax. The wax is frozen and then dusted with superfine graphite. The graphite makes the otherwise sticky wax very slippery. A mixture of one-half beeswax and one-half paraffin can be used in the same manner. The wax pattern is, however, more fragile and requires gentle handling.

Make your patterns at least 10% larger than the finished size desired. There is general shrinkage in any cast piece, and this is especially important to compensate for in ring shanks or any part of jewelry where tolerance is minimal.

The special materials needed for sand casting include a two-piece form or mold and fine casting sand (available from metal foundries). For heavier textured castings use river or beach sand. In addition, you need a parting powder (French chalk or superfine graphite) and a soft brush, a fine-screen sieve, a spatula, a C-clamp, two pieces of scrap wooden board, and the usual fire tongs, torch, and crucible.

Sand, other than prepared foundry sand, should be wet with glycerine, water, or oil to increase its packing capacity. If oil, water or glycerine is added, ram the sand, press the pattern, and remove it. Then allow the mold to dry before casting.

Richard Gompf has used sand casting as his major production technique for most of his professional life. It is well suited to strong, simple, elegant forms that emphasize the material's smooth reflective surfaces. The technique can also be used for limited repeat production as the pattern is permanent and therefore reusable.

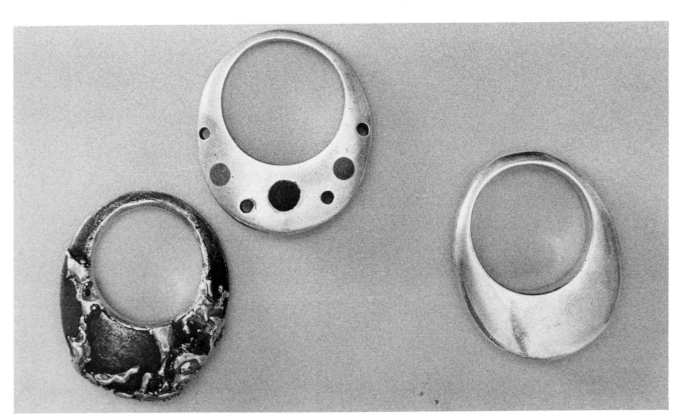

Ring Series by Richard Gompf. Sand-cast with epoxy and brass variations for limited production.

STEP 1. Place the cope—the side of the form without pegs—on a smooth working surface and sprinkle handfuls of sand into the form. Press or ram down the sand until it is packed tightly and the form is about half full. Ram sand in the drag in the same manner.

STEP 2. Set your sieve over the cope and drag and sift more sand into the molds. Then, remove the sieve and ram the loose sand down firmly. Repeat until the cope and drag are completely filled with hard-packed sand. Smooth the inside casting surface by shaving across the surface with the edge of a spatula. Sieving the sand in this manner is called *riddling*.

STEP 3. Place the open mold on the work surface, and dust both flat surfaces with superfine graphite. Either parting powder or French chalk is also used by many craftsmen. Both can be applied with a soft bristle brush.

STEP 4. Press the pattern halfway into the sand in the cope. Place it about an inch below the sprue opening. Some sand forms do not have a sprue opening built into them. If this is the case you will need to cut the sprue and a gate into the sand as a later step. Do not wiggle the pattern. Press it straight down firmly into the sand.

STEP 5. Close the form by setting the packed drag exactly on top of the cope with the pattern still in place. The peg keys will help assure an exact fit between the two pieces.

STEP 6. Ram the two pieces—the cope and drag—together until the frames touch. This will press the other half of the pattern into the drag's sand.

STEP 7. While the two halves are pressed together and the pattern is inside, shave the outer sand surfaces flat in the same way as the inner surfaces in Step 2.

STEP 8. Open the mold halves and carefully remove the pattern. Well-rammed sand will produce a smooth, perfect casting surface. The parting powder will have covered the separate surfaces so the sand will not adhere to the pattern or break away from the mold. If there is a broken area, gently press it back into place and dust with additional powder.

STEP 9. There is generally no need for vents when you use sand because it is so porous. When the pattern is complex, however, it is always safer to add vents. They can be gently scratched or pressed into the sand.

STEP 10. With the pattern removed, place the cope and drag together and clamp a flat piece of wood on either side of the mold. The hot metal will break out the sand if this precaution is not followed.

STEP 11. Stand the clamped mold upright with the sprue opening on top. When the metal is melted, pour it from the crucible into the sprue. Keep the torch heat continually on the metal in the crucible during the pour. Pour slowly but constantly.

STEP 12. Here the casting has been removed from the sand after it has set. Use fire tweezers to remove the piece as the casting will be warm for some time. The metal can be quenched in pickle immediately after removing from the sand. The casting sand is reusable but should be sieved to remove odd bits of metal and other possible contamination.

CORE CASTING. To sand cast a ring you will need to make a sand core within the mold to complete the form before casting. Prepare the flask in the same manner as you did in Step 1 of sand casting using only the cope. When the cope is half filled and rammed, place a 1½" long dowel the diameter of the ring size carefully on the sand about an inch below the sprue opening. (See the Appendix for corresponding measurements, remembering that there is a 10% shrinkage for cast metals.) Riddle and ram the sand firmly around and into the cope until it is filled. Shave the surface flat with the dowel in place.

Remove the dowel, place the ring pattern on the dowel, and reset it into the sand of the cope. The shank should be down and the ring crown out of the sand. Push the shank pattern on the dowel into the sand surface to make a cavity the size of half the ring to be cast. Dust the entire face of the sand including the pattern and dowel with parting powder.

Mate the drag with the cope. Riddle sand and ram the drag until it is filled. Then do Steps 7, 8, and 9 from the first demonstration.

You now need to make a sand core to replace the area previously occupied by the dowel. Use a short piece of tubing with the same inside diameter as the dowel's outside diameter. Ram the tube with sand until you have a length equal to the dowel used originally (approximately 1½"). Push the sand core out of the tube and use this to replace

the dowel in the sand mold. Place it (without the ring pattern) into the sand depression left by the dowel. You will see it bridge the ring cavity, closing both sides to complete the mold. Continue with the remaining steps for sand-casting.

If your casting flask is one that does not have a sprue opening, you will need to carve one with a thin knife into the drag sand. Instead of fine vents, you can also cut a riser (one larger vent) into the drag. Carve a funnel-shaped basin into the outer face of the drag sand and a sprue through the sand to the parting line. Carve the gate at right

angles and along the parting line directly to the casting cavity. Cut the riser, remembering that all vents are smaller than sprues, directly away from the casting cavity and immediately to the outside of the mold. Both the pouring basin for the sprue and the riser exit are on the surface of the drag. This means, of course, that you cannot clamp boards on either side of the flask but must pour your molten metal directly into the sand. The sand mold should rest flat on an asbestos sheet during the pour.

LOST WAX CASTING

Mold preparation is the same for either steam or centrifugal casting. In both instances, the mold material made of casting or investment plaster surrounds the wax pattern. The investment plaster is contained by a round metal flask. When the wax pattern is burned out of the plaster mold, an energy force—either steam or centrifugal—pushes the melted metal into the void. To develop the steam, a plunger is used; centrifugal force is developed by a motorized unit.

WAXES FOR CASTING. First and foremost, working with waxes has nothing to do with working directly with metals. They are two very different materials. However, the wax you use for jewelry patterns will be translated into metal, so you must always keep in mind the eventual metal effect.

In the casting techniques previously discussed, the mold material has imparted a distinct surface character to the metal, which in turn is deliberately used by the artist for visual design enrichment. Unlike tufa and sand, wax and investment plaster are both very finely textured. There will be little distinct surface character on the cast metal surface.

The waxes are plastic in nature, and are much softer and easier to bend, distort, melt, and drip. They do not have the resistant soul of metal. Investment plaster can take on an equally plastic form, thus reinforcing the ease of this process. Think of the enviable possibilities of being able to cast a bug without thinking of how it should look from an artist's viewpoint. But then, who is in charge: the artist or the bug?

THE ARTIST IN CHARGE OF THE WAX. There are hundreds of waxes on the market today that are derived from organic sources (insects and plants), petroleum, or plastic resins. Many of these are too specialized, are not readily available, or have a character that is not advisable for use in jewelry. In each of the three general categories, however, there are waxes that the jeweler can use for making a pattern for casting.

Jewelers' waxes have several qualities that must be considered when making a pattern. First is the maximum expansion temperature. You must know this tolerance to fit a ring or set a stone. At what temperature does the wax soften and melt? Hard or high-melting waxes should not be worked on top of soft or low-temperature waxes, and low-temperature waxes give the smoothest and best surface. You should also know its flash tempeature. The ideal wax has a low melting point and a high flash temperature. Ash from the wax, which occurs as a part of the burnout process, should convert at about 1300°F. Any ash left in the casting cavity can cause an imperfect casting. Waxes high in paraffin content have an excessively heavy carbon residue and should be avoided.

Does your wax "marry" with other waxes? Does it have "memory?" Many plastic waxes will not join or marry with either organic or other plastics that are not in their immediate family.

Other general considerations in using waxes are: Does the wax bend? Does it bend with or without heat? Can it be carved, filed, and sanded away? Will you drip it, which is an additive or building process, or will you cut, carve, and file the wax away to achieve your form?

You can purchase wax as both sheet and wire and, with certain limits, stick and bar forms. The latter are multi-purpose varieties and are made in different colors. The colors can help remind the wax worker of the individual characteristics of the individual waxes.

These jeweler's waxes have taken on the names of either the manufacturer or the originator of the wax formula as part of their identification. Bob Winston, a jeweler who now prefers to work waxes for production rather than constructing from metals, lists his wax preferences as: Corning pink sheet wax, Corning green wire wax, Peck's purple stick or bar wax, red Sierra wax, and workshop sculptor's wax.

Ring by Michael Lacktman. 14k gold with lapis lazuli balls.

MAKING A WAX PATTERN. You will need a selection of waxes, small steel modeling tools (some are dentists tools), a heat source (shown above is an alcohol lamp), your small files, and a waxing mandrel or stick if you are making a ring. The waxing stick is different from the forging mandrel. It is lighter in weight because it is hollow and it usually has a wooden handle. It has ring sizes marked on it in the same way as the forging mandrel.

The author is indebted to Theresa Baronowski, owner of San Francisco Casting Company, for the following points to consider in making wax patterns.

The best heat source for wax is a methanol alcohol fueled lamp. Carbons will be your greatest enemy in working and casting waxes so you should not use a lighted candle or any other source that produces hard carbons.

Establish a separate working area for using wax. It is too messy to be done at your design area and, if it is done at the workbench, metal filings can contaminate the wax and result in an imperfectly cast mold. Investment plaster can also be contaminated and explode during casting.

To build a wax form, drip the heated wax stick directly on to a cool surface or use a heated steel tool to feed the wax. Develop a more or less constant thickness in the form. An exaggerated variance from thick to thin can cause porosity in the cast surface because of stress from the uneven cooling of the metal. Remember, too, that there is shrinkage in the metal form as well as in the over-all form. For example, ring shanks become thinner as well as the ring becoming smaller in diameter, and prongs for stone settings may become too thin to complete a setting.

Even commercially produced carving slabs can contain air bubbles. These bubbles can fill with investment if left on the surface. If in the interior of the wax, they can fill with gas and explode during the burnout. When using carving waxes, be sure to check for air bubbles by holding your model up to the light. These bubbles must be eliminated or avoided.

The surface of a completed wax model should be as perfect as you want the completed casting. Every hump, bump, and fingerprint will reproduce in the casting. Waxes can be given the smoothest surface by passing the model through the heat. If the wax is soft and you think this will melt it, the surface can be smoothed with a heated modeling tool. On harder waxes, use a 220-grit sandpaper (or finer) and then pass the model quickly through the heat. All finished and tolerance measurements, such as ring sizes and stone mounts, should be measured when the waxes are cold. (You can keep waxes in the refrigerator.)

SPRUING. Every individual model in wax will be unique, and therefore the same is true of the spruing. Consequently, only the most general suggestions on how to sprue can be covered here.

Let us say your wax model is complete. Now you will need a sprue former and a round flask (both shown above), wax wires of at least 14-gauge or heavier, and thin asbestos sheeting. The sprue former, conical in shape and made of hard rubber, has several ridges on the base that correspond to the various inside diameters of the round flasks. The flask is usually of reusable stainless steel pipe but it can also be a tin can that is thrown away after a cast. The heavy wax wires will be used to make additional sprues.

Choose a flask that is the right size for your wax model. The distance between the inside wall of the flask and the surface of your wax model should not be more than ½" or less than ¼". This means that when the flask is placed over the model mounted on the sprue former, there should be no more than ½" and no less than ¼" between the top edge of the flask and the wax surface inside. If you use a tin can, you must have the ½" distance at all times.

You can cast several small jewelry waxes at once by using a larger flask and making a "tree" containing several waxes. Such a tree is prepared for casting in the same manner as a single wax. The individual wax models are mounted on a long main sprue at approximately a 45° angle. The models are tipped toward the top of the flask, away from the sprue former and base.

Your major concern in spruing is to get the hot metal from one point (the crucible) to another (the cavity) as rapidly as possible. When in doubt you should over-sprue. Here are some other check points to consider before pouring your investment.

1. Attach the main sprue of at least 14-gauge wax wire to the heaviest part of your model. Take into consideration that the sprue is either removed later or partially incorporated into the finished design.

2. Attach sprues to ring shanks at the bottom rather than to the top or crown.

3. Use the shortest spruing distance possible and widen the wax wire slightly where it attaches to the sprue base.

4. Tilt flat models on the main sprue rather than having them parallel to the base. The investment tends to collect air bubbles on flat surfaces and tilting will help reduce this possibility.

5. Crude, bulbous sprue attachments can produce porosity in your casting. Refine your sprue attachments for a smooth flow of metal.

6. Never place a sprue where it cannot be easily removed from the casting after the pour.

7. No part of the model should be below the point where the main sprue joins the model. A supplementary sprue could be added to feed molten metal directly from the sprue basin, but it would be better to re-plan the sprue system.

8. To assure an ample feed of the hot metal into the cavity of large or thick castings, add a button or shrink ball (an enlarged area in the sprue) on the main sprue between the wax model and the sprue base. It should be located not more than 1/8" below the model but not closer than 1/16". Generally, the larger the button, the better the cast. The button should not exceed twice the thickness of the main sprue.

9. The metals you cast will influence the degree to which you sprue. Generally, the longer a metal holds the heat, the fewer sprues are necessary. For example, casting with gold requires less spruing than bronze and bronze less than silver.

10. Whenever possible, attach sprues at the edge of a form rather than at the center of a flat area. The difference in metal volume between the larger flat area and the thin sprue can produce porosity in the casting.

Once the model with its spruing is complete and very smooth, clean it with a soft brush under cold water. You are now ready to treat the wax surface with debubblizer.

DEBUBBLIZING. There are surface tensions on the wax that interfere with the investment's holding firmly to it. To release these tensions you should paint on a debubblizer, either commercially prepared or mixed from equal parts of green soap and hydrogen peroxide. Completely submerge the model several times, or flow on the solution with a soft brush so bubbles do not form from the peroxide. You do not need to paint the sprues. Gently blow the model dry. A thin film of debubblizer should remain over the entire wax surface.

INVESTING THE WAX. Investment powder is an specially prepared compound called cristobalite that is similar in nature to plaster of paris. Because of the exacting demands of the dental industry, it has been carefully tested by the various manufacturers for minimum expansion and maximum strength in casting. Follow the manufacturer's recommended measurements very carefully in mixing investment with water. Jewelry supply houses have a flexible rubber bowl for this purpose that is easily cleaned, but investment can be mixed in any clean bowl.

Mix the investment to the consistency of heavy cream. Do not agitate the investment during this mixing as this will increase the possibility of bubbles. After mixing, gently bounce the bowl and its contents to bring any bubbles to the surface. Using a soft brush, flow the investment over the entire wax surface. Make sure that you do not create bubbles and that all surfaces are completely covered. The layer of investment should be ⅛" to ¼"

thick. Do not allow this layer to set before assembling the flask and completing the final investment pour. However, if you're using a sprue base that does not have a collar corresponding to the diameter of your flask, you should prepare the flask and then add the layer of investment. You have approximately 9 minutes to do the complete investment process as described next.

PREPARING THE FLASK. An optional step in preparing your flask is to cut a strip of thin asbestos long enough to line the inside of the flask. The strip of asbestos makes it easier to remove the investment after the cast. Moisten the strip with water and press it on the inside around the flask. Do not use too much water as it will dilute and weaken the investment: It should be only enough to stick the asbestos against the side, forming a wide "belt" around the flask. You should definitely use the asbestos if you are substituting a tin can for the flask.

Assemble the sprue base and lined flask. There are at least two types of hard rubber sprue bases. One type has graduated rings and the other has a rubber collar. The latter is self-sealing because the collar fits very tightly against the outside of the flask. The first type of sprue base is not leakproof and must be sealed with plasticene (an oil-clay mixture). Make a coil of plasticene and press it firmly around the flask base where it joins the sprue former. If the sprue former is too small for any of your flasks, temporarily attach it to a flat glass sheet with sticky wax, center the flask over the sprued pattern, and seal it with the plasticene. Whichever sprue base you use, be sure there will be no leakage when the investment is poured.

POURING THE INVESTMENT. Cristobalite, as discussed earlier, develops small bubbles as it is mixed and sets. You must reduce the potential of adding more bubbles not only during the mixture but also during the pour of the investment.

The investment must fill the flask completely to the top. You can place a paper collar around the top edge of the flask to keep the overflow in place. Remove the collar after the investment is set but not hard.

Pour the creamy investment down the side of the flask, filling it slowly from bottom to top. Tap the flask with your finger to bring any bubbles to the top. When it is set— about 15 minutes—remove the paper collar and cut away the excess investment so it is flush with the top of the flask. Use a sharp knife or hacksaw blade. The investment is soft at this time even though it is set.

BURN OUT. This wax process is referred to as "lost wax," and what the term is really saying is that the wax is wasted or lost and cannot be reused. The burnout is the removal of the wax pattern from the investment. You will need an electric or gas burnout kiln. Gas is better for production, but a small electric kiln is easier for the small studio workshop. You will also need small ceramic or Nichrome trivets to support the casting flask in the kiln during the burnout.

Let the investment dry for 24 hours or more, depending on the size of the flask. The burnout time will also vary but it generally takes 4 to 5 hours for single casting. The heat for the burnout should not exceed 1300°F. or the investment will break down, so your kiln should have a pyrometer. Small dental units only take 30 minutes to an hour, but burnout must be controlled by time and sight, a difficult procedure.

Start with a cold kiln. Place the casting flask mouth down on the trivets on the floor of the kiln. The wax will run out on to the floor during firing at lower temperatures and "flash" or burn at the higher ones. Heat the kiln to about 212°F. during the first hour, and 212°F. to 600°F. for the next two hours. Open the kiln. Using fire tongs, turn the flask over so the opening is up, replace it on the trivets, and close the kiln. Over the next two hours, raise the temperature to 1250°F. and hold this temperature for at least a half hour. Do not allow the kiln heat to exceed 1300°F. at any time as this will tend to break down the investment and result in a poor-quality casting.

The burnout and the casting process should take place in one continuous operation because reheating the flask also tends to break down the investment. You cast in a hot flask whether you use steam or centrifugal casting. For centrifugal casting, the flask temperature is directly related to the type of casting machine (spring-wind or electric)

Belt Buckle by Merry Renk. Centrifugal cast in sterling silver, 1974. The form was made by dipping cotton material into hot wax and then modeled. The fabric burned out as well as the wax during the burnout.

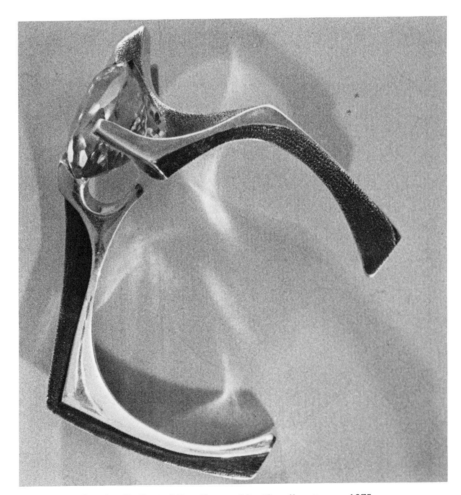

Bracelet by Cynthia Balloni. 14k yellow gold with yellow topaz, 1975.

and this affects the speed of the casting, the characteristics of the metal used, the fineness of your individual design, and the model size. The flask temperature is adjusted through experience rather than any rule. However, silver and yellow gold should be in a flask that is around 800°F. and other golds at around 950°F.

At this point you can continue with the other steps in centrifugal casting or you can steam cast the burned-out flask.

HOW MUCH METAL TO USE

When the void or cavity in the mold has a pattern of a given material, such as wood or wax, it is possible to establish fairly accurately how much metal to melt. This decreases waste and avoids repeated reheating of metal that can change its pure content. There are two methods of establishing the amount of metals to melt for casting. One is displacement and the other is by using mathematical factors.

Displacement uses a graduate beaker partially filled with water. Hold the pattern securely on stiff wire and push it into the beaker of water. Note the increase in volume on the marked scale. Remove the model and add metal to the equivalent measure. Remember to have all the metal accounted for including the sprue, sprue button, and any other feeder sprues, gates, or buttons. The metal must fill these as well as the jewelry cavity in the cast. Clean the metal by pickling and dry it well before casting. There should be no solder content on any of the scrap metal.

Using mathematical factors means calculating by the individual weights of each material you are using. If the model is made of wax, weigh the model, the sprues, and the button on a balance scale. Multiply this weight by the following factors: 10 for bronze; 12 for silver, 10K, 12K, and 14K gold; and 15 for 18K gold. This is the weight of the metal you will need. For

wooden patterns used in sandcasting and repeat production, cast one unit in your selected metal. Weigh the finished casting and divide the casting's weight by the weight of the wooden pattern. This will equal the multiple factor for each subsequent casting of the same metal and should be recorded for reference.

STEAM CASTING

With very inexpensive, modified, and improvised casting equipment, you can steam-cast a piece of jewelry as detailed as that done by centrifuge. The technique is limited only in that you cannot cast large pieces. The modifications and new equipment you need to make include a differently shaped sprue former and a steam plunger. The plunger creates the steam in combination with the hot metal which in turn forces the molten metal into the mold.

THE SPRUE FORMER AND PLUNGER. The modified sprue former (shown below) is domed rather than con-

ical as in other casting techniques. It can be made from 24-gauge copper with the dapping block and punches. There should not be any flat surfaces on this sprue former, especially at the bottom of the dome. Otherwise the molten metal will not flow easily during the cast.

At the bottom of the domed sphere, drill a hole just large enough for a 14-gauge round wire. This is one of two measurements for steam casting that are crucial. Too small a hole will not allow enough metal to flow and too large a hole will allow early leakage into the mold that will harden before the casting is complete. Set a short length of 14-gauge round wire through this hole.

The plunger can be improvised from a jar lid with a wooden handle securely screwed on to it. The lid must be large enough to fit over the round metal flask that contains the investment. At the time of casting, several layers of very wet asbestos sheets are placed inside the lid. The asbestos is re-wet and replaced within the lid for each subsequent casting. The author has also seen successful steam casting using a large baking potato as a plunger.

To steam-cast, have the plunger assembled with the wet asbestos inside the lid. Then, using fire tongs, place the hot (1200°F.) flask on an asbestos sheet with the sprue dome up. Fill the hemispheric depression with clean metal pieces and add a slight sprinkling of casting flux before you quickly heat the metal. When the metal is molten and fluid, press the plunger firmly over the top end of the flask and hold it in place for half a minute.

Be careful not to tip over the flask when clamping on the lid. Practice a little with the motions needed to hold the torch in place, remove it, and clamp on the plunger. The hand change between the torch and plunger must be quite rapid. If a film develops on the metal surface, it is too cool to be forced by steam.

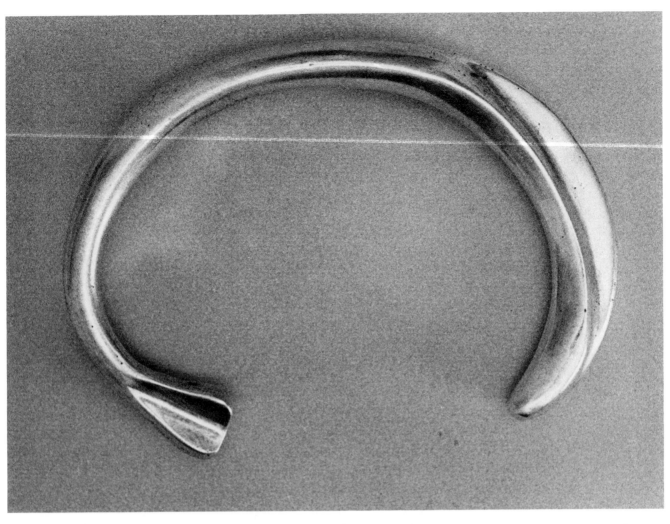

Bracelet (Above) by Richard Gompf. Sand-cast sterling silver for limited production.

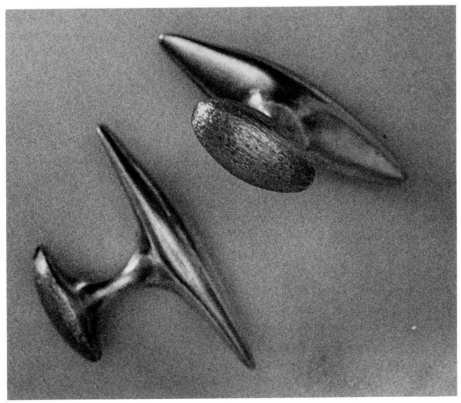

Cuff Links (Left) by Richard Gompf. Sand-cast in 14k yellow gold for limited production.

CENTRIFUGAL CASTING MACHINES

Casting machines come in a number of models. They have a straight or broken arm that varies in length depending on the size of castings. They are either spring-winding, which offers more pressure control, or direct-drive, which has no speed control; they are either horizontal or vertical. They have a balance mechanism that is adjustable to the weight of your casting flask. It is essential to have the casting arm balanced before you cast. Otherwise, the metal and machine will literally cast themselves off of the table.

MAKING A CASTING MACHINE. The casting equipment shown above is an example of a very satisfactory casting machine designed and made by ceramist Earle Curtis for his wife Merry Renk. It is electric and uses a straight arm in the casting unit. The component parts, including the motor (bought at a flea market), cost less than $25.00 in 1973.

The power motor is mounted vertically on a hinged board. A spring pulls the motor board against the drive belt which, in turn, drives the upper casting unit. Experimenting with the drive wheel, Earle finally chose a 3" one (a 4" one threw the melted metal violently outside the safety wall and a 2" one did not cast the metal with enough force). The motor is from an old washing machine (¼ HP at 1725–50 speed). Gas pipe and a flange fitting make up the center drive post. The fly wheel is made of two 16" diameter circles of solid 3/4" plywood glued together and a standard V-belt.

THE UPPER UNIT. The upper unit houses the casting arm and balance weights. The outer galvanized metal sheet acts as a safety guard from possible flying metal during the casting. A piece of garden hose was split lengthwise and slipped over the sharp top edge. The bottom of the tub ring is held together with a circular strip of plywood, and the inside is lined with 1/8" transite. Casting plaster seals the inner bottom seam. The Curtis casting unit uses a straight arm of strap iron held in a slot with a bolt and lock nut that is secured with a gas pipe cap. The arm is 24" long.

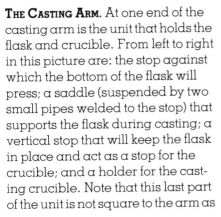

THE CASTING ARM. At one end of the casting arm is the unit that holds the flask and crucible. From left to right in this picture are: the stop against which the bottom of the flask will press; a saddle (suspended by two small pipes welded to the stop) that supports the flask during casting; a vertical stop that will keep the flask in place and act as a stop for the crucible; and a holder for the casting crucible. Note that this last part of the unit is not square to the arm as

are all the other parts. It is slightly tilted to accommodate the slight wave and possible splash of the molten metal when the machine is in motion. The same accommodation is reinforced in the shape of the crucibles.

To counter-balance the flask and crucible, Earle made a variety of cast lead weights that can slip on the other end of the arm (round discs with a slit provided to slip over the arm). A stop is welded to the end of the arm to stop the natural outward thrust of the weights when the machine is in motion. The weights are placed against the stop when the machine is set up to cast.

CRUCIBLES. These crucibles have been carved from refractory brick. The iron binding wire is a safety measure against their cracking from the direct heat of the torch. The groove in each side allows them to be slipped between the metal flanges on the holder. As you can see in the crucible at the top of the picture, the right wall is slightly higher and a little cupped to accommodate the wave effect of the hot metal as the casting machine starts. The fire tongs are adapted from kitchen tongs and have wooden handles added to extend their length.

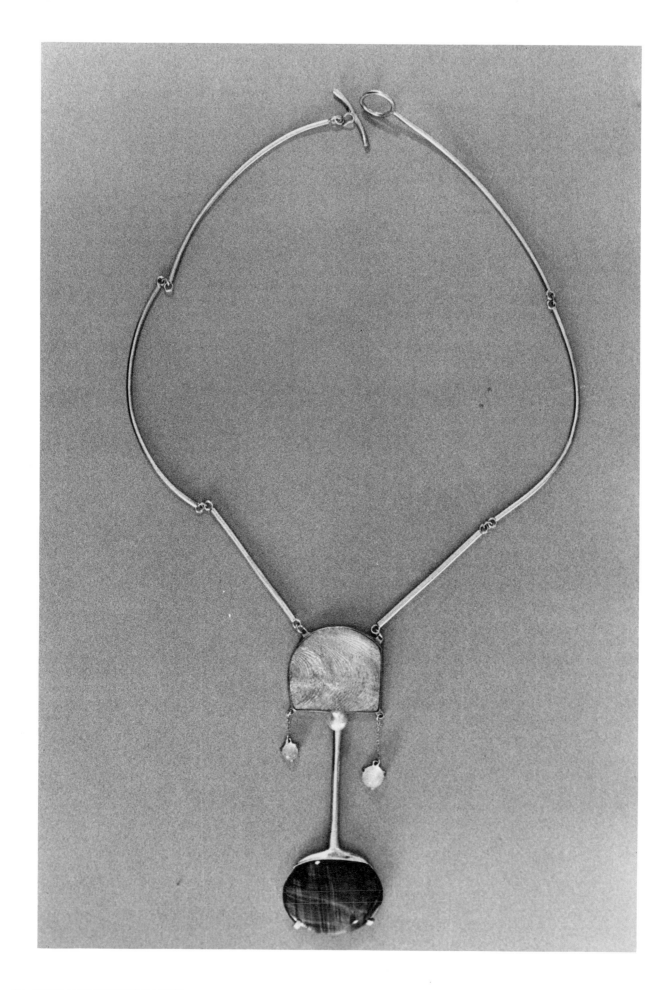

Necklace by Mary Ann Scherr. Silver, steel, brass, copper, and amber. Multi-metal, sandwiched and upset, forming spanned areas between split amber beads, coiled links.

Necklace by Florence Resnikoff. Silver gilt with cuttlebone casting, tiger-eye, pearl, moonstone and aquamarine, cast and fabricated, 1975.

CENTRIFUGAL CASTING

The steps in the centrifugal casting process are very simple.

1. Balance the arm. Adjust the weights to balance the weight of the casting flask and crucible before you begin the burnout.

2. Do the burnout. As the heat decreases (approaching 800°F. or 950°F.) preheat the flux-coated crucible to a point of glazing (glowing in appearance).

3. Take the hot flask directly from the burnout kiln with fire tongs and place it in the saddle on the casting arm without further cooling.

4. Using fire tongs, fit the lip of the crucible facing into the sprue opening as closely as possible. There should be no space between for the molten metal to shoot out.

5. Place your cleaned metal in the hot crucible with additional flux and melt it with your torch. Melt the metal, but do not bring it to a boil.

Add a small amount of flux to the molten metal. Release the stop bar if you are using a spring-wind arm or turn on the switch if your machine is electrically powered. Allow the machine to run down normally; do not stop it.

6. Remove the flask from the arm after it has stopped and allow the metal to cool and set before quenching. This will be about 6 minutes for silver and at least 12 minutes for golds. Quench the hot flask in cold water. The casting plaster will disintegrate and free your casting. If quenching is done too soon, the casting may crack.

7. Pickle the casting in a hot solution to clean it further.

8. Snip and saw off all unwanted sprues, then continue the finishing processes.

Many texts contain discussions and recommendations on auxiliary equipment pertaining to metal casting. As it is the intent of this book to provide procedures possible for the beginning jeweler, these major equipment investments have been omitted. If you wish to become a full-time production artist, they are

a must. If you plan to become directly involved with materials and their potential design possibilities for making jewelry, the investment is not necessary. Professional equipment that will speed up and eliminate some of the undesirable failures possible in centrifugal casting include a vacuum table with pump, an electric beater, and a vacuum bell. Actually, unless you are planning to start a serious production business, you are financially—in terms of time spent, equipment usage, and successful results—better off to send your wax pattern to a professional caster. Your designing time is worth four times theirs in actual money, and it will take you years to compensate for the equipment investment. You should, however, know and understand the problems of investment casting so you can intelligently understand its technical limitations. If you use professional casters, they will do all of the preparation of the model for casting; you only need to provide the pattern.

Necklace by Nancy Loo Bjorge (front piece only) Sterling silver, sheeps fleece; hammered, stamped, and fabricated, 1975.

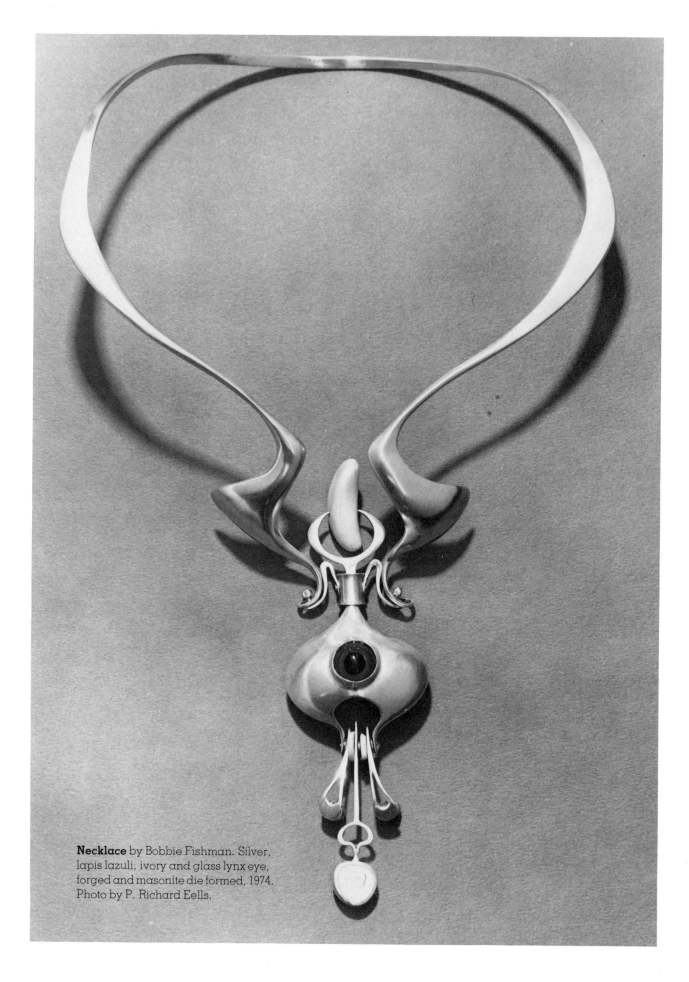

Necklace by Bobbie Fishman. Silver,
lapis lazuli, ivory and glass lynx eye,
forged and masonite die formed, 1974.
Photo by P. Richard Eells.

6

SURFACE TREATMENTS

Beyond the intrinsic beauty of the metal—its natural color or its capacity for a highly polished surface—there are a number of manipulative and chemical treatments that can add to the finish and enrichment of the jewelry form and your design. Of course, it is always your design and your practiced control of each of these processes that make them effective.

Techniques discussed in this chapter include: forming the surface character in detailed relief, both depressed and raised (repoussé and chasing); techniques that depress or cut-away part of the metal surface, such as punching, engraving, and etching; techniques that build up the metal form; filigree and electroplate; the inlay of one metal into another; and coloring with chemicals and heat.

In each instance, these processes are more delicate and must be done with care. You will usually, but not always, do these techniques last. Some, such as repoussé, are forming techniques; others, such as engraving or etching, can take place on one sheet of metal that is then cut

up and/or formed in another technique to be used with further construction processes.

REPOUSSÉ AND CHASING

Repoussé and chasing are terms used to describe surface modeling on sheet metal. They are done with a large variety of punching tools—many that you can make yourself—a chasing hammer, and a bowl of pitch to support your work. Repoussé is the term used when you are modeling from the back or reverse side of the metal, and chasing is the term when you are modeling on the top side or face of the work. In both techniques, repoussé and chasing, the tools do not cut through the metal; they simply indent it. You will use some of the tools more often for repoussé and other tools more often for chasing. Usually, the smaller, finer, and more detailed tools are used for chasing on the face.

There are five general groups of punches: tracers or liners, embossing or doming, planishing or smoothing, matting or background, and dapping or hollow punches.

HOLDING PITCH While cast-iron bowls are the professional tools for holding pitch, you can devise an adequate substitute by pouring pitch on a rectangular block of wood or into a metal pie plate. The iron bowl, wood, or pie tin should be supported by a leather padded ring or a sandbag. This allows you to comfortably adjust the angle of the pitch bowl as you work your design. The pitch can be purchased commercially prepared or you can mix your own, a messy process at best. The pitch is a basic mixture of pitch (3 pounds), plaster of Paris (2 pounds), and tallow (2 ounces). Varying the amounts of plaster to tallow will make the pitch softer or harder. Warm the pitch in a pail, mixing continuously. Slowly add the plaster and then the tallow.

Clean the back surface of your metal so it is free of all oil. Any oil on the metal will keep it from being held firmly by the pitch. Use a very soft, large flame and heat the surface of the pitch until it is soft. Be careful not to burn the pitch; this creates little bubbles in the pitch and the metal will not have complete support which means that you cannot develop a controlled metal surface. When the pitch is soft, drop the metal on it and wiggle it to assure a complete surface contact. Pull a little of the pitch over the edge of the metal to hold it in place while working. Cool the pitch and metal by running them under cool water.

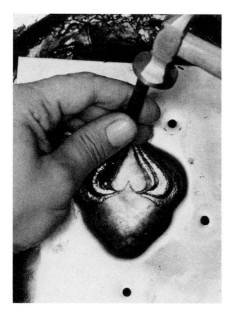

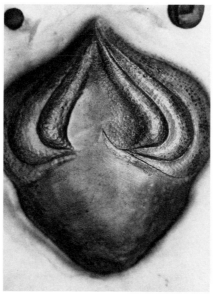

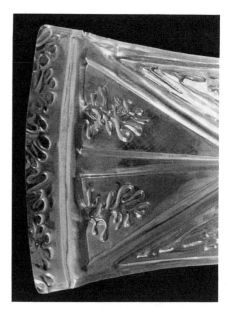

REPOUSSE. Draw your design on the inside or back of the metal with a felt pen. Heat the pitch block as described earlier and press the form, design-side up, into the softened pitch. The pitch forms a soft support for your work. Now use small dapping punches to further sink your select design areas. When the repoussé is complete, remove the metal from the pitch support, turn it over, and fill the sunken/raised bowl form with softened pitch before chasing.

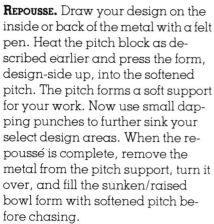

CHASING. Chasing is done on the top or face of the formed metal with punches. Here, still supported in the pitch block, is a partially completed form. On the left is an area still to be chased after repoussé; on the right is a completed chased area. One of the cardinal rules in using punches is to develop a rythmic controlled use of the hammer. You want an even, fine, dimpled surface—the better to reflect from the beautiful metal surface. An uneven surface means that you are not yet in control of the process.

Repoussé and chasing harden the metal surface. This allows thin-gauge metals to be successfully used in jewelry production because of the increased hardness/ strength that results from the surface treatments.

USING A LEAD OR WOOD BLOCK. A lead block or a piece of soft wood covered with felt can be used for small repoussé and chasing pieces. Beware of the possibility of surface contamination from the lead. If lead is left on silver, for example, it can result in pitting. Both the lead and the wooden block are softer than the pitch support, so do not expect the same crisp, defined surface when using them.

A beginning and easy project for repoussé can be done by gouging a few varied depressions in a piece of wood and covering it with felt. In the photo above, student Kathy Forrler, after making such a support and working with a nail ground to a round point, produced a repoussé surface in aluminum. She worked both sides of the meal to give the appearance of both raising and depressing the metal surface. All of this increased the strength and rigidity of the otherwise soft and flexible metal sheet.

REMOVING THE METAL. Reheat the metal and pitch with the same soft flame originally used to set the metal into the pitch. Lift the metal with tweezers and wipe off any excess pitch. Stubborn pitch adhering to the metal can be dissolved with benzine. You can also heat the metal to annealing temperature and the excess pitch will burn off as a white ash.

PUNCHING

Much the same process as repoussé and chasing, punching is usually associated with repeat designs. Much pre-Columbian gold has punched designs. Fundamentally, punching involves a matching male and female relief form between which thin sheets of metal are "punched." In this way, many like raised/depressed forms can be produced. The thin sheets are first cut out with snips, then placed in the female die and punched with the male stamp. Industrially, the punching and cutting take place simultaneously.

Another form of punching uses a sharp-edged punch and a single controlled tap with a hammer. The metal is compressed or stamped with a pattern. The fish scales on the old silver Ti ornament on page 121 are an example. Another example is the beautiful roe pattern of traditional Japanese metalwork called Nanako. They are created by using a beading tool in the background (Ishime) on the face side of the metal sheet as in chasing. The sharp-edged circles of the tool edge create a crisp beading effect.

Another punching technique frequently used on tin or thin brass uses the prick punch. Back the thin metal sheet with a soft material (such as wood) and tap the sharp point of the punch through the sheet. This raises a burr on the reverse side. If this side is to have any contact with the skin, the sharp cutting edges should be filed off.

ENGRAVING

Engraving is the cutting away of metal from the surface and is linear in effect. It produces a sharply defined line or, if lines are massed in a background pattern, a textured surface often referred to as a "Florentine" finish. Engraving tools are made of steel and have a square, lozenge, flat, round, knife, or onglette tip or cutting point. They

come in numbered sizes—the smaller the number, the thinner the tool. Their tangs are set in small, round, wooden handles that fit comfortably into your fist, and the cutting point rests against your thumbs and forefinger. The metal to be engraved is held firmly in an engraving block to free both your hands for engraving. Other devices used to hold the metal include your ring clamp, a small sandbag, or a shellac stick.

The shellac stick has a round platform top set on a handle. Shellac is melted on the flat top and the metal is set into the shellac while it is still warm. Cool and set the shellac under running water. This stick can be held against your bench pin and rotated easily as you engrave. You remove the metal by heating the shellac; any unwanted shellac on the metal can be removed with alcohol.

Secure the metal on any of the holding devices. The idea is to have your hands free for the push/pull action of using the engraver. Use your two thumbs: one to guide the engraver and one to check against the pushing pressure of your hand. Push gently against the handle in your fist with the heel of your hand. Don't get the rest of your other hand in front of the tool as you work. You can still jab yourself even while your second thumb is checking the push of the engraver against your cutting.

ETCHING

The simplest form of etching uses an asphaltum resist, which is a black varnish substance. It is painted with a brush over all areas of the metal where you do not want the acid to attack. Turpentine thins asphaltum (three parts turpentine to one part asphalt) and it cleans off the metal after the etch. It also keeps the brush soft while you paint. Paint the back and edges of the metal (the acid will eat there, too) before you paint your design on the front, and be sure the asphaltum is dry before etching in acid.

PHOTO PROCESSES ON METALS

Using etching and plating, a photograph can be transferred effectively on to a metal surface as a surface embellishment which, in turn, can be incorporated into your jewelry design. The etching is usually, but not necessarily, done first and the electroplating second when using a photograph. You can use either a positive or negative image in either process.

Etching eats away select portions of the metal plate surface. It is done with acids that cut or dissolve the metal when placed in the acid bath, thus lowering parts of the surface. The part that remains raised (the original metal surface) is preserved by various resists to the acids. In other words, the part of the surface that you want to keep is treated with resist; that part you want to depress or have eaten away will remain exposed to the acid bath.

Photo-electroplating takes this etched plate and, through controlled electrical currents passed through a chemical bath, deposits additional metal particles on the metal surface. Resist is used so the particles can deposit themselves freely on the exposed areas. If the plate is left in the plating bath long enough, there is a danger of the pits filling-in and obliterating the image. In electroplating, the particles tend to be attracted to the edges first.

The two sections that follow, one on photo-etching or photo-resist and the other on electroplating, were documented by the author in a day with printmaker Pat Waring Sherwood and jewelers Eileen Hill and Florence Resnikoff. Everything was happy, successful, and casual, with a picnic during the waiting times and an occasional sculptor or painter kibitzing. Pat Sherwood first discusses the photo-resist or photo-etching process that works equally well on copper and silver.

PHOTO-RESIST. Both the photo-resist and photo-electroplating processes that follow use a contact photo process. The desired image was not enlarged in any way, although it could be. All surfaces—the original photograph source, the photo transparencies, and the metal plates—were exposed with complete surface contact.

Photo transparencies were made on Kodalith Ortho #3, Kodak film No. 4556. This film can be used for both halftone and line shots. In this case, an 85 dot per linear inch halftone screen was contact-printed on a positive transparency. If the plate is to be manipulated or electroplated, use a 40 to 65 screen. A positive transparency was used because the photo image was to be the master artwork. The positive transparency can be prepared commercially from any dense negative or a print. The black areas must be strong and opaque, so a high contrast (high "gamma") negative should be used.

Two types of photo transparencies are generally used in this work: one in which the image is completely translated into masses and lines of black or white (line shot), and one in which grays are achieved by the use of a halftone screen in which the gray values are rendered by breaking up the areas into white and black dots of different sizes. The screens usually range from 40 to 133 lines to the inch for this work. The coarser or lower numbered ones are easier to work with (40 to 65 seems to work well). Most newspapers use 65. The lower the number, the larger and more visible the dots will be on the

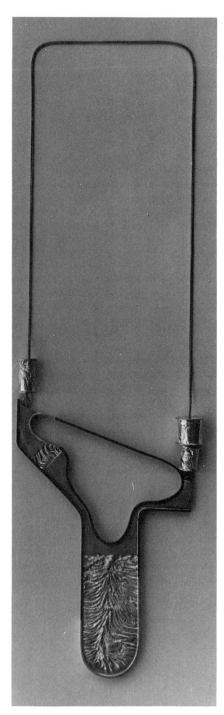

Pendant by Hiroko and Gene Pijanowski. This pendant is part of the wall hanging shown on page 120.

image. Each dot is actually dark at the center and gradually fades out toward its edge. More light passes through the edge of the dot than will pass through the center. Therefore, as more light passes through the black dot on the screen, the dot on the negative will enlarge. If there is less passing through the dot, the dot will be smaller.

One could also hand-make a transparency by drawing a design on clear mylar with "no-crawl" black ink. This would yield a line cut, all black or white with no gray or halftone areas.

MATERIALS YOU WILL NEED. You can do this process on any gauge copper or silver. You will need 1 quart K.P.R. Kodak Photo-Resist, and 1 gallon K.P.R. Photo-Resist Developer. Other chemicals include acetic acid (Glacial), phosphoric acid, and nitric acid. Equipment includes stainless steel, glass, or fiberglass trays (the developer will dissolve anything else including most photo and acid-resist trays), a 275 watt sun lamp (for the ultraviolet light to expose the plate), a piece of plate glass, and a piece of felt or foam rubber (for contact pressure with the glass during exposure).

Good results are achieved with the sun lamp, although most professionals use an arc lamp with a vacuum frame.

CLEANING THE METAL PLATES. The metal plate must be completely free of fingerprints, grease, and any commerical coating used to keep it from oxidizing. This is extremely important in assuring the proper adhesion of the K.P.R. photo emulsion.

STEP 1. Clean the plate by giving it a two minute bath in a solution of one part Glacial Acetic Acid to three parts water. Rinse with water, holding the plate by the edges only. Remember, too, in mixing acids, *always add acids to water.* Next, pre-etch the plate in a 2% by volume phosphoric acid bath for three minutes. Agitate gently a few times. This gives the metal a "tooth" to hold the emulsion. A nitric acid 2% solution can also be used. Rinse with water, again without touching the face. The plate should then be dried thoroughly on a hotplate or with a hand-held hair dryer to make it as free of water spots as possible. The plate is properly degreased when water runs off in sheets without sticking or beading.

When the plate is clean and dry, apply K.P.R. in the darkroom with only a red "safe" light on. (See Ap-pendix for a simple dark room arrangement suitable for either your bath or kitchen.)

Flow the emulsion down from the top edge of a vertically held plate. Hold the metal plate by the side edges in a clean tray so the excess emulsion can be caught for reuse. You want a thin, even coat so shift the plate around if necessary to get the flow. Next, stand the metal plate upright against the wall on a piece of paper towel and let it dry for an hour. Test the bottom—it dries last —with your finger before proceeding. If wet, the emulsion will stick to your transparency. The thin puddle line can be wiped away with your finger (you will probably be cutting the edge off for your jewelry design so this disturbance won't matter). Now you are ready to expose the plate.

STEP 2. Now you will begin the exposure and development. Still in the darkroom with the red safe light on, place the metal, emulsion side up, on a piece of foam or felt with the transparency on top. Place the emulsion side of the film (dull side) against the emulsion side of the plate. Cover both with a sheet of glass and a piece of cardboard. Hang the sun lamp 18" to 24" above the work. The larger the work, the higher the lamp should be. Here, Eileen has the lamp at 18". Remove the cardboard after the sun lamp has warmed up. Exposure time should range from 7 to 14 minutes depending on the density of the film. If in doubt, run a test strip and uncover the plate at 2 minute intervals. Remember the time is cumulative. Start with 7 minutes and work up to 13 or 15 minutes.

Development should run about 3½ minutes to 4 minutes without agitation. Develop face up in the tray with enough K.P.R. developer to cover the plate.

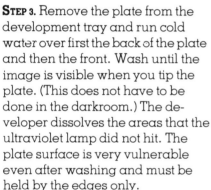

STEP 3. Remove the plate from the development tray and run cold water over first the back of the plate and then the front. Wash until the image is visible when you tip the plate. (This does not have to be done in the darkroom.) The developer dissolves the areas that the ultraviolet lamp did not hit. The plate surface is very vulnerable even after washing and must be held by the edges only.

After the water wash, put the plate on a hotplate set at 150° to 200° for about 5 minutes. Move the plate around to avoid getting hot spots. If you do not have a hotplate, use a fry pan or a pancake griddle, but always keep the metal plate moving. When the plate is cool, coat the back of it with lacquer or varnish.

STEP 4. To etch, immerse the plate in a bath of ten parts water to one part nitric acid for about 20 minutes. Very tiny bubbles (the acid working on the metal) show in the process. These can be gently brushed from the surface of the plate with a feather or the tray can be agitated as shown here.

Rinse in water and dry. The plate can then be inked with oil paint or oxidized with liver of sulfur and

lightly buffed to make the image more visible.

The chemicals needed for this process can be purchased at franchised photo graphic arts dealers, and more detailed information can be found through the bibliography.

Several plates were photoetched during our day and the next step took us to the studio of jeweler Florence Resnikoff to electroplate one of the photo-etched plates.

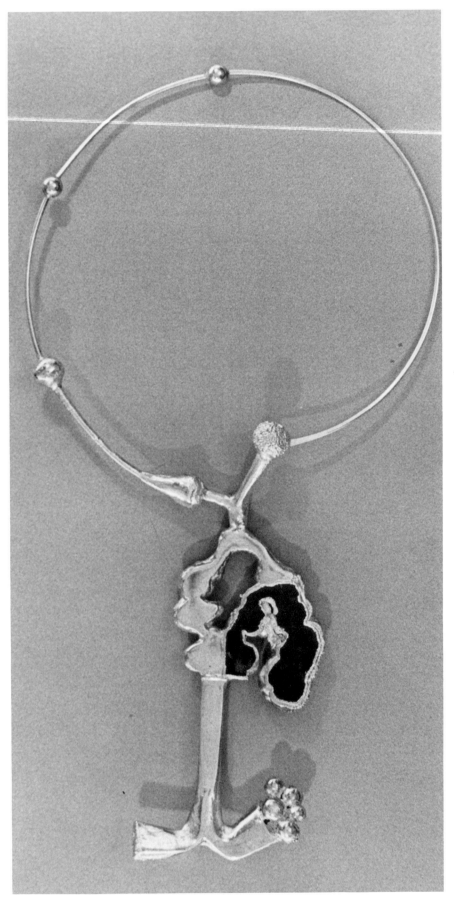

Pendant by Florence Resnikoff. Silver with moss agate slab, electroformed, 1974.

ELECTROPLATING AND ELECTROFORMING

While primarily used by industry, electroplating has now become of interest to the artist. This is due in part to a resurgence in historical and technical research. For example, in the Baghdad Museum you can see parts of a dry battery that worked on the galvanic principle, generating an electrical current 1600 years ago. Galvanizing is an electroplating process for coating iron with zinc to prevent rust.

Many electroplated products are familiar to us today. Automotive trim and bumpers are chrome-plated, originally on metal but now on plastics. Nostalgic moments can be recalled by the bronze-plated baby shoe, a thin metal electroplated on an old, worn, leather base.

In general, the term "electroplating" applies to the electrolytic disposition of metal. The term "electroforming" applies to the artists' extended use of the process—actually using it to create new metal forms regardless of the base material so the object itself is electroformed. For example, the artist can create a form of wax, use a modified electroplating process, melt out the wax leaving a thin metal shell complete or ready to work further. This is not a direct way of working metals, but it allies itself with such processes as lost wax casting.

As the name implies, the process uses electrical current either converted directly from AC to DC from the traditional 115V–220V main or from a battery that must be recharged for continued use. By passing the current in one direction, metal ions deposit themselves on an attractive surface; by reversing the charge, ions of metal can be removed from a previously plated surface. The latter is one way in which precious metals are retrieved from scrap and is called electrostripping.

THE COMPONENTS. Below is a schematic diagram of the process for electroplating. These components can be purchased separately (flea market, etc.) or neatly assembled from a distributor. They include: a transformer that reduces the main's voltage from 115V AC to a maximum of about 12V AC. A variable alternating current control called a *Variac* that controls the output from the transformer from 0 to 12V AC. A *rectifier*, either selenium or silicon, that changes the low voltage alternating current (AC) to direct current (DC). Two meters: a *voltmeter* to indicate the voltage being used; an *ammeter* to indicate the current in amperes passing through the electrolyte. Too much voltage will burn the plate and it will powder off. Florence Resnikoff provided the following background as we were processing the photoplate.

This is an electrochemical process based on Michael Faraday's Law (1810) that relates the amount of metal deposited to the amount of electrical current. There are two kinds of conductors of electricity: negatively charged particles, called electrons, and positively charged particles, called ions. Electrons carry current in wires, but in the electroplating process the ions exist as molecules of a metallic salt in fluid, called an electrolyte. When a negatively charged voltage is applied to the work (jewelry) immersed in an electrolyte, the positive ions are attracted to the nega-

tive work, carrying the metallic particles to deposit them on the surface of the work to plate it.

Copper sulfate in solution is the metallic salt in the acid copper bath that we are using. In addition, bars of positively charged copper put in the bath also contribute their ions to the electrolyte. These are called anodes and they are made of pure copper. Distilled water is used in making the bath because it is free of metallic ions. (Tap water is contaminated and should be avoided.) The copper acid bath has the advantage of low cost, quite high plating speed, low stress, and is simple to control.

There are two small electroplating units useful to the shop craftsman on the market. These can

be purchased independently or in combination. One is for dipping small objects and the other is for brush-plating. Both use the penlite batteries as a source of current.

Brush-plating is used for small areas where only one place in the metal is to be plated or when the work is too unwieldy to be placed in an immersion bath. A plating anode in contact with the battery anode is contained in a small brush, and a lead wire in contact with the battery cathode is connected to the work. The brush is dipped into the plating solution and applied to the area to be plated. This is in reality a miniature plating bath, a duplicate of the larger and more complex immersion bath demonstrated in this chapter.

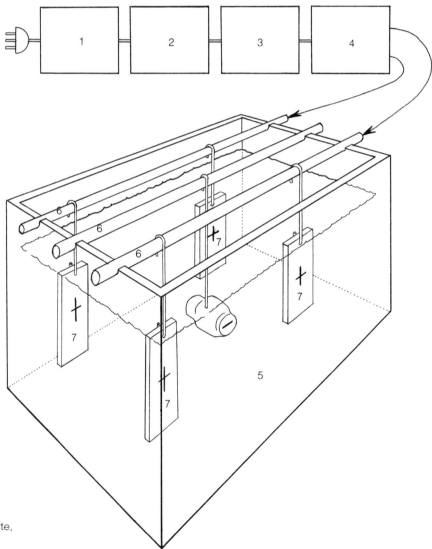

Electroforming Unit. This is a schematic presentation of the component parts of an electroforming unit. It includes: (1) transformer, (2) variac, (3) rectifier, (4) voltmeter and ammeter, (5) the electrolyte, (6) the bus bars, and (7) the anodes.

ADVANTAGES AND DISADVANTAGES. There are many advantages to this process not found in other fabrication techniques. First, tolerances are very precise—less than 0.1 mil under controlled conditions. You do not need to compensate for bend allowance or shrinkage. Second, the surface finish can be so fine that it does not require polishing (again, under controlled conditions). Third, the finished properties of metal (its brightness and smoothness) can be determined by controlling the plating conditions. There are, however, limitations as to shape, keeping in mind high and low current density areas. Size is limited to the tank capacity and, to some extent, the design is limited depending on your use of a permanent or expendable matrix material. Fourth, a single piece can be made or there can be production runs. Fifth, the cost per piece is lower, primarily due to the controlled amount of metals used. Sixth, the work can be quite lightweight yet strong because the metal is thin and the form can be hollow.

If you are in a hurry, however, one of the disadvantages is that the rate of deposition of metal can run into days if it is a large piece or if you are electroplating several pieces at once. The other major disadvantage is that imperfections on the master mandrel will be duplicated in the plated surface.

DEVELOPING A MATRIX. The photo-etched plate used in the demonstration electroplates copper on copper. The plate is serving as a permanent matrix holding the additional metal ions; it will later be used by jeweler Eileen Hill in combination with other fabrication processes. A matrix or mandrel, the base on which electroplating and electroforming take place, can be made of permanent or expendable material. The appendix lists possible matrices that can be used. In all cases, the matrix must be scrupulously clean. This means scouring with caustic soda as well as using

the appropriate cleaning solvents or acids relating to the matrix material.

Electroforming can only be done on conductive surfaces, for example copper, silver, or gold. If you wish to coat a non-conductive material (such as paper, wax, plastic, or wood) the surface should be thoroughly dry. It should be painted with a coat of plastic lacquer to prevent its absorption of acids at a later time. When the sealing coat is dry, paint or spray the matrix with conductive paint (usually made of finely powdered silver, copper, or graphite held in suspension by quick-drying lacquer) that is available at electronic supply companies. Allow this to dry before proceeding.

Some matrix materials are better sealed with waxes than with lacquer. For example: if the conductive paint is lacquer based, it could dissolve plastic. Therefore, you would use wax to coat the surface before painting it with the conductive paint. The matrix should be soaked in the wax at 212°F. until all bubbles of steam or air have ceased. Remove the matrix, allow it to drain, reform it if necessary, then cool it completely. Larger matrices can be painted with a solution of wax and carbon tetrachloride. The conductive coating must be compatible with the matrix regardless of its material. You should use paraffin on leather and higher-melting waxes such as beeswax on other animal or vegetable matrices.

Necklace by Peter Blodgett. Silver, forged and electrofabricated.

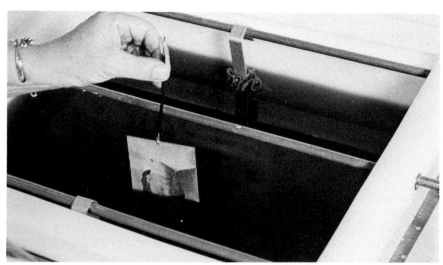

STEP 1. Once the matrix or mandrel is prepared, you are ready to electroplate. Check that all surfaces are absolutely clean. To attach a hanging wire, drill a small hole at the top of the metal plate as shown here. Block out all areas, including the hanging wire, that you do not want to have receive the metal ions with asphaltum. Let the block-out dry before going on to Step 2.

STEP 2. Attach the length of copper wire to the matrix. It should be long enough to hook over the bus bar and to suspend the matrix, fully submerged, in the electrolyte. The copper bath is at room temperature here but some baths are heated. It depends on the matrix, the bath's chemical make-up, and the plating

material. Hang the matrix from the central or negative bus bar and turn on the current. A general rule for adjusting the current is that you need 20 to 40 amps to a square foot of surface. Industry uses between 1½ to 2 V. Here, Florence uses ¾ to 1½ V. Too much voltage will burn the plate and powder it off.

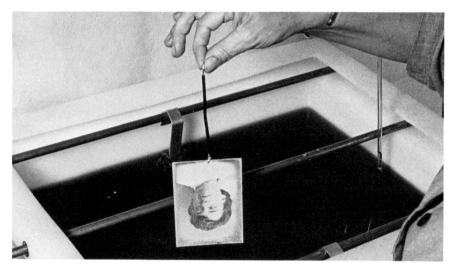

STEP 3. The copper ions move within the electrolyte. Agitation will improve the deposition of ions; the pump above the tank demonstrates the bubbling, moving action within the bath. Time the process, checking to see how the deposit is developing. It is best to start with a low voltage and to increase it as needed. The plating here took about an hour's time and the voltage was gradually increased from ¾ to 1½ V.

STEP 4. Electroplating on a photo-etched surface requires care. If too fine a screen is used in the etching process, the electroplating can quickly compensate for the etch and begin to fill in the recessed dots. That is beginning to happen here as you can see by the "halo" appearing around the edge of the plate. It has not yet happened on the remainder of the plate so the image is still intact.

COLORING BY CHEMICALS

The coloring of metals can be done by applying chemicals or heat or a combination of both. Chemical coloring is most common to silver, while heat coloring is often used with ferrous metals such as iron and steel. Chemical coloring, because it lies only on the surface and is not a part of the metal base, will eventually clean or wear away. A coating of beeswax or lacquer can be applied to preserve the colored surface for a longer time.

Using chemical coloring is generally an esthetic choice. Its main use is as an accent or emphasis. Because it can be easily polished away, most of the color deposit lies in recesses on the finished jewelry. For example, if the forms are rounded or curvilinear or the joint angle too closed for complete polishing, you could color the metal surface. The color would be in the inaccessible areas and act as an accent to the remaining brightly polished metal.

Coloring the metal surface will not correct or cover any blemishes such as scratches, pits, or faulty soldering. In fact, it will accent the blemishes and show up bad craftsmanship immediately.

Coloring with chemicals is always done last, after all finishing and buffing have taken place. Once the jewelry is colored, you can rebuff the exposed surfaces to enhance the metal highlights in your design or to discharge the chemical oxidation from surfaces that normally would not be oxidized.

CLEANING METALS. Jewelry must be completely constructed and polished (but stones not set) before any coloring is used. Coloring is the last process you do except for a final polish to remove unwanted color from the metal surface. The metal must be free of all fire oxides and polished with both tripoli and white diamond in areas where you do not plan to color. (See Chapter 9 for polishing.)

Wash your jewelry with liquid soap and water. Rinse, using a small, soft-bristled brush to assure the removal of any polishing compound. Repeat this several times. Clean the jewelry in hot pickle. Wash, repickle, and wash again to assure that the metal surface is free of any oils and grease. Do not handle the metal excessively; even your fingertips hold skin oils that can affect ability of the chemicals to hold evenly on the metal. If you are coloring sterling, use a brush with pumice to clean the metal surface free of the pure silver resulting from repeated pickling.

To apply the color solution or paste, you can brush it on, dip it in a bath, let it stand in the bath or do repeated dippings, and, in some instances, apply it with the metal hot. You should not handle the jewelry during the coloring process. Suspend it with a silver wire for the dipping baths. You can use tweezers but do not use iron wire—it conditions the chemicals and thus changes the formula. See the Appendix for an annotated table on chemical coloring formulas, the colors obtained, the metals on which they are used, and specific comments on their application. Almost all coloring or oxidation of metal surfaces follows the same procedure as for potassium sulphide, commonly called liver of sulfur.

LIVER OF SULFUR (POTASSIUM SULPHIDE).

The most commonly used chemical coloring for silver, copper, and bronze is liver of sulfur dissolved in water. Liver of sulfur will deposit a near-black color on the surface of the metal. Dissolving barium sulphide in water will produce a similar coloring bath.

To prepare the coloring solution using potassium sulphide, add a small chunk of the chemical to water and wait until it is dissolved. This solution will deteriorate when exposed to oxygen in the air so it must be used immediately or stored for a short period of time in a tightly covered glass jar. The solution can be used either hot or cold.

If you use the coloring solution cold, first clean your piece in pickle. Then, drop it into the jar and let it stand for 15 minutes to an hour. The time depends on the strength of the solution, the extent of the surface of the jewelry piece, and how dark you want the coloration.

For a much faster coloring, heat the sulfur solution to just below the boiling point and immerse the cleaned jewelry. Remove the piece immediately with tweezers and rinse it under cold water. The longer silver, copper, or bronze remain in the solution, the thicker the coating and the darker and richer the color. However, a heavy coat may flake off if you choose to shade the coloring by rubbing with pumice powder.

VARIBLES. With some of the chemical coloring formulas, you can achieve a series of colors or values of one color through successive dippings. For example: by using a liver of sulfur bath in combination with separate baths of water and household ammonia combined with detergent, a series of colors ranging from gold to rose to blue to violet to charcoal gray can be developed. After thoroughly cleaning your jewelry, dip it first in the ammonia and detergent, then directly into the liver of sulfur until it turns golden. Remove the metal and put it immediately into the water bath. This acts as a stop similar to that used in photo-developing. By repeating this process you can build successive color coatings until you reach the color you want. Charcoal gray is the last color possible.

As chemical coloring affects only the surface of metals, any abrasion will eventually remove it, and it is always affected by the chemicals in the air. This can be somewhat retarded by applying a layer of beeswax diluted with benzine, most automotive waxes, or lacquer. Lacquer will peel with time and moisture, and gives a shiny surface to the oxidation rather than the usual soft matte finish. Waxes have a soft luster and deepen the color somewhat.

COLORING WITH HEAT

A few metals—such as copper, golds with high copper content, and steel—can be colored by use of heat alone. The end results are not too permanent nor practical for jewelry production. However, they warrant experimentation, either alone or in combination with other coloring practices. The pioneer research work of jeweler Mary Ann Scherr on stainles steel using heat and a combinationof vegetable oils, water,and flux to create her "growing" surface is an ideal example of the possibilities for experimentation. She writes about the effect:

"The combination of vegetable oil and water applied to the flux-coated surface of stainless steel causes a constantly altering pattern of colors, textures, and forms. These changes continue to 'grow' and mature regardless of the various vegetable oils used. The only difference is color, as the colors are unique to the oil type; corn oil grows whites to grays to intense, dark gray. Other oils will produce oranges, tans, blues, and whites."

Tempering steel, usually hardening the working end of a tool, also colors the metal. The metal must be clean and polished to reveal the color change during the process. Hold the steel in the air (not rested against a surface) while you heat it. It will go through the following changes in color: light yellow, straw yellow, bronze, light blue, and dark blue. You can stop the process at the color you want by quenching it immediately in water or oil.

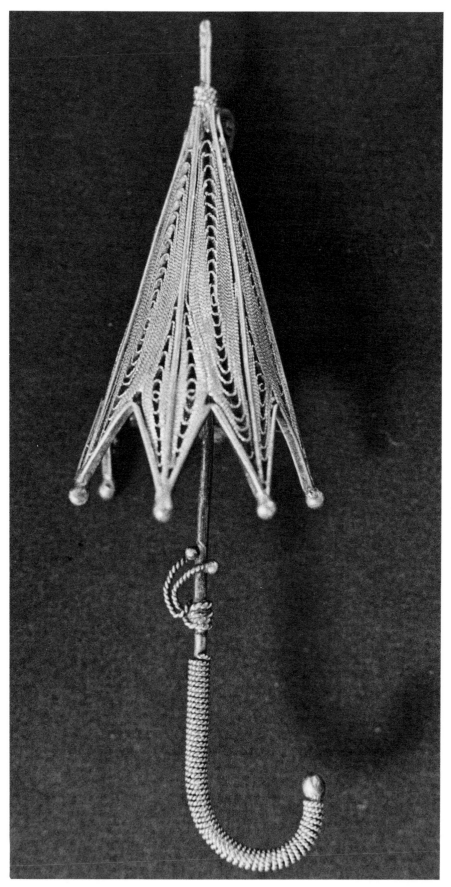

Umbrella Pin. Filigree of fine silver, French nineteenth century. Collection of Helene S. French.

When heated in the same manner, copper produces pale yellow, red, violet, and black. Again, you can stop at any of these colors. Let the metal cool some before quenching it in water or in oil for a deeper color. Care should be taken to build the oxide layers gradually and repeatedly for more permanence. Rapid overheating can cause the oxides to become too thick and they will flake off. (Rapid overheating is one quick way to clean copper; dirt and oxides will chip off leaving a bright surface.)

FILIGREE

Filigree is a process using extremely fine wire, 22- to 28-gauge, soldered to more fine wire or on to a thin metal background. Fine silver or gold wire are most commonly used because the metal is more malleable. Sterling can be used if it is thoroughly annealed.

Flat wire is traditional because it will stay in place, but round wire is easier to use for a contoured surface. The wire is bent with tweezers or your fingers. In doing filigree your drawplate will be in constant use to reduce short lengths of standard-gauge wire to fine, hairlike wires. You can also twist or braid your fine wires together as shown in the petite umbrella pin. Remember to anneal your wire as you draw it smaller and use a lubricant to ease the drawing process.

In designing filigree, the traditional method is to work in units—to form one section of filigree, solder and form a second unit and join it to the first, etc. The wires and units are quite tightly packed and allow only occasional small open areas. This increases the strength of the completed work, which otherwise would be very fragile.

Assemble your pieces of fine wire bent to your design on a metal backing. The backing can be a permanent part of the design or it can be a

clean iron sheet that will not take the solder when you join the wires together. Everything is very fine in scale in filigree. The solder is in the form of filings held in place with gum tragacanth. The solder-gum is applied with a small camel's hair brush as you assemble the wire units. No flux is used but all metal and solder surfaces must be absolutely clean. The moisture of the gum is evaporated—let it set and dry—before soldering or everything will bubble out of place. Solder the assembly in a burnout kiln or, if you have become proficient in soldering, lay the assembly on a wire soldering trivet and heat as you do when soldering wire on sheet using a very small, soft flame.

NIELLO

Niello, a mixture of various sulfides of silver, copper, and lead, is inlayed and fused to the metal's surface. Because it is fused to the metal base and therefore durable, you can use large design areas of the dark blue-black niello.

The preparation of niello reminds one of medieval alchemy. It requires some time and a tendency toward making witches' brew. Formulas vary but the process of making niello (it is not available commercially) is basically the same. For equipment you will need two crucibles (one larger than the other), fire tongs, a charcoal stick (a burned length of dowel will do), a steel slab or a large, deep container filled with water, a mortar and pestle, a #80 sieve (available at ceramic supply houses), a scotch stone, and a burnisher. A kiln is preferable to your torch for fusing as any flame touching the metal will burn and pit the surface, which is almost impossible to remove or correct.

There are many similar formulas dating from Pliny to contemporary times, but the major portion dates from the Middle Ages and the Renaissance where the process was used successfully on armor. Basically, the formula consists of using

silver, copper, lead, and sulfur. The simplest formula and procedure for the process is used at the Metropolitan Museum of Art for repairing historical works. If, after trying this one, you want to expand your alchemy, a number of the bibliographical references have other formulas. All of the steps should take place in a well-ventilated area.

1. In the smaller crucible, melt 1 ounce of silver and 2 ounces of copper. Then, add 3 ounces of lead, stirring and mixing it with the charcoal stick.

2. Put 6 ounces of sulfur in the larger crucible. When Step 1 is accomplished, pour the metals into the sulfur crucible and mix with the charcoal stick. Cover and let cool. Do not breath the fumes.

3. Re-melt the mixture. Pour it into a large, deep container of water or on a lightly oiled steel slab. Pouring it into water will break it up into pieces. If it is poured onto the slab, you must break it up into smaller pieces after it has cooled. Wash the pieces in cold water until the water runs clear.

4. Grind the pieces of niello in a mortar until it will pass through a #80 sieve. Generally, the finer the grains, the more consistent and blemish-free the finished surface will be. Store the grains in a stoppered container until you are ready to use it.

The design to be inlayed can be etched, engraved, or be pierced work in 24-gauge metal backed with 18-gauge metal. The niello area can have other metal inlay areas that can be held in place by the niello rather than solder. They can be soldered. The edges of the surrounding metal do not have to be angled. However, if you do have inlaid metal pieces that are not soldered, the edges of these must have a bevel (the larger surface tangent to the background or base). All

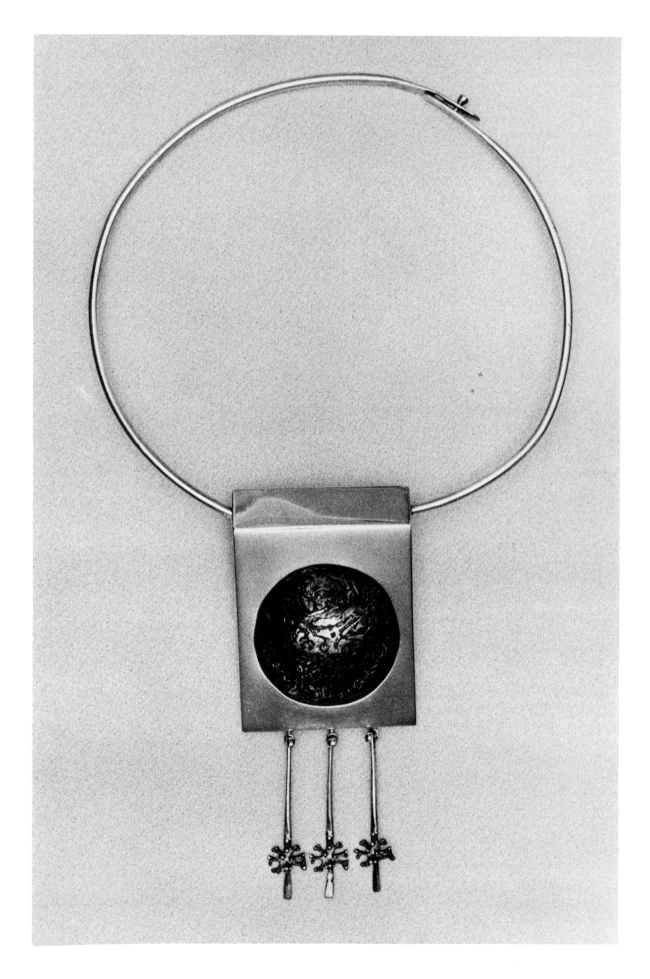

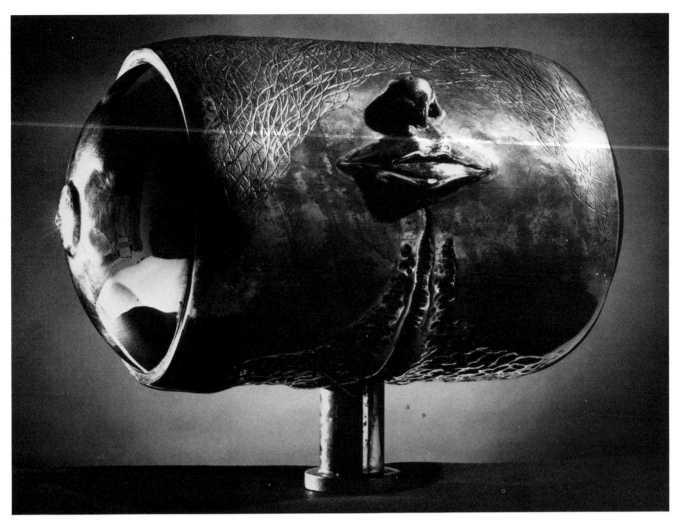

Brassy Body Pot (Above) by Jed Krieger. Brass, forged and chased. Photo by William L. Stonecipher.

Bracelet (Left) from Indonesia of silver and fine silver filigree. Museum of New Mexico Collection. Photo by David Donoho.

Pendant (Opposite Page) by Florence Resnikoff. Silver, 14k gold, copper, etched, cast and fabricated, 1975.

Pendant by Gene Pijanowski. Copper, brass. bronze and silver, silver inlay, chisel texture, Mokume and Rokusho.

metal surfaces, surrounding and inlay, should be of equal height. Once the base design is complete, pickle it to free it of oxides and contamination. To keep the metal clean before inlaying, store it covered with water but dry it before you begin the inlay.

Mix a paste of niello with a saturated ammonium chloride-water solution. Dilute paste flux with water until it is milky, and wet the areas on the metal where you will apply the niello. Lay in the niello paste on the parts to be covered to a depth of not more than $1/32''$. Make the area higher than the surrounding metal surfaces as some niello shrinks up to 50% and will sink down when fused.

Niello is a low-temperature alloy, melting at 700° F. on the average. It can be used on silver, gold, copper, brass, or any metal that will hold up at this temperature. Lay the work on a slab of steel. Fuse the piece in a kiln (700° F. for this formula), or heat the steel slab from beneath with a torch until fusion takes place. (Make sure the open flame does not touch the work.) Do not quench—let it air cool. It should be fired only once; a second firing will usually result in pitting. Remember that you are working with lead, which ordinarily will pit silver when in contact with it. You are combining them under controlled conditions that are tenuous at best.

FUSING

Fusing is a decorative process that joins small particles of metal to other metal surfaces without the use of solder. The particles, in snippet or ball form, are coated with flux and set on the support surface which is then heated. Heat just to the point where the surface bits are in a molten state (not flowing) and before the larger base metal falls. Remove the heat immediately. Related processes include reticulation and granulation.

Granulation, perhaps one of jewelry's most difficult and oldest processes, is a form of fusing. Minute grains of precious metal, some as small as $1/160''$, are carefully placed in a planned design and joined by heat without solder. Using solder on such a small shot would flood them and thus destroy the very sharp, defined quality of the grains. The process of granulation is not detailed here, but you can research it further with such authors as Philip Morton, Robert Von Neumann, or Oppi Untracht. Larger balls, called shot, can be soldered to your jewelry surface as an accent.

MAKING SHOT. Shot are small balls of metal that can be made easily by melting scraps of metal on your charcoal block: use a very low-pressure flame as shot can easily be blown away by the pressure of the flame. You can either make a selection of various size shot and sift them to sort, or you can cut evenly measured wire lengths for equal-size shot. An easy way to measure the wire is to use very small jump rings (See Chapter 8). One caution: too large a piece of scrap will produce more of an egg-shape than a ball because of its weight.

Score the surface of your charcoal block and set the scrap in the scoring. This tends to keep the tiny balls in place. For larger shot, carve out small semi-domed forms in the charcoal. This will compensate for the metal spreading out of round. Very small shot can be made by using metal filings. It is best to make shot with a reducing flame as it creates a smoother surface and one free of oxides. Store shot in water to maintain this oxide-free surface.

RETICULATION. A major characteristic of this process is the semi-controlled distortion of the metal surface. It is done with the torch flame and essentially roughens the metal skin while leaving the major portion of base metal intact.

Metals have individual melting points, the principle behind reticu-lation is to have a metal base that is lower-melting than the skin metal, but that is also an integral part of the same metal. Silver alloyed to grades below sterling and 14k gold are used. Use 18-gauge in a larger sheet than you need. The metal shrinks up to 10% and you will inevitably burn holes in it. You need to pull the fine silver or gold to the metal surface and have the lower melting alloy remaining below the surface. This is done by repeatedly bringing the metal to 1200°F. (annealing) and pickling. It will take four or more successive annealings to bring a durable coat of fine silver to the surface. You may want to coat both sides with yellow ocher and let it dry before starting.

Lay the metal on a flat, clean, dry, pre-heated asbestos block. Using a hard, even flame, heat the metal in one spot until wrinkles appear. Once this effect starts, move on over the entire surface without stopping even if you burn a hole. You can somewhat control the direction of the wrinkle with the flame. Reticulated metal cannot be formed, bent, or twisted because it is brittle and the deformed surface adds to its rigidity. Always solder with low-melting solder as reticulated metals have a low melting point.

INLAY

Inlaying metals or other materials offers the jeweler an opportunity for a hard-edged area of color or a textural accent that is not possible in any other decorative process. Basically, the term describes the laying-in of an accent material as opposed to chemically treating or mechanically changing the metal surface. Inlay is a mechanical process. It can be slightly depressed from the established surface, flat or flush with the surface, or slightly above or raised. The inlay is primarily linear, done with wire or narrow strips of metal. In the case of damascene and nunome zogan

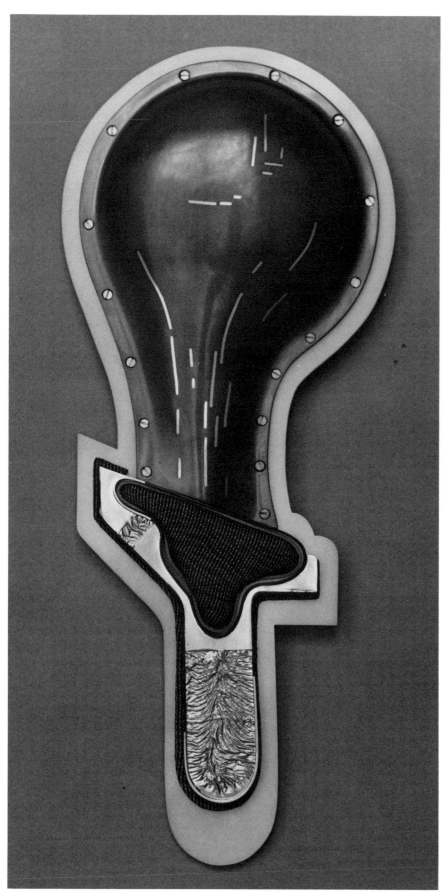

Wall Hanging Pendant by Hiroko and Gene Pijanowski. Copper, silver, Shakudo, fabric, brass, and plastic, inlayed, formed, reticulated and fabricated.

(cloth inlay of Japan) it is done with pure gold or silver foil for broader areas. These metals are the most malleable and are worked into other metals that are hard, most notably mild steel, copper, brass, and bronze.

DAMASCENE. Taking its name from Damascus where it is a major decorative metal process, damascene is most often seen in the metal work of Toledo, Spain. It is done on steel using gold and silver in both wire and leaf forms. Essentially, the design is cut away with a scorper or an engraving tool, the encised area is given a tooth or roughened, the wire or foil is layed in and tapped into place with a very small punch, and the excess foil cut away with a sharp knife. The wire is placed in an undercut groove and tapped flat at the surface. This splays the wire, fitting it into the undercut, and, at the same time flattens and levels the top edge to lock the wire in place.

Most classic damascene processes are still practiced in Japan where each specific variation has a given name. The above description, with modifications in finishing, refers to nunome zogan or "cloth" inlay. Honzogan refers to true inlay that has a flat surface, and Taka zogan is raised inlay.

MOKUME. Gene Pijanouski, together with his wife Hiroko, are jewelers in the United States. They combine in their work both the occidental and oriental metal processes. Gene has provided the following discussion on another traditional oriental metals technique called *mokume*, the lamination of metals which are then repousséd.

"The lamination of various colored alloys, and the various methods employed to expose these layers, was and still is a technique used by the Japanese craftsman and falls under the general heading of mokume-hada or wood-grain body.

"This technique had its origins in the iron forgers' art in which layers of iron or varying types, sometimes interlaced with washes of various metal oxides, were forged into pieces or folded again and forge welded. At times the finished piece was immersed in an acid bath so the strata of metal was attacked by the acid. This resulted in a surface that closely resembles wood grain or burl.

"The edge of the Japanese sword blade when properly polished is the traditional example of mokume used by the iron forger. The Tsuba (sword guard) and other parts of the Japanese sword "furniture" were also embellished with mokume. Ferrous and non-ferrous metals are used to produce a foil or background for other techniques done in sheet metal and attached to the mokume. This technique has shifted from the use of ferrous to non-ferrous in application.

"This technique and other Japanese ways of working metal were demonstrated by Professor Unno Bisei of the Imperial Fine Arts College, Tokyo, Japan when he gave a series of lecture demonstrations at the Royal College of Art, London, England, about 1910.

THE LAMINATES. "The selection of alloys should be considered from the standpoint of color variations— using the greatest contrasts available, using new alloys or those of historical importance.

The Common Base Metals: Copper, brass, bronze, and any other commercially available alloys with melting points as close as possible to each other and higher than the solder being used.

The Non-ferrous Precious Metals: Gold—recommended by karat and use, listed best to poorest with regards to workability. Fine (pure) 24 karat. Green— 18 karat (30–40% silver or silver plus cadmium). Red — 18 karat (more copper than silver). Yellow— 10 to 18 karat. White— 18 karat (25% platinum or 12% palladium) has a higher melting point than pure gold, very brittle (recommend the use of fine silver of a lower karat, such as 10K).

Grooming Ornament from Thailand. Traditional, old Ti silver, Courtesy of Taylor and Ng, San Francisco.

Headpiece from Sudan.
Silver gilt (punched), filigree.
Museum of New Mexico Collection.
Photo by David Donoho.

Anniversary Metal by Merry Renk. Engraved sterling silver and porcelain, 1972.

Japanese Non-ferrous Alloys.
Shakudo—copper with 3% to 10% fine gold, when polished and colored it produces a range of color from reddish brown to blue-black. Shibuichi—one part silver to four parts of copper, when colored produces shades of gray. Rogin— "misty silver." Shibuichi with a higher percentage of silver. Aokin —85% copper, 15% gold, and a very small amount of silver. When polished and colored, a dark purple (eggplant) color is achieved.

SOLDERING. "After the initial selection of the contrasting alloys has been made, take two of the alloys (preferably 18 or 20 gauge in thickness, approximately 2″ × 2″ inches) that are very flat and free of oil and grease and make them ready for soldering. Medium silver solder is recommended throughout the soldering sequences. The pieces are fluxed on all surfaces, being careful that only enough flux is used. Any excess can cause the metal not to solder and form pockets of flux.

"Evenly distribute small paillons of solder so that, when they melt, the surfaces are completely 'tinned' or covered with solder. Two or three sheets of metal can be done in this first stage of sweat soldering. Apply heat evenly using a neutral flame. This will cause the solder to flow quickly before the flux has been exhausted. Have an old file or some other implement handy to press down the sheets when the flow point is reached. Flat sheets soldered on a horizontal surface seem to fall into place easily (or should I say *should*) by capillary attraction, gravity, and surface tensions.

"The laminate should be cooled slowly because the heat is contained within the mass. Pickle in the standard sulfuric acid solution to remove flux and oxides. Then boil in bicarbonate of soda (one small handful in a quart of water) to neutralize the acid. If the solder has competely flowed, the edges of the laminate will not contain any holes. If not, apply flux and solder paillons to the edges where necessary and solder again.

"Roll the laminated sheets through the rolling mill, annealing as much as needed. The laminate will curl because of the different stress or work hardening of the alloys contained within. This can be avoided to a certain extent if the laminate is rolled in as many directions as possible. Cut the laminate in half and solder again, following the steps noted above. In the final rolling it is advisable to stop at 16 or 14 B&S gauge to allow enough thickness for clean-up and the next steps. Twelve to forty-eight layers seem to be the best, but many more can be done if your strength holds out or if you are fortunate enough to have access to an electric rolling mill. Any forming of the laminate should be done now.

"Place the laminate on any semi-hard surface: pitch bowl, lead block, wet leather, etc. Make depressions in the metal from the reverse side (as in repoussé) with a variety of punches. Some experimentation is recommended at this point to get the feel of how deep and what kind of patterns can be created by the different tools employed. One rule seems sound: don't bump-up beyond the center of the thickness of the laminate. Slowly file all the bumps, examining what has happened in this technique, which has been referred to as the "planned accidental." An alternate method of exposing the resultant laminates or layers is to carve into them from the front surface (if a front or back has been predetermined) with chisels, engraving tools, burs, drills, etc.

"A two-part to one-part nitric acid etch produces interesting effects, attacking the different alloys at subsequent intervals. If the laminate is left thick, 10 to 12 B&S gauge, thick strips can be cut off and arranged in patterns.

FINISHING AND COLORING. "Bright-polishing will kill many of the subtleties within this technique. A satin or matt finish by brass or steel brushing, steel wooling, or use of a lea compound are some of the possible ways to retain the contrasts created.

"A cold, weak solution of potassium sulfide (liver of sulfur) can be used. Ammonia and detergent in equal amounts with a few grains of table salt rubbed into the surface will work as will natural aging (atmospheric), the fumes of ammonia, or a combination of two or more of these. Many other patinas are available that are endless in nature and concoction with built-in variables of application, alloys within one variety, molecular or grain structures within one alloy, atmospheric conditions, etc."

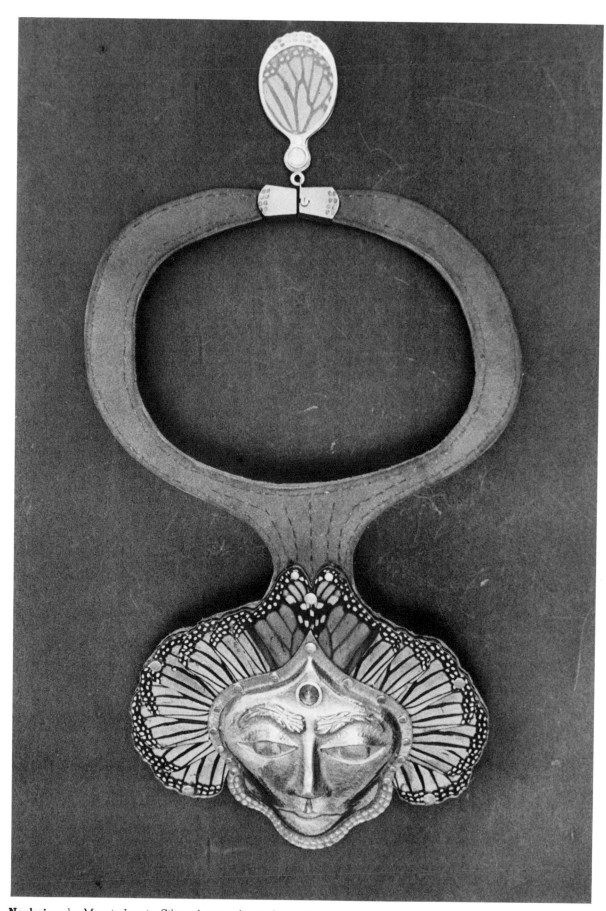

Neckpiece by Marcia Lewis. Silver, brass, plastic, butterfly wings, leather, topaz, fabricated, 1974.

7

COMBINING METAL WITH OTHER MATERIALS

Solder or spelters bond two metal pieces together. Bonding two or more dissimilar materials, however, must be done in a different manner. There are both mechanical and chemical means available for the jeweler to use. Mechanical means, which can be used to combine metals as well as dissimilar materials, include riveting, bolting, screwing, and clamping. Clamping includes using bezels, prongs, or pegs. Chemical bonding includes the use of adhesives and is not used to join metal to metal.

RIVETING, BOLTING, AND SCREWING

A rivet is a permanent bolt with a head, stem, and another head forming one piece. There are no threads on the stem. A rivet is used either for permanent rigid joining or as a pivot. Once in place it cannot be removed without being destroyed. Rivets are available commercially in various metals or you can make them from round wire. Depending on your design and the stress of the joint, the head may be mushroomed, countersunk, or flat. Mushroom and flat heads are stronger than the countersunk ones. All rivets should be annealed

before putting them in place. Once a rivet is in place, you will be upsetting and shaping the other head and the metal must be malleable.

Rivets may be decorative or functional or both. If decorative, it does not matter what their diameter is. However, if they have any functional stress, there are a few rules to follow. First, the length of the rivet stem depends on the thickness of the materials to be joined and the shape of the head to be formed. A countersunk head must have an amount equal to ¾ of its diameter sticking out above the metal's surface; a round or flat head will need slightly more than its diameter. Stems that are too long will bend and the head will form off-center. Second, the diameter of the rivet should equal twice the thickness of the materials being riveted.

PLACING THE RIVET. Match the pieces to be riveted and drill the hole. This assures their alignment. Rivets that are not aligned are weak and the head may shear later under tension. It is better to drill the holes than to punch them. Punching creates a burr on the underside of the metal that must be filed away before the rivet can be set. The stem must fit tightly in the hole. Other considerations for the placement of rivets are: hammering the head too much will cause spreading and the formation of too thin a head; rivets too close together or too close to the edge will cause the material or metal to break or split, either between rivets or between the rivet and the edge. Always have a true right-angle cut on the wire to be used for making the head. Any irregularity will cause an irregular, imperfect head.

When upsetting the second rivet head, it is always necessary to support the first. There are commercial heading tools or you can make a comparable-size depression in a hardwood block or use your steel dapping block. The latter, of course, can only be used on mushroom or button heads because they are round. Flat and countersunk rivets fit a different profile and therefore must have a different support.

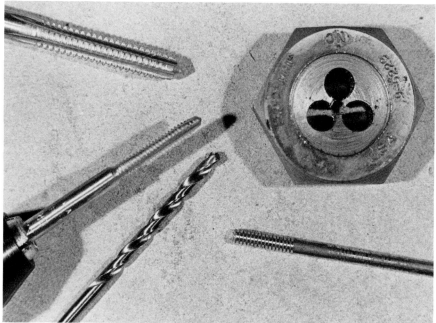

USES FOR RIVETS. As shown above even plain rivets can be decorative. Here, Marcia Lewis has used flat-headed rivets to join mixed materials. Semi-precious stones, most notably pearls, that are drilled through to form a bead can be riveted. If you have access to the back of the mounting material, a length and gauge of appropriate wire is given a head, then passed through the hole and through the backing. Support the pearl when making the other head or, if you are using a bifurcated rivet, insert a knife in the split and lay each leg over. If you have used a metal background, solder the length of wire, slip the pearl or bead on, and upset a head on the top of the bead.

Pin-stem joints, are riveted. Commercial pin stems often have the wire for riveting assembled in them. First the joint is soldered. Then the stem is inserted and the rivet ends upset, locking it in place. Do not close it too tightly as the stem must still pivot.

BOLTS AND SCREWS. These join metals and metal with other materials, either permanently or temporarily. Blind nuts are bolts that thread into a stock material without piercing through. In this case the stock material, usually quite thick, is serving as the nut. For secure fastening, there must be more than three full threads used in any bolting combination. A tap and die set as shown above is used to do the female and male threading for nuts and bolts. A tap drill (upper left) is used to make a threaded hole that acts as the nut for bolting. It can be a separate unit (nut) or in the metal stock itself for a blind bolt. First, drill a hole slightly smaller than the inside diameter (or core) of the threads of the tap. The tap drill is held with a tap wrench and twisted clockwise into the hole. Light machine oil is used on steel and kerosene on other metals to make thread cutting easier. Turn the drill about two turns and then back the tap out of the hole to clear the chips. Continue until the tap is completely through the material or as deep as you want it for a blind bolt.

The die makes corresponding threads on the bolt. It should be done on stock that is slightly larger than the outside diameter of the threads of the tap. Cut the threads in the same manner as you cut the nut. The table in the Appendix offers a guide to the correct tap, tap drills, and corresponding B & S wire gauges.

Screws have a head, a threaded stem (core), and a threaded nut. The sides of the core are parallel and the threads are cut at varying angles, spiraling down the stem.

Screws serve the same purpose as bolts except that they do not have the closing nut and the threaded sides are usually tapered. They do not go all the way through a material and are designed to be used on softer materials and metals. They join with less pressure than bolts. Screw heads vary in design: they can be countersunk (flat or oval) or rest above the surface (button or hexagon).

BEZELS, PRONGS, AND PEGS

Bezels, prongs, and pegs are the mechanical means used by jewelers to attach most gemstones to a jewelry design. They rely on pressure and counterpressure to clamp the stones securely in place for strenuous, continued wearing. The type you choose depends on several considerations beyond the design. With softer stones and fragile materials you need to use a bezel. It surrounds the stone and assures the maximum, evenly distributed, clamping necessary. Bezels are traditionally used with opaque materials, such as ivory and wood, and are occasionally used with transparent gemstones that have extreme internal stress such as opals. This type of mount does not give full benefit to the stone's light qualities, however.

Prongs are traditionally used with transparent stones. Transparent stones are normally higher on the Mohs scale of hardness, which means they do not need the complete support or protection of a bezel. Prongs raise the stone from the surface. This allows light to pass around and through it, thus displaying it to its best advantage.

A peg—a single prong—is inserted in a drilled hole (most often in a pearl) and used in combination with cement or a similar chemical bonding agent.

In every case, your concern is to mechanically clamp the stone in place with even pressure.

BEZELS. A bezel holds a stone in a closed setting and is most common to cabochons, irregularly shaped stones, or softer materials such as wood. It is like a small collar that surrounds the stone base. It should be high enough to assure a secure closing around the sloped sides and, at the same time, allow maximum visibility of the stone or other material. The drawing shows the correct relationship between the bezel height and the stone. Too

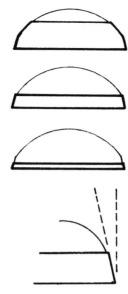

much (top) will obscure the stone. Too low may not hold the stone in place. The bezel must fit the base or widest part of the stone exactly. It is usually made of 20- to 26-gauge fine silver or 18K gold because these are most malleable and easier to burnish around the stone.

To make a circular bezel, measure the circumference of the stone's base, determine the correct height of the bezel, and cut a strip of fine silver that length and width. Solder as you would a ring band using hard solder. True the ring on a mandrel or, if irregular in shape, roll it on a flat surface with the stone fit loosely on the inside. (Bezels can also be stright or rectangular). This presses the bezel into shape. If the bezel is slightly small, it can be stretched with a burnisher. If the bezel is too large, it must be redone by snipping out the old solder joint and resoldering.

Next, with a fine, flat file or emery paper, clean all burrs from both edges of the bezel and true them if necessary to assure parallel sides. There are now varying solutions to completing the bezel.

If both the backing metal and the stone are flat and you are mounting an opaque stone, drill a small hole in the center of the backing area that the bezel surrounds. This will make it possible to remove the stone later if you need to. In using a transparent or translucent stone, cut a hole in the backing the shape

of the stone and about ¾ its size. Set the bezel around the hole and solder it in place. Use ready-flo solder, placing it on the inside of the bezel. With as small a flame as possible, concentrate the heat on the outside of the bezel. Gravity and capillary action will assist in a successful soldering.

If either the backing or the stone are not flat: this irregularity can be accounted for by making an inner shelf or bearing bezel. Without this shelf it is impossible to set the stone firmly. The bearing is an inner bezel, lower than the outer bezel and just high enough to keep the irregular stone base off the metal backing.

When the stone is flat-based but the metal backing is not—in a ring, for example—then both the bearing and outer bezel must measure higher to allow for filing and fitting on the bottom. Assemble the two bezels before filing and soldering to the back metal.

In placing bezels, make sure you have enough room around the bezel for burnishing. The stone is set after all polishing and coloring. Set the stone into the bezel and, using either a burnisher or a stone pusher, carefully push the bezel closed around it.

For round, irregular, or oval bezels, start pushing in the bezel at the top of the longest axis, then at the bottom or opposite the first push. Crimp the right quadrant, then the left. Next push between each of the quadrants, alternating oposites. You will have made eight evenly spaced pushes around the stone. To complete the closing, move successively around the bezel, pushing in with overlapping pressures. When the bezel is closed, use the burnisher to remove any marks. Straight-edged bezels are set in a similar manner, but the corners must be filed out in a tiny "V" to allow their closing.

A reverse bezel is one where the cabochon is fitted from the back into a hole with beveled sides made of

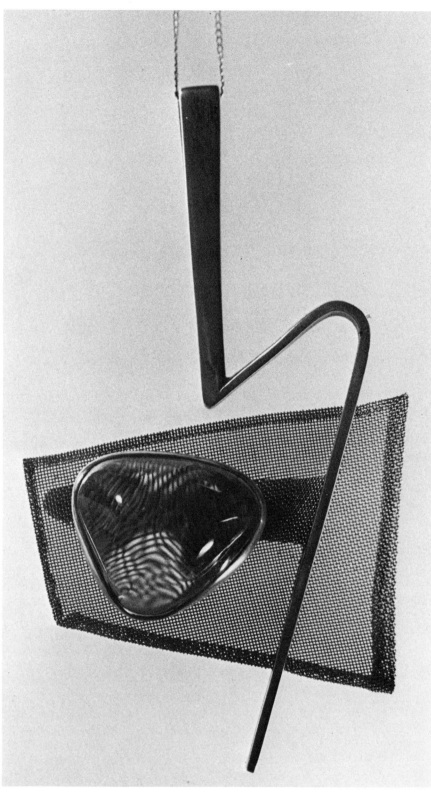

the base metal. For transparent or translucent stones a narrow bezel is soldered on the reverse side. It is closed sharply while, at the same time, pressing and holding the stone in place. If the stone is opaque you can use tabs of 22-gauge fine silver that are soldered on the reverse side. Do not place them too close to the edge of the hole or they will not bend back to admit the stone, nor will they close neatly to lock the stone in place.

PAVED AND GYPSY SETTINGS. These types of stone settings do not involve either bezels or prongs as added mechanical units. They involve developing the pressure and beading needed from the metal base itself.

In a paved setting the stone is set down into a cavity that is cut or drilled to the gem size. The surrounding metal edge is then chased or beaded over the edges of the stone. This type of setting is done on small, transparent stones that are very often set closely together (thus its name, "paved"). Gypsy settings, used to set faceted stones flush with a metal surface, have a beveled seat and a grooved channel for the stone that is made with appropriate-size burs. The edge of the channel is chased or beaded over. First, drill a very small hole where you want the stone as a guide for the other drilling. Be very careful when using chasing tools in either the paving or gypsy setting. Use very light taps of the hammer and small tools or the stone can shatter. You can chase a channel around the stone in the paved setting before chasing the edge. This gives a bit more metal to move toward the stone, but it also gives a slight indent around it.

To create beads after the seat and channel are drilled, set the stone temporarily in place with sealing wax (removed later by soaking in benzene). Make a series of four to six cuts radiating toward the stone with a line engraver. Cut them deeply and stop short of the stone. Tilt the engraver to lift the small

Pendant (Above) by Margaret de Patta. Sterling silver, stainless steel screen and crystal. From the Collection of the Oakland Museum, California. Lent by Eugene Biewlawski.

Pendant (Opposite Page) by Hiroko and Gene Pijanowski. Copper, Shakudo, brass, moonstones, silver, silk thread inlay. Formed, coiled, and fabricated.

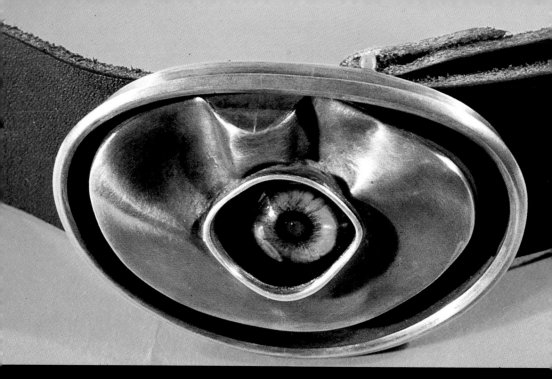

(Top) by Bobbie Fishman.
pper, sterling silver, glass eye.

Pendant (Bottom Left) by Gary Upton.
Brass, wood, and enamel bead.

Pendant and Necklace (Bot
by Karen Ehrardt. Sterling
garnets, black jade, jet bea

Neckpiece by Eileen Hill.
Silver and bronze. Fabricated.

Necklace by Ben Nighthorse.
Silver, turquoise. Fabricated.

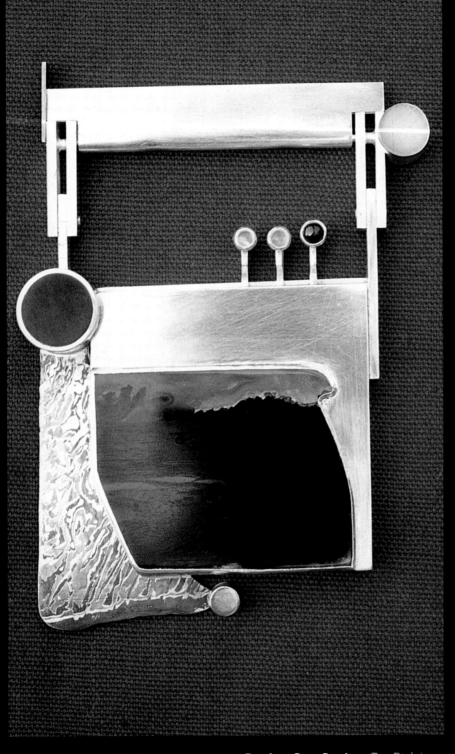

Pendant (Above) by Hiroko and Gene Pijanowski. Silver, copper, brass, Shakudo, moonstones, garnet, agate. Mokume and fabricated.

Rainbow Drop Pendant (Top Right) by Ruth Laug. Silver, copper. Raised and formed.

Bracelet (Bottom Right) by Peter Blodget. Nickle-plated brass, black-plated nickle silver, acrylic.

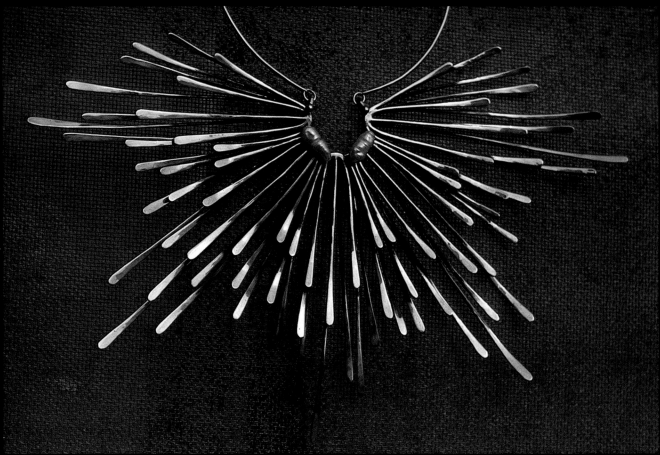

Pendant (Top Left) by Bob Christiaansen.
Enamel, sterling silver, white coral.

Bracelet (Top Right) by James Barker.
Sterling silver, yellow gold,
ivory, lapis lazuli.

Necklace (Above) by Merry Renk.
Sterling silver. Forged and oxidized.

Vest Clasp (Opposite Page)
by Marcia Lewis. Silver, ivory, ebony.

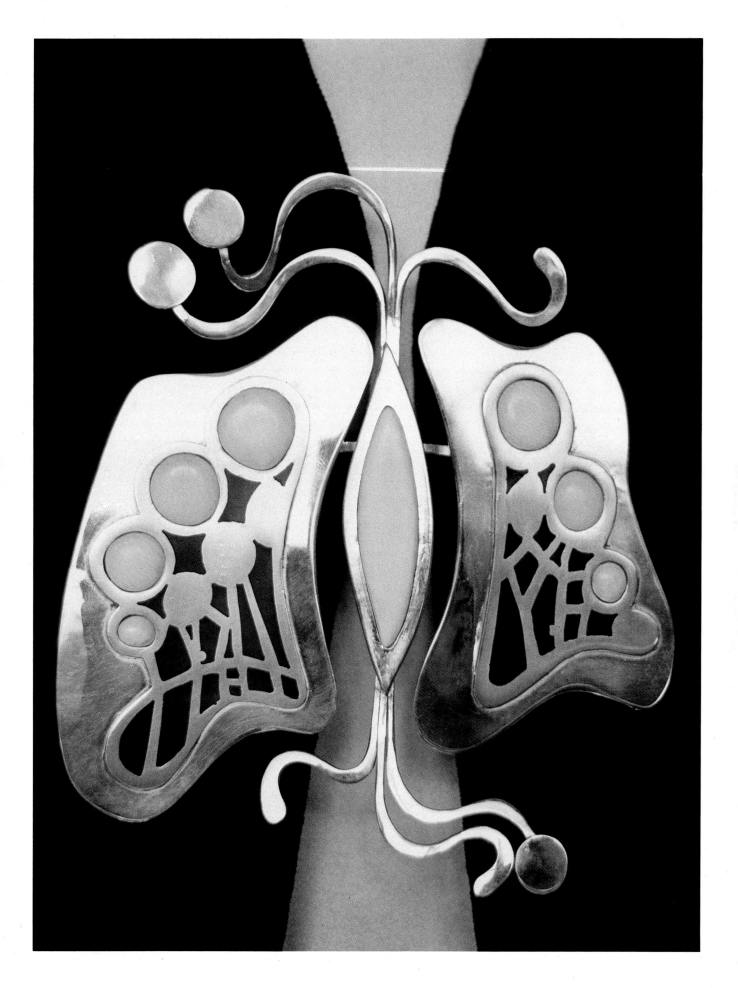

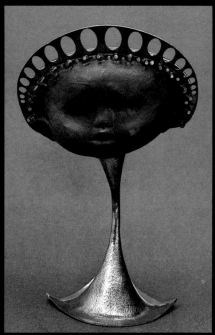

Pepsi Generation Badge (Top)
by J. Fred Woell. Copper, brass,
steel, glass, silver. Photoresist
and fabricated.

Infantasia Hand Mirror (Bottom)
by Marcia Lewis. Silver, brass,
leather, mirror.

Peacock Pin (Right) from the
Philippines. Base metal in gold plate.
Die punched and filagree. Collection
of Dr. D'Arcy Hayman, Paris, France.

prongs. Select the appropriate size tool from a beading set. By rocking and turning the tool on the prong, work it into a small, round grain. This is then closed around the gemstone.

It is sometimes impossible to use any of the aforementioned means of securing a stone, especially the irregular, baroque, or natural forms. In these cases your imagination must take over. Very slight irregularities on the bottom of stones set in a simple bezel may be compensated for by using a bit of fine hardwood sawdust or hot sealing wax on the floor of the setting before dropping the stone in place. Place the stone immediately if you use the wax, while it is still impressionable. It is also possible to use an alternate mechanical way of setting a stone: a combination of bezel and prongs, the traditional and symmetrical crown setting, or prongs used asymmetrically. For such shapes as square, rectangular, and oval stones you need four or more prongs for a secure setting. Baroque and small round stones may be set with as few as three.

Prongs. Transparent stones are faceted to increase their brilliance. Therefore, faceted stones are best displayed by prongs or in crown settings. These lift the stone from the backing and allow a maximum of light to reach the stone surface from all sides. Commercial crowns in many sizes and shapes corresponding to traditional gemstone faceting are available in silver and different karat golds. Visually they are seldom compatible with individual jewelry design by an artist.

There are three steps to making a crown setting, each designated by name. First the *collet* is made, then a *bearing* or seat is cut, and finally, the *prongs* are cut. The refining, finishing, and polishing follow in the fabrication process. The last step to completing your jewelry is to set the stone.

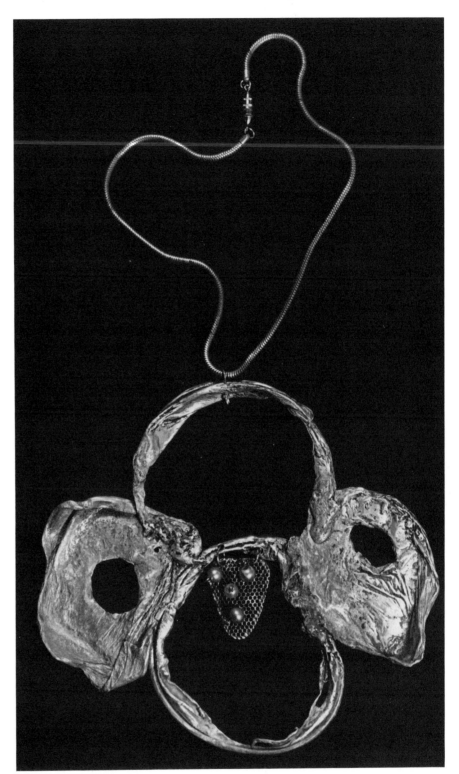

Pin by Anne Brown. Melted and fused aluminum, old pin part.

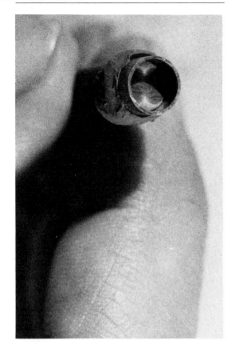

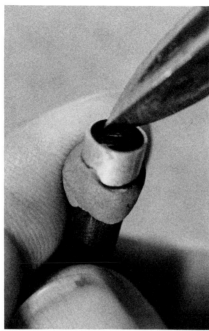

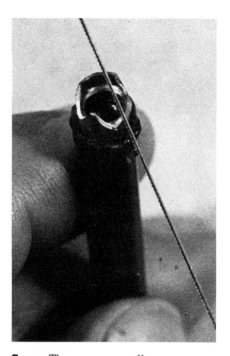

STEP 1. The collet is a tube of 16- to 18-gauge metal—thinner if in gold —that is the same diameter as the cut stone. It is the height you want the completed setting. Attach this with sealing wax to the end of a pointed piece of wooden doweling. This stick is a temporary handle that can be held in a vise or in your ring clamp for more ease in working.

STEP 2. Cut a bearing 1/16" deep on the upper inner wall of the collet. This will form a seat for the stone. You cut the bearing with your scraper, a drum bur, or your narrow, flat engraver. Caution: do not make this too thin as it will weaken the prongs that you will cut next.

STEP 3. There are usually an even number of prongs in a classical crown setting. This does not mean that you have to cut an even number. What you must do is cut and distribute them evenly around the collet. Measure and scribe whatever number of prongs you decide in terms of the size stone and the necessary grace in your design. Use the finest saw blade. By tilting the saw frame you can saw away the negative spaces, leaving the designated number of prongs. Refine the setting by fine filing, emery paper, and polishing with tripoli. Solder the collet to the metal backing. After the entire work is finished the stone is set.

Bend the prongs slightly outward by pushing the crown over a dapping punch slightly larger than the stone girdle. The collet is still not the actual diameter of the stone until this is done. Drop the stone in place and hold it with the forefinger of one hand while the points of the prongs are pressed over the girdle or edge of the stone with the stone pusher. Alternately push opposing points. Use a curved burnisher to close the tips of the prongs down so they will not catch on clothing.

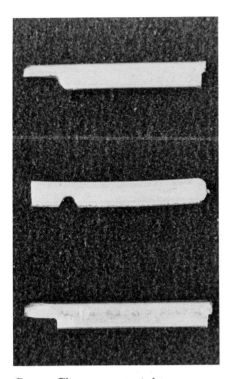

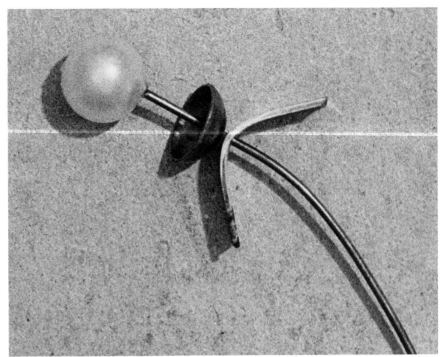

CLAWS. Claws are straight prongs that are usually a bit heavier and larger, and have a notch filed toward one end that the girdle of the stone fits into. There can be fewer claws than prongs because they are heavier and because the clamping action involves more of the stone at its widest girth. The setting does not need a seat and therefore the stone is fully suspended above the metal surface. The notch on which the girdle rests is called a *shoulder*, and it can be flat—for stones cut with flat bottoms—or beveled to fit the angle cut of the pavilion.

PEGS. Pegs are used primarily to secure pearls. The pearl has a hard outer shell and a softer interior. Above is a pearl being set with a peg and a small cup. Drill a hole half way into the pearl (they may also be purchased this way). Then enlarge the interior end very slightly using a dental drill. The peg is made of two pieces of 18-gauge, half-round wire. Partially solder the two together, spreading one pair of the ends slightly so that the peg is actually bifurcated. An alternate to this is soldering two round wires together and processing them through your drawplate as described in Chapter 3.

Drill the correct size hole in the jewelry and solder the peg in place. Cut the peg to its correct length—the depth of the hole. Make a tiny wedge to fit between the two half-round wire ends that will spread then when fully in place. Place a small amount of bonding in the

pearl hole and insert the peg with the wedge loosely in place. The wedge will press into place, widen the peg end slightly and bond with the cement, locking the pearl in place.

Larger pearls can be set in small, shallow cups (as shown above) made in the dapping block. Make sure the cup is no more than ¼ the height of the pearl or you will obscure it too much. Drill a hole in the center of the cup and solder a 20-gauge round wire through it for the peg. Solder from the interior of the cup. The bottom of the peg can be riveted or soldered to mount the pearl. The top peg is cut to length and given a slight bend. Place a small amount of bonding cement in the pearl's hole and insert the peg. A bend in the peg will clamp the pearl securely once the cement is dry.

CHEMICAL BONDING

All chemical bonds have greatly improved as a result of expanded research in plastics. Epoxy bonding agents, while esthetically not as satisfactory as mechanical joining, must be used at one time or another. The bonding cement used to reinforce pegging pearls is an example. Riveting is the only alternative for setting but the method can obscure much of a tiny pearl. Jewelry supply houses stock the most successfully tested cements of the hundreds made. Each bonding agent is compounded to join specific materials in the strongest way and it is foolhardy not to accept the experts advice in selecting an appropriate cement.

You must take into consideration the physical properties of the materials you are using when making your selection. Is the surface of the material absorbent—will some chemical in the adhesive penetrate the fibers of leather, for example? What are the solvents appropriate to its dilution? Is it flexible or rigid? Will it be affected by heat, acids, water, etc.? Will it stain or discolor? Can it be cleaned if necessary? Will it deteriorate with age? Check whatever qualities are necessary with the dealer and if any answers are negative to your individual purposes—don't buy it! Look for another answer.

Wax. One type of bond—actually a natural plastic material—is worth mentioning in terms of setting soft stones such as turquoise. These softer stones can be polished with simple jewelry tools and polishes. You can make a low bezel, solder a metal backing, and set small, irregular scraps of stone in hot sealing wax. When the area is completely and solidly filled, the surface can be finely filed, rubbed with carborundum stone, and polished with white diamond. Many of the mosaic stone designs of the Southwest Indians and silver and turquoise work from Mexico use this process. You can use a closely colored wax or one of great contrast to emphasize the random mosaic stone pattern.

This surface must be polished slowly as friction will heat and soften the wax surface. Also, the wax is brittle so it should be worked in small settings rather than wide expanses. The outer bezel should have a slight slope inward, from the base toward the top. This will allow hot wax to spread at the base, thus offering more support and less surface tension.

GEMSTONES

Gems and semiprecious stones have been used throughout history as an integral part of jewelry. Valued for their color, texture, pattern, and brilliant transparency, they have been held in high esteem, given great monetary worth, and attributed with magical powers. Until the 1500's, gemstones were carved or cabochon-cut. The discovery of faceting transparent stones at that time increased their value tremendously.

Stones are identified by hardness on a relativity scale developed by a mineralogist, Mohs. The system measures the ability of one material to be scratched by being rubbed against another. It is not an exact scale, but one that gives the relative hardness of one stone to another. Glass has the hardness of 5½ on the scale and a steel file has 6½. Glass imitations of stones can be easily tested since the file will scratch glass.

Toughness is the ability of a stone to withstand breakage. Toughness and hardness are not the same so one may be rated high and the other low in the same stone. For example, the diamond is the hardest material known, yet, it is not tough. It can easily be cleaved, fractured, or chipped. Jade is considered a soft stone, yet it is the toughest of all the stones.

Cameos are examples of carving. These are made from select portions of a seashell, carved and polished in such a manner as to expose successive layers of color in the shell in a relief design. An intaglio has the design cut or engraved into the shell or stone and a cuvette has a hollow background with a raised design.

A *cabochon* is the oldest cut and can be made from any rough, hard

material. They are cut round, oval, rectangular, or square, in heights of low, normal and high. Some stones are always cut cabochon— the opal, for example—because their internal stress will not allow them to be faceted. All softer stones on the Mohs scale are cut in cabochon and they are set in more protected designs because of this susceptibility to surface scratching. *Doublets* and *triplets* are stones that are sandwiched: the gem on top and less precious material underneath. Hard stones and most transparent stones are faceted.

Faceting stones has one purpose: to establish reflecting planes in such a manner as to allow light to enter the top and to be reflected back through the top. It concentrates the light or fire in the stone and gives full power to its color. This is called the refractory index of a stone. Three stones have a single refractory index: the diamond, spinel, and garnet. All other transparent stones have double refractory indices, some greater than others. The zircon and peridot have the greatest (their edges appear double when viewed from the top).

When light passes through the facets of a stone it is separated into its component parts: red, orange,

yellow, green, blue, and violet. The facets are acting as a prism. This is called chromatic dispersion in gems. The separation can be very great, as in a diamond, and the fire or pure colors can often be seen separately.

On traditionally faceted stones, the individual parts are identified as the top or table, the crown, the girdle or the widest part of the stone, the pavilion, and the culet or the bottom tip. Hard stones are cut by cleaving, thus creating symmetrical facets on the surface of the crown and the pavilion.

Besides being round or oval, traditional faceting takes the form of single-step, emerald-cut or multi-stepped, baguette or rectangular, and marquise or almond-shaped.

Lapidary is the art of gem cutting; several fine texts are listed in the Bibliography for reference and for more extensive study. The table in the Appendix lists some of the gemstones most popular for jewelry and their corresponding hardness on Mohs scale.

ENAMELS

Enamel is a vitreous glaze of finely ground glass that is fused by heat to a metal surface. Oxides are added to the powder to create numerous colors. The enamel may have a high-gloss or a matte finish when fired. It can be opaque, translucent, or transparent—the latter offering great visual depth to the work because the base metal shows through. Copper, fine silver, gold, and steel are most frequently used as the base metal for enameling. Enamels are much like ceramic glazes, and there are historical examples where enamels decorate large ceramic and brick wall tiles at Tell el-Yehudia (Egypt) and in Babylon. The major classifications of enamels are cloisonné, champleve, basse-taille, plique-a-jour, and Limoges.

In cloisonné, narrow strips of metal, called *cloisons*, enclose each area or color of enamel. These cloisons are bent to shape and fastened to a metal ground with solder or enamel Champlévé is another process used to fill metal recesses with enamel. The recesses are chiseled or etched into the surface of the metal. The expanse of metal left between the recessed areas can be wide or narrow. Basse-taille is very similar to champleve except the cut away areas are sculptured and chased. This low relief is left visible through the use of transparent enamels. Plique-a-jour is a process in which only the cloisons hold the transparent enamels; there is no metal base. Light is able to pass through the areas of colored glass—thus its name which translates "light of day". Limoges is a surface technique in which none of the enamel goes below the surface nor is it contained within walls. The entire metal surface is covered with enamel without interruption and relies on painting techniques.

Enameling with vitreous glazes is a complete discipline in itself and is much too extensive for inclusion here. Only a short digest of technique will follow. The bibliography suggests several fine texts devoted exclusively to this process.

THE WORK AREA. As with jewelry production, a separate work area with segregated and well-organized spaces is necessary to assure quality production. Enamels are stored in glass jars and shelved by individual color and by grit, wire, and chunk. The jars should have a small fired sample attached as part of the label for easy recognition of color and opacity. You will need a very clean table with a stack of clean paper and a jar for leftover, scrap enamel. Stored next to the table are 80-mesh sift screens, tools and brushes, glycerine, light machine oil, salt water, and gum tragacanth. Then you need a Nichrome fire screen, an enameling kiln or soldering tripod with torch, a spatula or loading fork, and an asbestos sheet.

The variety of tools you may need for the various techniques include scribes, stylus, leather modeling tools, crochet hook, tweezers, pallette knife, pliers, files, ball-peen hammer, carborundum stone, mica sheet, drills, vise, a large glass bowl or pie plate, and small glass jars. Chemicals and materials include nitric acid solution (5%), asphaltum and turpentine, steel wool, and emery cloth. Punched blanks of copper are available or you can cut your own from 18-gauge metals. You will also need 20-to 24-gauge wire for cloisons, and an assortment of other metals to supplement your individual design.

PREPARING THE METALS. All metal surfaces must be clean before the enamels are applied. The metal can be cleaned with pickle, steel wool, emery cloth, or a file. Once the metal is clean, handle it by the edges to keep your fingerprints off the surface. To protect copper from developing firescale on the non-enameled surface, paint it with a salt-water solution (made one tablespoon salt to a cup of water) or a commercial masking preparation. Wash this off after the first firing if you are counter-enameling.

In general, enameling follows this sequence. First the metal is

Pendant by Bob Christiaansen. Sterling, enameled, white coral and carneallian, fabricated.

cleaned, then the type of enameling process is developed. For example, cloisons are prepared and soldered, the metal surface is cut, etched, or chased, or holes are pierced, cut, or cloisonnéd. The enamel can be applied dry by sifting, painted wet, or layed on in a paste form. There are small enamel chunks and threads available that can be used in that form or in combination with powdered enamel.

A thin layer of enamel is applied and fired and then a second applied and fired. It is better to have several layers than one thick one because enamel builds stress on the metal surface. To relieve this stress, the metal should be counter-enameled on the back or reverse side. The design can chip off if the work is not counter-enameled. Counter-enameling is a good place to use scrap enamels because the mix of colors also offers a mix in firing temperatures. Enamels do not all fire at the same temperature. When sifting enamels, place the metal on a clean piece of paper. When you have finished sifting, remove the covered metal and return the powder to its container. If you applied several colors without clearing the individual colors from the paper, dump the mixture in the scrap jar for counter-enameling.

FIRING ENAMELS. Firing enamels—the fusing of the enamel or glass to the metal surface—is done either in an enameling kiln, over an electric hotplate with a Pyrex dish serving as a dome, or on an open kiln. The open kiln is made of a soldering tripod or two firebricks stood on end, both with a Nichrome wire screen on top. The latter arrangement is fine for small jewelry and accent enameling, while the kiln offers a larger firing space and more professional heat control. When the enamel is fused, the surface will appear shiny and smooth. The temperature varies with individual colors and the base metal used. Occasional over-firing produces very unique colors in non-

repeatable variations. The work is supported on a metal or ceramic stilt as it goes through the firings. Apply and fire enamels in the following sequence: one coat of counter-enamel, one base coat on the face, one coat of counter-enamel, then a design firing. This will place the tiny stilt marks on the back of your work, not marring the front. It is not necessary to do additional counter-enamelings if you do more than two firings of the design.

Very fine enamels may need as many as 20 firings to build up a quality surface that can display great visual depth, especially in basse-taille.

Glycerine slightly diluted with water, or light machine oil can be painted over a first or ground coat to hold sifted enamels within a given painted area when designing Limoges. Shake the excess off onto the clean paper and pick away any stray grains. With care you can scratch through—graffito—the powder to make a fine line. You can also dust over a paper stencil and remove it with tweezers. Again, clean up stray grits. One thing enamel will not do: it will not mix into a third color when firing. Each individual grit retains its own color integrity. For example, sifting yellow and blue will not fire out green, only a mix of yellow and blue specks.

Mix enamels and water to a paste when doing cloisonné. This paste is dropped in the areas to be filled, allowed to dry, and then fired. This is repeated until all the enamel areas are flush with the cloisons. For champlévé and basse-taille a similar charging, firing, and re-charging takes place in the depressed areas. Traditional enamels, when completed, should have a flat surface that is flush with the surrounding metal. If there is irregularity in the final enamel firings, the surface can be ground smooth with a carborundum stone using a rotary motion under water. This matte finish can remain or the piece can be given a final firing to return the gloss.

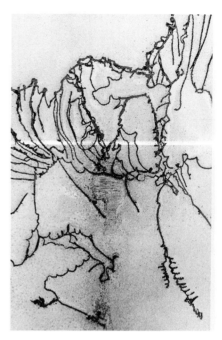

NEW TECHNIQUES. This photo shows a detail of an enameled panel by June Schwarcz, an innovator with an international reputation for working with vitreous enamels. Here, she uses electroformed wires as cloisons embedded and held in place by enamels. A number of firings used both opaque and transparent enamels. The electroformed wires were burnished with a scotch stone as a last step. Over-firing of the basic white enamel in combination with the copper wires created a number of subtle green variations throughout the design.

A few jewelry supply houses carry a low-temperature hard-curing enamel. It is actually a bi-system plastic. The colors are mixed with a catalyst and can then be painted, sprayed, or applied with a spatula or squeeze bottle. It is not vitreous. It does not fuse with the metal surface but is similar to a bond. The work is fired in your cooking oven at 200°F. for an hour. There are forty colors available—opaque or transparent—and the colors can be mixed to obtain an infinite variety. It will adhere to metals, wood, some plastics, and ceramic materials. It can be filed, stone-ground, and polished in the same way as vitreous enamels.

Pendant by Eileen Hill. Silver, brass, ebony and ceder, cast and fabricated, 1975. Photograph by John Thompson.

PLASTICS

The term "plastic" is a general one referring to any substance that at sometime and by some applied means passes from a soft, malleable material into a hard, durable one. Plastic materials exist naturally in such materials as clay or the gums and resins that ooze from growing trees. Heat is the most common treatment applied to plastic materials to bring them to a hard stage.

Plasticity is the ability of a material to flow like a liquid yet take a shape of its own upon hardening. Natural resins mixed with coloring agents form sealing wax, which is one of our earliest compounded plastic materials. Heat a rigid stick of sealing wax until it becomes plastic or soft and putty-like and drop it on a surface. This molten sealing wax flows sufficiently to take up the impression of anything pressed into it. The design will become permanent and the plasticity of the wax disappears when the wax is cool and hard. Only reheating will put it back into its plastic stage.

A few other natural plastics include glass and bituman (mineral); shellac (animal); and amber and rubber (vegetable). All of these— although we have practical uses for them—are weak, tend to be brittle, soften at a low temperature, and burn readily in their natural form.

Two industrial developments during the nineteenth century started what we today call our plastics industry. First, rubber was vulcanized. Once sulphur was combined with the masticated rubber, and heat and pressure were applied, rubber lost its plastic quality. Reheating would not return it to its original malleable form again. The second industrial change was the conversion by chemical means (nitric acid) of wood cellulose and other plant products into a clear, tough, hornlike material. The initial result of this was an explosive called nitrocellulose. Soon after its invention, however, a young metalworker by the name of Alexander

Parkes in Birmingham, England, became interested in the new plastic. Prior to this, he had been electroplating natural objects. These included a silver-plated spider's web and a bunch of roses, both of which were presented to Prince Albert and Queen Victoria.

Working with nitrocellulose, Parkes found that it would dissolve in molten camphor. As it cooled it passed through a puttylike plastic stage during which it could be molded. When it set, it was hard, hornlike, and flexible in thin sheets. We now call it celluloid.

Today plastics are essentially classified in two basic groups: thermoplastic resins and thermosetting plastics. The first group becomes soft when exposed to sufficient heat and hardens when cool, and they will do this repeatedly. Thermosetting plastics achieve their final shape when heat and pressure are applied during the forming process. Reheating does not soften these plastics. For the jewelers' purposes, plastics come in liquid, foams, paste, powders, sheets, rods, tubes, and solid volumes. It also comes in emulsions and pellets. They may be cast, formed, molded, carved, laminated, and fabricated. You can join plastics to plastics, plastics to different materials, or use it as an adhesive. Mechanical linkage using rivets, nuts, bolts, self-tapping metal screws, hinges, or clips are all metal techniques that may be adapted to plastics. Adhesive bonding joins material(s) together without dissolving or otherwise affecting the surfaces. Solvent bonding of such thermoplastics as acrylics is done with ethylene dichloride or methylene dichloride applied with a dropper, brush, hypodermic needle, glass tube, or rod. The solvent softens the surface and fuses the plastic pieces together.

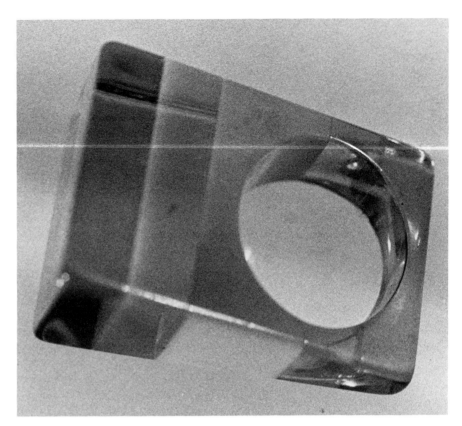

CHARACTERISTICS OF PLASTICS. It is believed that plastics are lightweight. Maybe! Because it is strong, durable, and stable, it more often takes a hollow form or is given a cellular form (foamed). Therefore, for the volume represented, plastics are lightweight. However, a sheet of clear acrylic plastic, square inch for square inch, has a relative atomic weight that is between gold and lead.

Besides its weight, there are other properties of plastics that are valuable for the jeweler to know. Many plastics are transparent, with clear acrylics (such as the ring shown above) having the unique ability to "pipe" light. Light is captured, passes through the material, and is refracted toward the edges. The edges, and any surface carvings, seem to glow. In general, plastics have a low abrasive index—a fingernail file will cut through many of them and all scratch very easily. Some foamed plastics will vaporize and can therefore be used as patterns in bronze casting. The foam form is embedded in sand or casting plaster and then gravity-cast, whereupon the hot metal vaporizes the plastic. A traditional wax mandrel can be invested, melted out, and liquid plastic cast in the cavity instead of metal. This can be done with gravity casting, but not with centrifugal. There are plastics that can be tooled using metal lathes. Also, inclusions can be added to some polyesters.

Plastics are easily worked because of the low abrasive index. Wet, fine-grit emery paper or cloth in progressively finer cuts is used by hand or on a sander for finishing. Water is used as a lubricant to keep down the toxic dust. It should be worked to a 660 cut and then given a final buffing using an unstitched muslin wheel with tripoli and then rouge. Do not use the same buffing wheels for plastics as you use on metals.

BONE

The principal bone material used for carving today comes from cattle. Bone from either a horse or a sheep may also be used. Sheep bone is harder than the other two; the color of horse bone is less white. The marrow bone is the one used most frequently.

CLEANING AND PREPARING BONE. Prepared, dried bone slabs may be purchased. To clean and prepare bones yourself, first select a marrow bone, saw off the joints with a hacksaw, and remove the marrow. Then, make a solution sufficient to cover the bone using proportionally one teaspoon of alum and one teaspoon of soda to one quart of water. Place the bone in the solution and boil for one to three hours depending on the fat content of the bone. Change the solution several times, washing the bone each time. After all fat content and miscellaneous meat materials have been boiled from the bone, remove it, rinse it, and dry it.

You can cut the bone into rough slabs at this time or continue with the whole bone. Place it or its pieces in a 40% bleach solution of hydrogen peroxide in a glass or Pyrex container and leave it for 24 to 48 hours.

Great caution should be exercised when using the hydrogen peroxide solution because it can burn the skin. Use tongs or rubber gloves to protect your hands. You can reduce this hazard slightly by using a 20% solution and heating it to a boil, then simmering the bone in the solution for a few hours. Remove the bones from the bleaching bath with tongs and rinse them well under cold water. Let the bone air dry. An alternate to this bleaching is to place the cleaned bone in the sun and open air for several days. The chemically bleached bone will be slightly whiter.

TOOLS AND MATERIALS. All of the jeweler's tools previously mentioned can be used on bone. Be forewarned that working with bone, even after it has been cleaned, is somewhat unpleasant because it has an objectionable aroma when it is sawed, drilled, or filed.

There are a few precautions you should take when working on bone because, unlike metal, the material is structurally grown in hard, dense layers. It also has a grain or direction similar to that of wood. This means you must always use a support block when drilling holes or the underside will chip or splinter. This, of course, means more finishing work and depreciates fine craftsmanship.

Bone meal will build up rapidly in the teeth of either a saw or a file. It is sticky because of the fat particles and so clings to the tool. Use the file card to clean the teeth of both often. If fine files still hold the bone meal, heat them slightly and then use the card. Be very careful not to overheat the file or you will damage it. Gouges used for working wood may be used carefully on bone to scoop out depressions. They should be very sharp. Bone is harder and more brittle than most woods and should be worked with more care.

Do not clamp bone pieces directly in the metal vise. You will need to devise "helpers" for your vise to hold the small pieces of bone while filing or sanding. Make these of hardwood to avoid marring or exerting too much pressure on the material. These can be small wooden triangles or a square length of hardwood with a rabbited slot. Your bench pin can also be used as a holding support.

Always sand in one direction on the bone—with the grain or lengthwise. Any other direction will produce visible scratches on the surface. Use Numbers 1, 1/0 and 2/0 papers. Fine steel wool (0 to 00) can be used after the sandpaper.

To complete the polishing, use whiting, Paris white, or water-ground whiting. Do not use any of the polishing compounds traditional with polishing metals as they will discolor the bone. Polishing compounds used for horn or plastic can also be used on bone. Generally, a well-polished surface can be obtained using hand rubbing only. There is no need to use a polishing machine but, if you do, always use a wheel for these compounds that you do not use with any others.

Bone can be joined to other materials by using rivets or epoxy-resin glues. Remember that bone has a grain or direction of growth very similar to that of wood. Cross-sections of bone are more fragile than those cut the long way and you will need to work with thicker pieces of cross-cut bone than with lengthwise cuts.

Bone can be dyed, or it can be engraved and inlayed with colored wax. To color bone, use a strong aniline dye. Boil the bone in the solution for about an hour or until your color preference is reached. It will be slightly lighter when dry. Dye the bone after you have completely formed and polished it.

To inlay color into bone, cut your design 1/16" into the bone surface

HORN

Horn consists of a usable outer shell and an inner membrane that must be removed before working. The outer shell is made up of two other layers, one very hard and a second slightly softer one. Horn will vary in thickness depending on the animal source. Horn from a cow is much thicker than horn from a steer. There are also multi-colored variations in the material that should be taken into consideration during your designing. The horn of domestic animals differs from that of wild animals. Wild animal horn is generally solid throughout its length, while only the tip end of domestic horn is solid.

To obtain horn you must go to the slaughterhouse or purchase it already processed at specialty suppliers. If you do secure it from the slaughterhouse be sure to check for external flaws resulting from barbed wire or fights. Vickie Pipes used the following general procedures for working horn.

CLEANING THE HORN. To remove the inner core from a horn, boil it in water for at least an hour. The inner core will fall free. Do not boil too long as this will tend to stress the horn in later processing. If you do not remove the core as soon as possible it will begin to decompose (with obvious side effects). Dry the horn completely before you begin working or it will warp later.

Horn is shaped by using heat in combination with press molds or with the simple handtools of jewelrymaking. Forming horn is a slow process because it is a strong, tough material.

with a sharp knife. Break up sticks of colored sealing wax (it sometimes comes with a wick that creates unwanted soot as it burns) and place the wax in a small pan or crucible over heat to soften. Heat the tip of a small screw driver over the alcohol lamp or use one of the improvised wax tools mentioned in Chapter 5, and force the softened wax into the carved grooves. Excess wax can be removed later in the sanding and polishing process. If you polish with a machine, be careful that the heat it generates does not melt the surface of the sealing wax.

SCRIMSHAW. This is a fine example from the Taylor and Ng collection of a bracelet with scrimshaw—the scratching or engraving done on whalebone or walrus tusks. The lines are either scribed directly into the material or a drawing can be transferred by pin pricks through a pattern on to the surface and lines cut to join them together. The cuts are very shallow and are brought out by rubbing ink or lamp blacking into them and then polishing the excess off of the surface.

FORMING HORN. Select a horn that has a general form that corresponds to the shape you are making. To get a slab of horn, first cut off the thick point and then cut the horn shell longitudinally with a jeweler's saw or hacksaw.

There are two ways to heat your horn. The first is to use a soldering torch with a flame similar to that for annealing. A solution of water-glass (sodium silicate dissolved in water) should be brushed over the horn before it is heated to prevent burning. The second way is to boil the piece of horn again. With this method you do not run the risk of burning or scorching the horn. You do, however, have to be careful of boiling the horn too long because it will be more susceptible to marring or it can raise little flakes on the surface that take time to remove later in the finishing. You can form horn relatively easily in a softened state and it will retain the new shape when air cooled.

Make a paper pattern or a leather one if there are compound curves in the shape. Lay the pattern on the horn and carefully trace around it using a sharp pencil or your scribe. Allow excess material around your pattern if you are using a torch as the edges will singe and need to be filed off. If bending the horn in a simple curve, bend it further than you want the final bend as it will have a tendency to uncoil slightly.

Compound forms with compound curves can be pressed with a wooden mold that has parallel concave and convex faces. These can be carved with chisels, files, and rasps. Sandwich the heated horn slab between the two faces and

clamp it firmly into your bench vise or with a C-clamp.

Horn stretches in only one direction, not in all directions as does metal. This is due to the directional growth pattern of the material. For example, if you have a round, cross-section of horn, you can

stretch its diameter by using a wood reamer. Press the reamer down into the heated horn circle, revolving it in the same way you would a juice squeezer. Making horn thinner will allow you to form it more easily and allow light to pass through it.

FINISHING HORN. Cut away the excess material using either the jeweler's saw or a file. Be sure to use the same even strokes as in filing metals, and to select the file profile most compatible with the horn's edge profile. The horn is very easy to sand and should take little time.

To polish horn use powdered pumice and water. After rubbing vigorously, rinse and then polish further with a wet cloth and powdered coal. A final protective polishing using soap and Paris whiting will result in a fine, warm, soft, deep surface shine. To get a different surface texture after the initial filing and sanding is complete, drop pieces into household liquid bleach. The bleach will eat away the horn and create a very uniform and slightly whitened surface. Be sure to rinse and dry each piece after the bleach treatment or the bleach will continue to eat away at the surface.

Tortoise shell is worked much in the same manner as horn. The best shell for your use comes from the Hawksbill turtle in plates about 7" by 12". It is harder, less fibrous, and more brittle than horn. When heated in boiling water, the surface softens and liquefies. Two softened pieces can be laminated to increase thickness by joining and clamping them while they cool and dry.

Tabletier-Cornetier (Horn Workshop). Eighteenth century, from Vol IX, Plate 1, "L'Encyclopedie, ou Dictionnaire Raisonné des Sciences, des Arts et des Metiers" of Denis Diderot.

WOOD

Wood is often used together with metal in jewelry production. It has a rather open grain in comparison with more popular materials and is not conducive to very fine, detailed work. However, many exotic hardwoods are very tight-grained with singularly unique patterns in their growth rings. They also offer a wide color range within a small piece. Woods are classified as hard or soft, which actually has nothing to do with hardness but is based on whether they come from deciduous or evergreen trees.

Less interestingly marked, even-grained, hardwoods can be inlayed (piqued) in the same manner as horn, bone, ivory or other dense, soft materials. It can also be inlayed into a metal surface. Wood is held in place by bezels, pegged, or riveted. Be sure the piece is sound and without cracks. If it has a knot, it should be tight. Woods should have a light oiling from time to time; only a few, like teak, have natural oils. Many will get fine hair cracks if this is not done. The exotic coloring of some hardwoods is not fast (a few are even dyed) and you can expect the wood to change and darken with age.

Many hardwoods are so dense that jeweler's tools will work on them very well: the saw, files, drills, emery, and polishes. Do not use the rouge as the red will discolor the wood.

Individual pieces of wood, used as alternate units in a bracelet, for example, must have findings that work but do not detract from the material effect. Wood pieces are usually pegged with a small loop. The hole is drilled 1½ times the wire gauge and as deep as possible. Kink the peg, thread it, or rough it up with a file. Very dense woods can be tapped and the peg threaded and then blind-screwed in place. Drill the hole straight and at right angles to the surface for small wood pieces. If the piece is heavier, drill the hole at an angle and correct the loop angle by bending it after the cement is set. Put a little bonding cement into the hole, insert the peg, and let it all dry.

Bits of hardwood can be pegged to metal or set in a bezel. When pegging it is essential to align the pegs with the holes in the wood by temporarily rubber-cementing the wooden shape in place on the metal. Then, drill your holes through both. Remove the wood and clean the rubber cement off of both surfaces. Solder the wire pegs in place, and using a bonding cement to replace the wood on the pegs. Most cements can use a little clamping (use a clothespin) to assure a close bond.

Close bezels normally around wood pieces. Be sure of two things: first, that all soldering on the piece is completed and, second, that the wood has been given a slight slant to the edges as in a cabochon shape. In this way, the bezel will lock the wood on to the surface.

Inlaying wood into metal is best done with cross-grain cuts rather than horizontal-grain cuts. Use two sheets of metal, one as a backing and one with a hole or holes cut the same size as the wood inlay. The angle of the inlay edges should be chamfered. Sweat-solder the two sheets together, checking to be sure the bevel slopes inward. Fit the wood piece exactly; wood that is a bit larger can be hammered in place by setting the assembly on a steel block, placing a second steel block on top, and hammering. End-grain (cross-cut) wood cuts give and fit into the cutout better than running-grains. File the wood and metal together to achieve a flat surface.

Pendant by Aimée Johnson. Silver box construction, wood inlay, 1975.

FRAGILE MATERIALS

We have a funny thing in our heads about jewelry. We casually wear very brittle stones, delicately mounted in almost hair-like prongs —stones that may also be worth hundreds of dollars—without a care because we have been conditioned to accept them as wearable. And, they are. Yet, there are other fragile and beautiful objects that have not been accepted for contemporary personal adornment. It cannot be the material value of a gemstone as opposed to a sea shell, for example, for there are indeed rare and beautiful sea shells worth thousands of dollars. It has just been assumed that gemstones are good and shells are bad because they will break and the stone will not.

On the Mohs scale, sea shells rate within a half point of such accepted materials as pearls, amber, and ivory. Could it be that throughout history, shells, teeth, fossils, pebbles, and fish vertebrae—the objets trouvé—have come to be regarded as trivial, and thus the original pride in their wearing is lost? The shell is just one of a number of fragile objects that you should consider possible enrichments, counter-points, or accents in your original jewelry design.

We are now becoming more and more aware that the intrinsic beauty of things is what make them "precious"—not the predetermined economy of a given material. Contemporary jewelers are incorporating many fragile and precious natural materials and objects into their designs. We see feathers, butterfly wings, or quills as possible adjuncts to our work with metals, provided that the piece is designed for wear on special occasions or to be worn on more protected areas of the body.

Consider, too, that materials of small ready-mades in metal can be

successfully re-oriented toward jewelry design. The general hardware store, the miniature hobby shop, the marine hardware shop, or even the stationers are all great supply sources of ready-mades if you are on the alert.

LEATHER

The subject of leather is included here not because it is a direct jewelry process but because it has proven a very complimentary material to metal. The combined use of leather and metals has, historically, gone through cycles of popularity. At this time it appears to be on the rise again. While natural leather is much in demand but not in great supply, synthetic leathers have supplemented the popular demand to a point where there are greatly extended design pos-

sibilities. Jewelry is now becoming quite an integral part of the body and body covering. Since having large portions of the body covered with leather rather than metal is certainly more practical than the reverse, integration of the two is also more practical.

Leather from small animals is called skin, while leather from large animals is called hide. Both are sold by the square foot in whole or half skins and hides. They are also sold by the square inch, but this is more expensive. Scrap leather is sold by the pound. Some hides are split, which produces two

full hides, one weak and one strong. Various animal hides and skins have more durability than others. Many of the exotic leathers, such as ostrich or pigskin, are not as durable as cowhide but their natural surface beauty and softness is such that it should not be embellished. There are areas of hides and skins that are stronger than others, so your use and design should take this into account. The strongest part is down the spine or center and the weakest at the extremities, for example, belly and leg areas.

Belt "Rapunsel," by Marcia Lewis. Brass and carved leather, masonite die-formed, chased and fabricated, 1974.

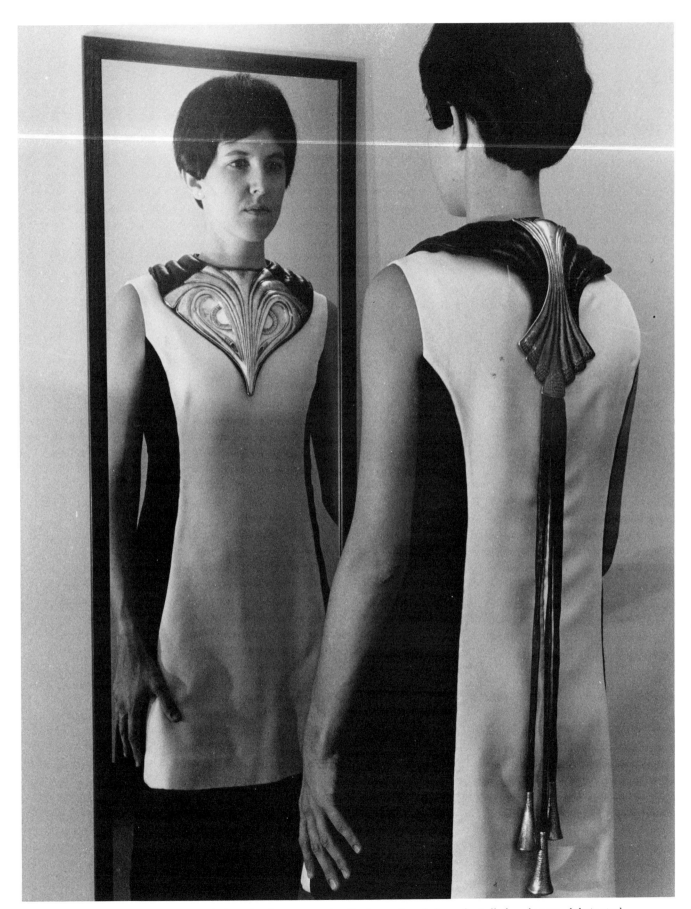

Big Bird by Marcia Lewis. Silver and glove leather, masonite die-formed and chased, stuffed and sewn, fabricated.

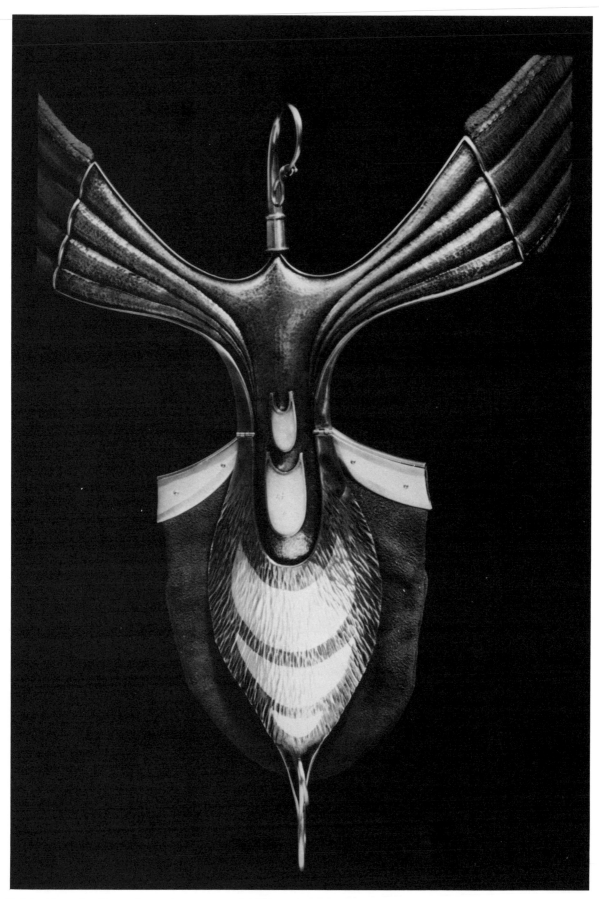

Holster Purse by Marcia Lewis (ornament only). Silver, brass, suede, carved leather, and resin, 1974.

LEATHER TOOLS. Heavy leather is cut with a sharp knife; thin leather can be cut with scissors. You may need to thin the edges of a piece of leather for seaming or turning. This is done with a very sharp blade, usually with a razor held in a skiver or by using a matte knife held very carefully.

Leather is quite sensual and beautiful in itself. However, if you must, design and patterns can be applied to it by carving, stamping, inlaying, onlay, and dyeing. All of these parallel the metal processes very closely except that the material is much, much softer and more flexible. Leather pieces are held together by lacing, sewing, riveting, or with an adhesive. Leather can be worked dry or wet-formed.

All procedures are best done on leather before a dressing or finish is applied. Most dressings have oil in them. All of the processes here use water, which means that these operations cannot penetrate an oiled surface. Leathers with naps, suedes, and splits do not receive a finish. Generally, finishes are grouped in the following manner: conditioners, soaps and cleaners, waterproofing agents, and polishes. They each come in liquid or semi-liquid, pastelike, or cake-form compounds.

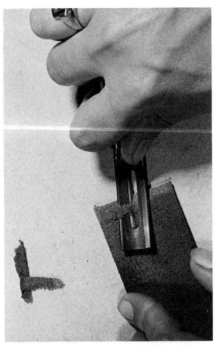

CUTTING. Cutting leather should be done with a very sharp knife. Use a metal rule as a guide for straight lines. Always back the leather with a resilient cutting surface. The cut must be made with one, heavy, deft stroke. If you take several strokes you run the risk of a multi-cut edge rather than a true, crisp one. Thin edges on leather make it easier to bend over or hem. To thin leather edges, you can shave or skive the back or underside of the leather as demonstrated here. Do this on a hard surface. Shave a little at a time to safeguard against cutting through the leather. Pick up the scraps because they can mar the face of the material if they get underneath.

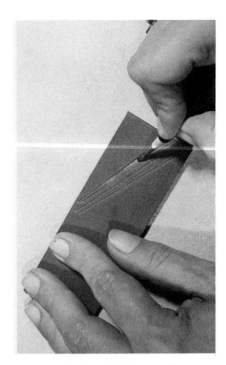

TOOLING. Tooling leather is done on wet material, dampened on both sides with a sponge. The tool looks very similar to a combination scribe and burnisher and does essentially the same thing. Here the scribe or narrower end is quite dull and a little curved so as not to cut or mar the leather face. Using a guide—a steel rule or cardboard templet—trace the edge with the narrower, smaller end of the tool while pressing firmly to make an indented line. Larger areas are depressed by using the broader end of the tool in the same manner as in burnishing.

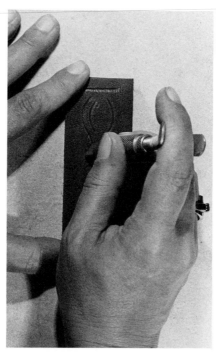
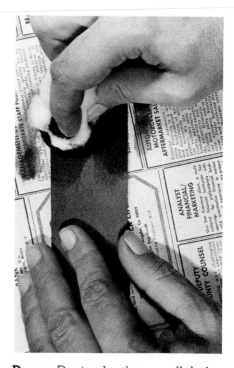

STAMPING. The repeated stamping of leather produces a depressed design or pattern. The process is identical with that for metals. The stamps are interchangeable with those for metal stamping, but caution must be used because the metal stamps are sharper and can cut into the softer leather face. Dampen the leather on both sides. Place it face up on a hard surface and wait until the face is almost dry before punching. If the leather is too damp it will not retain the impression.

CARVING. Carving leather is sometimes called incising and is best done on calf, cow, sheep, or goat hides. Lightly draw your design directly on the leather face with a pencil. Use a hard backing board. Dampen the leather on both sides with a wet sponge. The carving is done with a swivel knife, held between the thumb and the middle and fourth fingers with the index finger resting in the saddle on top. Hold the knife upright; do not tip it in either direction. Cut with the corner of the blade. Begin each cut using light pressure and end the cut in the same manner. Do not cut more than halfway through the hide thickness at any time. You do not cut away leather; you incise a cut line that is further emphasized by using the broad end of the modeling tool (burnisher) to depress one side of the cut.

DYEING. Dyeing leather parallels the chemical coloring of metals except that it deeply affects the material by penetrating into the porous fibers. The dye can be applied with a brush or dauber (or lamb's wool), or the material can be sprayed or dipped in a dyebath. The surface must be very clean before dyeing. This can be done with a mild solution of oxalic acid—one teaspoon acid to one pint of water. Oxalic acid is available at most drugstores. Dye may be applied to wet or dry leather, but penetrates best on damp leather. The most permanent dyes are specially prepared for use on leather. There are two types: oil and spirit solvents and water-soluble dyes. They do not mix together. Leather should be dyed after punching holes, etc., but before attaching findings or lacing. Use a hard support surface and apply the dye, spreading it rapidly before any of it dries to avoid streaking. If you immerse the leather in a bath, prepare enough dye for one dip. Place the leather on a clean surface to dry. If you spray dye, the leather must be damp. Do several light sprayings rather than one heavy one to prevent streaking.

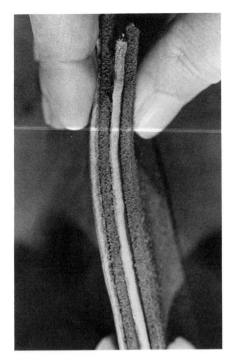

LAMINATING. Bonding and laminating leather is done to increase the thickness or volume and to create contrasting layers of color or texture between various leathers. Hemming is a bonding process, too. It creates an effect similar to that of mokume in metal. There are two types of bonding agents, wet and dry cements or glue. The surfaces to be bonded are roughened with a wire brush, coarse steel wool, or sandpaper. In wet-bonding, the adhesive is applied to both roughened surfaces and joined immediately. In dry-bonding, the adhesive is allowed to dry before the pieces are joined together. Wet glues are generally not flexible; a few tend to stain and are hard to clean up; all of them require weights or pressure while drying. These factors must be taken into consideration for each of your individual purposes. Master's and Barge's Cements are especially made for the leather trade and offer strong and flexible bonding. To assure complete contact in using dry bonds, tap the bond area with a mallet or roll with a rolling pin. This eliminates air pockets and forms a complete surface contact.

PIERCING. Piercing leather produces holes that are used for decoration or for lacing and grommeting. Care should be taken not to place the holes too close to the leather edge or it will tear away. A rule of thumb would be not closer than ⅛". The holes are made with a number of different cutters that come in a variety of sizes. The drive-punch is useful for punching holes too far from the edges for the revolving punch to reach. The revolving punch has a selection of tube sizes on a single gripper. A thonging chisel cuts narrow slits, and an awl is used to pierce small holes to make it possible for a needle to pass through the leather for sewing.

Valentine Pendant by John Leary. Silver, brass, ivory, and black onyx, enameled (upper box), constructed, and fabricated, 1975.

8

FINDINGS AND FASTENINGS

There must be some mechanical way of adapting your design for wearing: to keep it in place, to get it around your neck if it is smaller than your head, or to keep it on your ear or on your clothing. These bits of engineering design are called findings. They make it possible for you to fasten the jewelry to you or your clothing.

Very closely associated with findings are the means of fastening one part of a piece of jewelry to another. Linking several units together to form a bracelet is an example of a fastening, as is the finding on a necklace that joins the two ends together temporarily.

There are many commercial findings of varied designs available to you. It is often advisable to purchase some of these that are well made of either sterling silver or karat gold. These are the most expensive to buy, but cheaper ones often cause damage to good fabric or physical injury or discomfort in the case of earrings. Acids in the body may react to lesser low-grade metals and fabrics can discolor.

FINDINGS TO PURCHASE. Many findings have parts that you can make with a well-equipped workshop. How-

ever, it is generally best to purchase such things as those on the right: pin stems and catches, tie-tack backs, cuff-link backs, earring wires, clips, or screw-backs, spring-rings, and box-catches. The box catch is the largest mentioned, so it is the fastening you might first

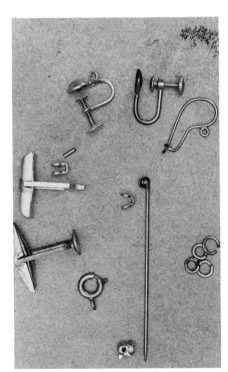

try building yourself. Ultimately, you probably will want to design and make many of your own findings and fastenings, especially ones that are more visible and that can add to the unique design factors in your work.

It is also probable that you will need to invent special findings once you start thinking of jewelry as something beyond decoration hung around your neck or your wrist. Once it becomes more of an integral part of your body, you will need to identify more closely with "joints" and the necessity of articulation. That is what fastenings and findings are all about.

Commercial chain is very handy, as are braided cording and leather thongs for hanging pendants. However, it very often detracts from the art of your jewelry. Chains are made up of an intricate series of links and, by varying each link design very singular and beautiful chains can be made. This is the more professional approach to jewelry: that of making the entire design and having concern for the total appearance on the body without any commercial imposition.

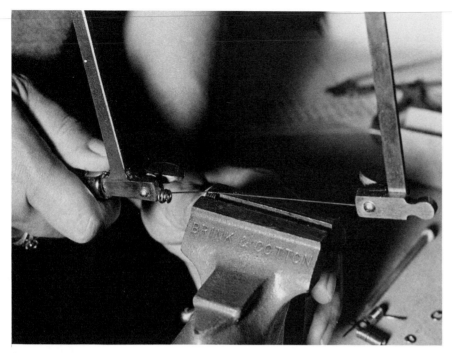

THE JUMP-RING. The most elemental link you can make is the jump-ring. It can serve as a link in multiple numbers for a chain, it is used in combination with the spring ring as a fastening on a necklace or bracelet; it can serve as a single unit of wire measure so you can make shot; or it can join (or jump) a series of units together to form a necklace or bracelet.

Most often a jump-ring is made of round wire, although it can also be made of square wire. Usually you make a number of them at the same time. They are made of many different gauges of wire and in varying diameters. There is, however, a tolerance correlation between the heaviness of the wire and how tight a diameter you can bend.

Select a nail or dowel to serve as a mandrel and clamp it in your bench vise. It should have the same diameter as you want to make your jump ring. Hold the end of your wire against the mandrel and wind it tightly around the mandrel as if you are coiling a spring. Clip off the wire after about eight turns. Remove the coil from the mandrel, clamp it in your vise, and saw through the first coil at a very slight longitudinal angle. As you cut through each successive coil of wire, a ring will loose itself. The slight angle of the cut gives a larger solder surface when you close the ring.

It is best if jump-rings are soldered closed. In a chain this is done by pick soldering (see Chapter 4). After making the chain of jump-rings or equivalent links, suspend the individual ring to be soldered on a hook. Carry the solder on your pick to the heated ring. Because the soldered joint is separated from others, there is little possibility of the chain and links becoming unsoldered.

A single ring can be used in combination with a hook for a fastener. A slightly larger one makes an adequate fastener when used with a toggle. You may need two rings of different sizes for a necklace fastening, the first one for the spring catch and the second to be tied or bound in some manner to the jewelry length. Jump-rings, then, are part of the simplest fastening, or catch.

CATCHES. A catch is a fastening that temporarily closes the jewelry so you can put the piece on and keep it there. The most familiar commercial catch is the spring catch and ring used in closing a necklace. The catch is opened, the ring slipped on, and a spring re-closes the loop. Usually, the action is against the expected pressures of normal wearing positions on the body. Besides the spring action, other possible closures include a hinge with a removable pin, a twist by means of a screw, a slide or twist with a locking tab, and a radial rotation or locked pivot.

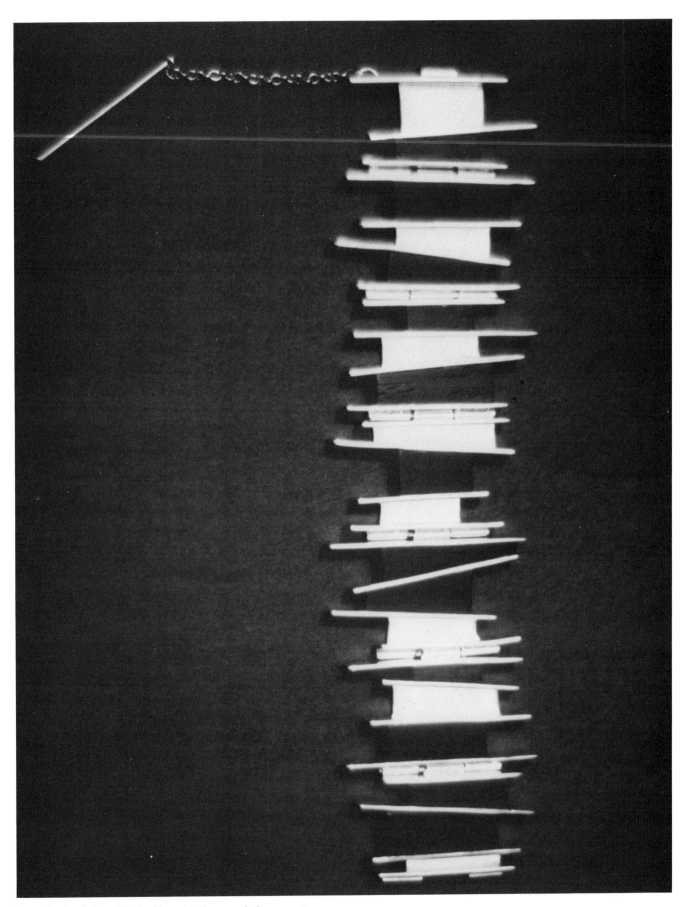

Bracelet by Arlene Fisch. Hinged silver and ebony units.

HINGES

The simplest hinge unit is the single rivet, which allows one unit to pivot in a given manner while permanently attached to another. Hinges are usually made up of a pin and cheniers (knuckles) that are soldered in place on the units or links you are hinging. You can make the hinge of tubing and wire or rod. The latter must fit exactly inside the diameter of the tubing. There must be an uneven number of cheniers to assure that the hinge stays in line. All saw cuts on the tubing must be true right angles. The pin can be permanently riveted after soldering or it can be a temporary one to serve as a catch.

STEP 1. Measure and saw the cheniers for the hinge. File off the burrs left by sawing while they are still in the jig to assure that their ends are at true right angles. Insert the pin rod or wire and cut off a length that is easy to handle. This is later shortened to the proper length for riveting, or it can be replaced with a pin and loop for a catch. Lay the temporarily assembled hinge in place where it is to be soldered. Accurately mark both of the links or units to be hinged where the cheniers will be soldered to them.

STEP 2. Remove the pin and coat it with yellow ocher. Coat the ends of each chenier completely with ocher and paint ocher where the cheniers will not be soldered on the links. Every second chenier will be soldered to the same link and the alternate chenier to the opposite link. All areas where solder should not flow are painted with ocher to minimize the possibility of freezing the hinge when you solder. Now assemble the hinge.

Step 3. Put the links on your charcoal block and lay the assembled hinge in place. Check to see that the hinge touches the links and that the links are parallel. Carefully paint each joint to be soldered with paste flux. Do not allow it to flood along the hinge or into any of the ocher-painted areas. Lay a snippet of solder at the center of each chenier where it touches the link to which it will be soldered. Be very careful during the soldering not to overheat the hinge areas.

Check to see that each chenier is soldered completely. Then, disassemble, pickle, and clean all ocher from the pin and hinge parts. Do not file or polish between the hinge sections or the ends of the chenier. This will make the hinge wobble or slide when assembled again. When all intermediate work is done on the units, reassemble the hinge. Trim the pin to its correct length and upset the head. If the pin is to be a removable one, finish it appropriately. Remember that a loose pin must have some safe way of keeping it with the hinge. This is usually a small safety chain permanently attached to the end of the pin and to a separate link.

FINDINGS YOU DON'T SEE

Pin assemblies, earring backs and clips, cuff-link backs, and tie-tack backs are findings that are not frequently in view. Because they are more or less behind the scenes and only their correct function is of the utmost importance, commercial findings serve best. The special placement and soldering of these tiny units is discussed in detail in Chapter 4 under special soldering conditions. Under most circumstances it is best to complete all finishing—stripping and polishing through tripoli—before riveting pin stems in place or adding earring backs. You should use easy-flo solder on the latter. Keep any spring-designed finding away from heat as it will destroy the spring quality in the metal.

BOX CONSTRUCTION

For a fastening that is part of your over-all design, a box-spring clip is very attractive. There are several ways of building the box, each with a slightly varying effect especially at the edges. The box is made differently depending on whether you want a soft or a crisp-angled edge on it.

A box with a soft-angled edge is made with a long strip and one or two sides. A hard-edged box is made with five or six individually cut pieces of metal. Both are soldered in the assembly. Generally, one box receives a springlike tongue that is permanently soldered to another box end. The spring is inserted into the thin slot at the end of the second box and the clasp closes when the shorter tab falls in place inside the box wall. There must be a release in this case so there is a permanent peg soldered to the short tab.

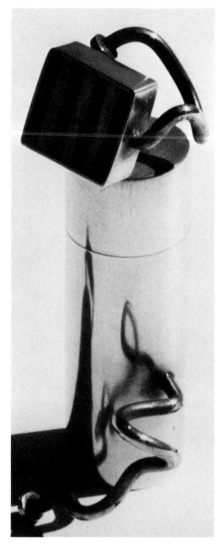

Bottle by Eileen Hill. Silver, brass, ebony and cedar, fabricated, 1975. Photo by John Thompson.

A Hard-edged Box. To construct a hard-edged box, every individual piece of metal must be carefully cut, filed, and decorated before soldering. In Marcia Lewis's clasp, shown above, the slots were cut and the punching completed before the soldering. In this instance there are only five sides to the boxes. The sixth is open to receive the leather neckpiece. This was later glued in place in the clasp after all polishing was complete.

The tongue of the clasp on the spring of the catch was made and soldered last in the box assembly. It is made of two metal pieces, filed and soldered at a fairly closed angle, and then closed more by hammering after soldering. Hammering, as you remember, hardens the metal surface. Metal can be spring-tempered by tapping or hammering. The interior of the metal has a little give, but the surface tension is built up. The spring clip for a tie-clasp is made in a similar manner. The metal is partially bent and then the angle closed further by hammering. Remember, too, that this should be the last step in the process because any heat will anneal the metal, thus destroying the spring.

A Soft-edged Box. Soft-edged boxes have mitered edges. The corner metal is filed away and the metal strip bent to close the angle as shown above. The more metal that is filed away in the angle, the more acute the closed angle will be. The deeper you file the metal, the sharper the edge—but never as sharp as if it was constructed from individual pieces. Measuring and scribing the lines for the angle is done on the inside of the bend angle. The two filed surfaces of the angle must be exactly equal and flat to assure a true corner. Do not file more than ¾ through the metal. In closing the angle, bend the metal once. Do not attempt to rebend it or it will break. Be sure the metal is annealed. Bend wider strips of metal over a square mandrel with a mallet; narrower strips are usually bent with pliers. The angles should be soldered for rigidity.

One of the major problems in filing an angle on a wide metal strip is that there is a tendency to file deeper at the edges than in the middle. If this happens, a gap will remain at the edges when the strip is bent.

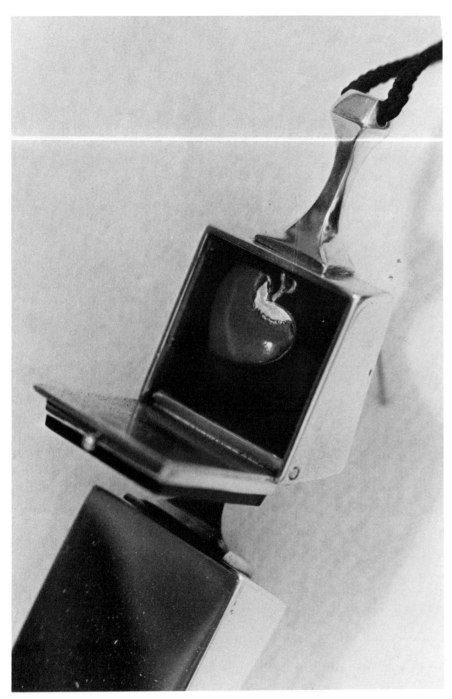

Valentine Pendant (detail) by John Leary.

BOX CONSTRUCTION. Boxes are certainly not confined to fastenings and findings. The principle can easily be extended into design possibilities as you can see by the work of John Leary shown here. There is one caution you must heed when constructing a completely enclosed, totally constructed form such as a box. Be sure that there is an escape for the gases that build inside the form when soldering. It does not matter how large this escape is, but it must be there. Often it is hidden within the design. If there is no way to incorporate it into your design, be open about it. Drill a small hole, well-placed in one of the sides, before you solder. This also relieves the surface tension of the metal that develops in such a form.

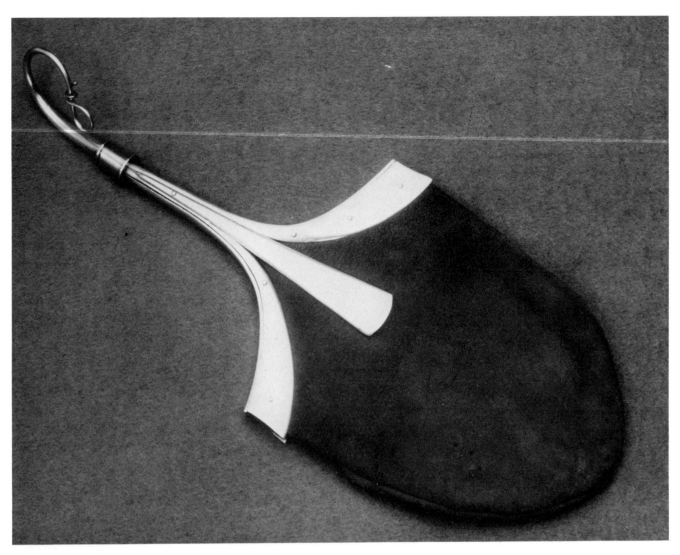

Pendant 142 (Far Left) by Albert Paley. Silver, copper, 14k gold, delrin, tourmaline, lens, fabricated, 1975. From the Exhibition "The Goldsmith," presented by the Renwick Gallery of the National Collection of Fine Arts, Smithsonian Institution, Washington, D.C., and the Minnesota Museum of Art, Saint Paul, Minnesota. Purchased for the Permanent Collection of the Minnesota Museum of Art. Photo by Bradford Palm.

Purse (Above) by Marcia Lewis. Split inlayed silver and suede, 1975.

Belt (Left) by Nancy Loo Bjorge. Copper, brass, rabbit fur, fabricated, 1975.

Bracelet by Sandi Miller. Sterling silver, 18k yellow gold and ivory, fabricated and sandblasted, 1975.

9

CLEANING POLISHING AND FINISHING

Polishing is the final process in making jewelry. It is that last touch in your designing process that puts the spotlight on your work. In polishing, you gradually wear away the metal surface until the deepest working blemishes and firescale are removed. This is done by using various coarse to fine grit compounds, often preceded by an acid bath and followed by the minor assembling of a pin stem or stone setting. As polishing is predominantly prescribed by how or when the jewelry is to be worn, first consider these points:

Jewelry that is to get constant wear will get minute scratches on the metal surfaces in that wearing. As metal is exceptionally reflective in its very refined state, these scratches will tend to reduce that reflection and luster. Other types of jewelry—for special costumes, select occasions, or worn in non-stress areas such as the hair or around the neck—can receive and maintain the most refined polishing. It will require only occasional brightening with a rouge cloth.

Essentially, it is not a good idea to lacquer metal surfaces. Not only is laquer foreign to the natural character of metal, but it is also softer than the metal you are trying to protect. It scratches and chips very easily. This exposes the metal surface, which only emphasizes the discoloration. To remove discoloration, the lacquer must also be removed and the whole process repeated.

Of course hard metals do not scratch as readily as softer metals, but most precious metals and their alloys are not that hard. Alloys with nickel are fairly hard, but sterling, copper, and yellow golds will all become scratched with wear.

In the long run, the more careful you have been in all of the preceding fabrication processes, the easier your cleaning, polishing, and finishing will be.

CLEANING

Wash your jewelry thoroughly with soap and warm water and dry it carefully before beginning the final polishing. Your scraper will cut away solder and smooth out deep scratches and coarse file marks. These can also be removed with emery paper or cloth which comes in various grits. Always work from coarse to fine grit. Emery paper can be purchased mounted on an emery stick (you can mount your own) or as a cone that slips on to a wooden mandrel for the buffing lathe. Generally you rub the metal against the emery on its support, stick, or mandrel. The metal is moved in one direction on the coarser emery and in the counter direction on finer-grit emery. This way you can see the scratches being removed.

FIRESCALE. Emery will remove firescale—a buildup of cupric oxide that you can see on this pendant. However, in work containing more than simple angles, you can remove the firescale by either a nitric acid dip (stripping) or by reversing the charge in your electroplating unit with the jewelry in it. The latter is certainly the safest if you have made the investment, and the recessed areas will keep their very bright finish. The nitric acid dip is more hazardous but much faster.

Cupric oxides (firescale) lie just below the thin surface of metals with copper content and show up as a dark blue-grey film when you begin cleaning and polishing. If left this way, metals will tarnish very rapidly. For the most permanent polish, these oxides must be removed completely or buried below another thin film of pure metal. To bury or hide the firescale on sterling silver and karat golds, heat the metal to about 1200° F. and let it air cool. Pickle in a hot sulphuric acid solution for one or two minutes and then wash under tap water. Burnish with a fine brass wire brush, using soapy water as a lubricant, until a soft luster appears. Repeat the sequence three or more times. This process is sometimes referred to as "frosting" and it develops a thin skin of fine silver or pure gold that is resistant to tarnish. Polish your jewelry using a sequence of Lea compound, tripoli, and rouge. (Avoid using any abrasive as scrubbing can remove the fine or pure metal film and you're back to firescale and discoloration.) The rouge polishing will bring to light any remaining firescale, and you must repeat the sequence if it appears. Wash with soapy water and a soft bristle brush and dry thoroughly to ensure removal of all compound residue.

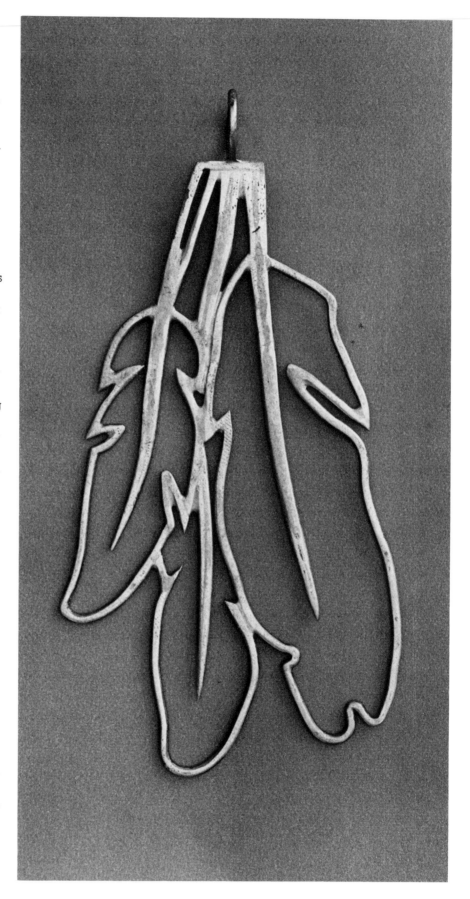

ACID STRIPPING. Although more dangerous than other cleaning processes, nitric acid stripping, done in a well-ventilated area and with the care all acid handling demands, is the most satisfactory.

The stripping solution is one part nitric acid added to one part water. Store, as with all acid solutions, in a marked covered glass container and locked away when not in use. Put enough stripping acid in a Pyrex dish to cover your work. Attach a stainless steel wire securely to your jewelry. Bring the bath to a low boil. Do not have findings such as pin stems and ear clasps in place because the acid will destroy them. Wire, other than stainless, will also be attacked by the acids.

Dip your work into the hot solution and count to 10 slowly. Remove the metal and wash it under tap water. The action of the acid removes surface metals. The longer it remains in the acid, the more metal is removed. With some imagination you can visualize the results when the jewelry is left in the dip too long.

COMPOUNDS AND BUFFING WHEELS

You will be using three buffing compounds. The first is Lea compound, used for cutting down pits and deep scratches, as well as firescale if you choose not to use a nitric stripping solution. The second compound is tripoli or White Diamond compound, and it is used to further refine the surface, removing small, light scratches. Both Lea and tripoli are known as cutting compounds. The third compound is rouge, which is more of a burnishing compound because it does not cut the metal but gives a high polish to the surface. Its use is optional.

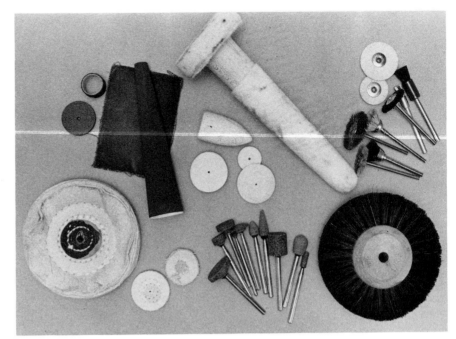

WHEELS AND BUFFS. The majority of buffing now takes place with motor driven wheels or buffs as shown above, on to which the compound is fed. This may be a large motor lathe or a handheld motor or flex haft. Ideally these motors should have variable speeds. The lowest or slowest speed is for using Lea compound, medium speeds are for using tripoli, and the highest speed for using rouge. Do your polishing in an area totally separate from your general workbench. The dust, lint, and flecks of compound fly. Protect your eyes and face with a shield. Under the best conditions, your polishing lathe should have a hood that further confines the contamination. You must have individual wheels or buffs for each

compound and they must not be mixed in their use. As subsequent compounds are finer and finer in grit, you will find yourself putting scratches into the surface rather than polishing them out if you mix the compounds. Also, always scrub your jewelry with a soft bristled brush in warm water and soap between each change of buffing compound.

Buffing wheels come in a variety of materials: wool, muslin, felt, and leather. All except the felt should be stitched. The wool and leather wheels are used with the coarser compounds and the muslin and felt with the finer ones. They are measured by diameter except in the case of felt (this also comes in cones for use on the inside of rings). There are also brush buffs used with tripoli and rouge compounds that reach into irregular and difficult areas.

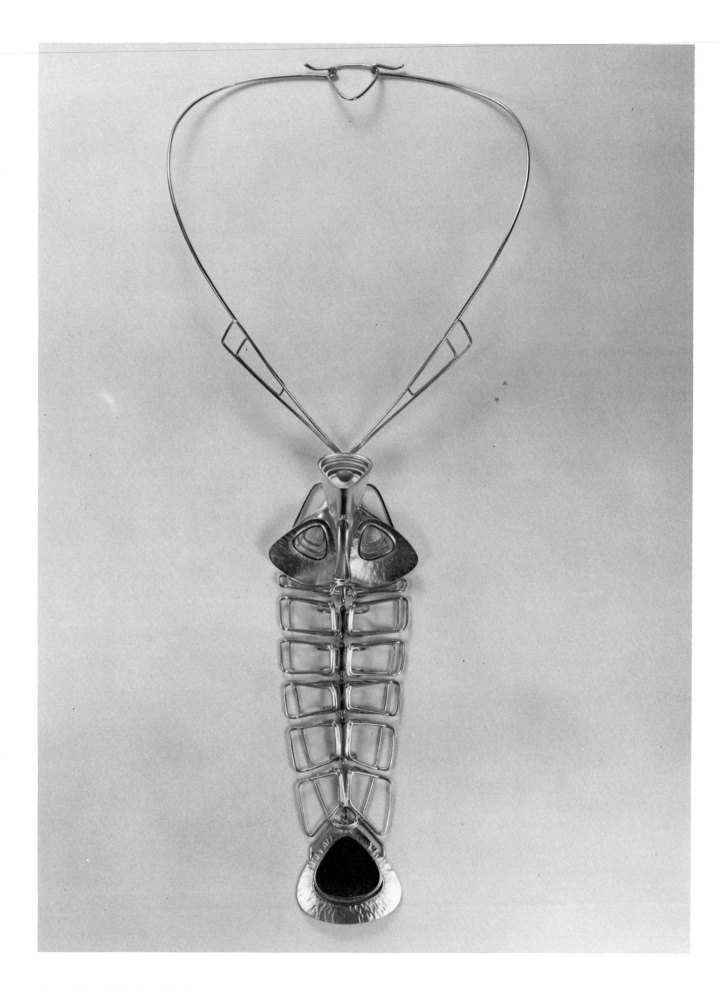

Snail Ring by Arlene Fisch. Silver, snail shell, Egyptian Mummy beads.

Neckpiece by Michael Pinder. Silver and lapis lazuli, fabricated so the rib sections are individually linked to mold to body contours.

Box by Eileen Hill. Silver, ebony and cedar, fabricated, 1975. Photo by John Thompson.

POLISHING

Polishing lathes revolve the buffs toward you. For this reason you must always hold your work slightly below the center in the lower quadrant of the drive shaft and buff. Holding the metal on the upper half is dangerous for it can tear your work out of your grasp if any metal edge gets caught in the buff. Long hair must always be tied back and kept away from the revolving wheel, also.

Charge the buffing wheel frequently with small amounts of compound. The compound, not the buff, does the polishing. Hold your work with both hands and keep it moving at all times in all directions. Do not hold it in one place. Avoid having corners or edges of metal projecting into the buffs. Always polish from an edge, never on to an edge. Beside the safety factor, holding the metal any other way will wear down the sharp edges that may be a part of your planned design.

Lathe polishing chain and long jewelry such as fine necklaces and bracelets can be dangerous. Long chains should be wrapped around a flat stick with rounded edges for support. Shorter lengths should be held completely closed in your hands with only an inch exposed between your fists. Support this short length with your forefingers against the buff and in the lower quadrant. Any chain length caught in the buff acts like a sharp whip, slashing out as the wheel revolves.

Fine chain lengths may not be able to withstand the pressure of buffing on the lathe and should be hand polished. A soft cloth can be charged with the polishing compound and, while the cloth is held in your fist, the fine chain is repeatedly pulled through it with the other hand. Be sure to completely wash off excess compound before proceeding to the next finest compound.

Use small felt buffs on a mandrel powered with the flex shaft or hand unit. These can get into inaccessible areas like the inside of rings, etc. Be sure to keep the small buffs moving evenly over the surface to avoid polishing dents that may create a wavy, uneven surface.

Use nylon bristle brushes when polishing filigree. Whiting and water will work as a compound for this delicate work.

The chemical coloring of metals take place at the end of the tripoli polishing. After coloring, polish the exposed surface with tripoli and complete the sequence with rouge if you so desire.

PUMICE POWDER AND BURNISHING. Fine-grade pumice powder will give metal a soft, subtle finish as opposed to the bright luster achieved with compounds. Its most popular use is after chemical coloring where it brings back soft highlights but allows most of the coloring to remain in the recessed areas.

Burnishing metal gives it a smooth, pressed surface. It is frequently used on bezels when setting a cabochon. Burnishing compresses and smooths only the metal surface. It is not often used on larger surfaces (although there is no reason why it should not be).

SAND BLASTING

A matte finish or frosted surface can be given to any metal by blowing it with a sharp, fine grit (sand or carborundum) using compressed air. There are professional units available, but an air-brush using mixed grit to avoid clogging can substitute. Areas that you do not wish to be affected by the sand blasting can be protected by painting them with rubber cement or hot wax or by laying on plastic electrician's tape.

Steel wool, sizes 1 to 000, can be used for hand polishing a matte finish. Always rub in one direction. Coarser or finer steel wool will not create the matte. Nickel wire, fiber, or nylon bristle wheels on the polishing lathe also give a matte finish. A polishing compound of fine pumice mixed with soft soap and water is used as a lubricant with the brushes. Reverse the brushes from time to time to assure the even scratches from the bristle ends that are necessary to create a consistent matte.

AT LAST

The last and final step before you put your beautiful jewelry on is to add stones or other accent materials in setting and any findings needed for completion such as pin stems or earring clips.

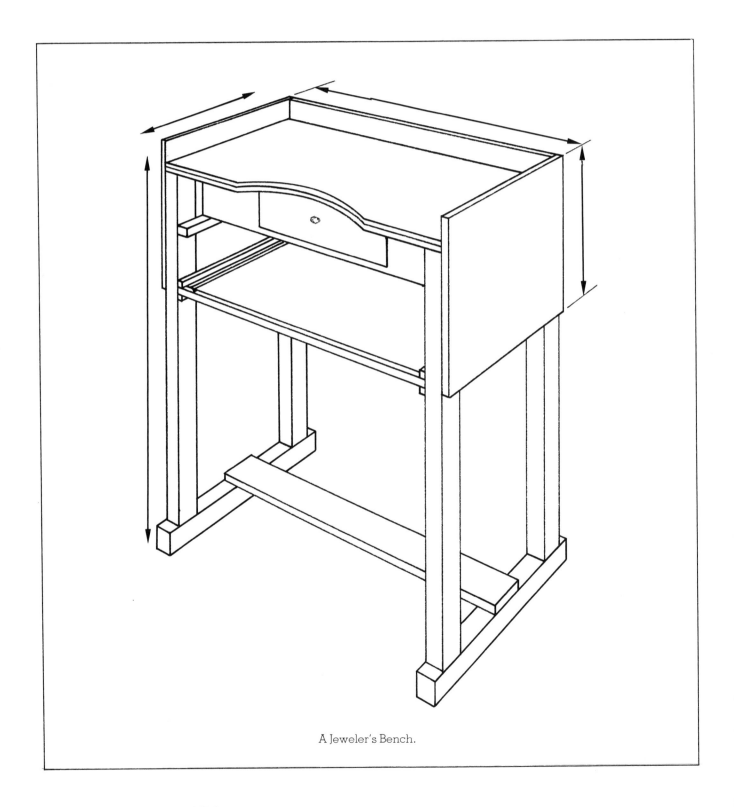

A Jeweler's Bench.

A WORKSHOP OF YOUR OWN

Just as in designing any personal portion of your home—the kitchen, the bath—your personal habits dictate to a large degree your workshop organization. This includes the storage areas for tools, supplies, and equipment as well as all working areas. It also includes grouping related services, for example activities needing running water or extended heating of chemicals. As with your kitchen, in the beginning you will have fewer tools than after you become a more sophisticated craftsman.

The drawings in this chapter are only suggestions for your workshop organization. They are arranged so you may expand your working space as you expand your equipment inventory.

IN THE BEGINNING

In the early chapter on tools and equipment, it was mentioned that the beginning set of tools would fit into a tool box, a storage size equiv-

alent to a fishing tackle box. Along with this you will need only a *sturdy* work table. It must be one that will not move across the floor or bounce as you hammer, for example. One possible solution to your worktable needs is a jeweler's bench.

A JEWELER'S BENCH. A plan for a jeweler's bench that can be moved out of the way when not in use is shown at the left. Note that the table surface is a few inches higher than a standard table height. This brings your work closer to eye level and provides more working comfort in long hours of use. Note, too, that this plan includes drawer storage for hand tools and a sliding tray under the bench pin area to catch filings. The thickness of the top is important. This one is two sheets of ¾" solid-core plywood, making a total

thickness of 1½". It is very rigid and firm. Any model bench pin, with or without the holder or anvil-holder combination, may be used. The tongue of the wooden pin can be slipped easily into a small groove carved between the two sheets. While any solid, even-grained wood will do, hardwoods will last longer and give a more sturdy construction if you build it yourself.

NEED MORE WORKING SPACE?

You have learned by now that some jewelry procedures are dirtier than others, that time is lost by having to clean up the same area before going on to the next step in construction, or you have too many tools to fit into a portable box. You have also discovered a place, perhaps in your home, that can be left as-is to give the workbench a permanent location.

Now You Have a Room. The first studio or workshop room the author built was in a walk-in closet about 5' × 10' in size. Other than the obvious advantage of being able to close the door on the work area, this small space had all of the necessities for a good "efficiency" workshop. The service areas were divided as shown above. This included a super-clean designing area with small storage units for stones, findings, and metals as well as the necessary designing tools and records for cost accounting. It also included a clean construction area with the hand tools on the wall at eyelevel, a soldering area, a hot-plate, and a sink arranged in that order around the walls. Locked storage was below the sink area. Major remodeling included the insertion of a venting fan into an existing window, bringing the water and gas lines through a wall from the adjoining bath, and adding electrical outlets on a separate service line.

ADDITIONAL BASIC TOOLS

In this workshop plan you will find several pieces of large equipment not discussed in Chapter 1. Their main advantage is to decrease your working time and increase accuracy and refinement in your production. These additions are the *drill press* and the *polishing machine*.

The drill press can be purchased as a totally assembled unit or it can be a sturdy stand on which a portable electric hand drill is mounted. An auxiliary tool used in conjunction with the electric drill press is a drill vise. Usually of heavy steel with a flat bottom, this vise holds very small pieces of metal—too hot to hold with your fingers—firmly in its jaws while you drill the hole.

The polishing machine is a large motor, ½-horsepower or more, with shafts on one or both sides. These shafts hold various types of buffing wheels or ring cones made of muslin, leather, or felt. You will need a complete set, three of each type, to complete the unit. Remember, it is just as important not to contaminate one of these polishing wheels with a different polishing compound as it is when you are polishing by hand or with the flex shaft units. Your polishing machine should have a hood to keep the compounds from flying out over the entire work area.

Both the drill press and the polishing machine require electricity. It is wise to check your workshop space for extra power as well as for other general service factors. Whether you have a portable tool box and table-bench, a wall-bench, or a room organized into a workshop, use the following checklist for both

your general comfort while working and, especially, for your own safety.

WORKSHOP NECESSITIES

Making metal jewelry is a greatly satisfying pleasure for many material and emotional reasons. However, there can be frustrations in the fabricating process if the general working conditions are inadequate. Any working area should have good light, sufficient electrical power, and good ventilation. In addition you should have running water, appropriate wall and floor surfaces, and various types of storage.

One of the most satisfactory lighting arrangements is a combination of soft, over-all natural light (north exposure) and off-white, matte wall surfaces with no general artificial overhead lighting. Each work station or area is then supplemented with individual incandescent, adjustable lights. This lighting system provides maximum illumination and minimum eyestrain. It also makes it easier for you to notice that you have left the Bunsen burner, alcohol lamp, or torch on and to adjust the torch flame tip.

You should have a separate electrical line for the supplementary lights and motor-driven tools in the workshop. Overloading the circuits and the excessive use of extension cords is hazardous.

Another unit that may be drawing electrical power is the venting fan. A fan may not be necessary if your local climate allows for enough open windows. However, this is not usually the general condition you will find yourself in throughout the year. It is a very serious consideration when you

remember that you are working with various acids and toxic materials.

At best, you should have running water in your workshop. At the very least, it should be in the immediate vicinity. This is important since you will be working with acids and many of your polishing compounds must be washed off your work.

Your working surface and all other structural surfaces—floor, walls, and ceiling—should be smooth, light in color, and non-reflective. Most of your work is very small and the pieces are easily lost in cracks and on other types of surfaces. It is also best that the floor not be concrete but more resilient. Brittle, tempered tools and gemstones will chip when dropped on a hard surface. Light walls and ceilings reflect, diffusing a soft over-all light needed throughout the workshop. The workbench top should also be easy to sweep clean. As indicated in the section on workbench construction, a good optional surface to the sealed plywood is a piece of ¼" transite (asbestos composition) sheeting.

Open storage for jewelry tools is the first essential. Other storage includes closed and locked storage—protection from dirt and security. The latter is very important when you consider both the value of your materials and the hazards from such toxic chemicals as acids. These should be kept securely controlled at all times, especially if there are children around.

Pectoral (Above) by Arlene Fisch.
Silver, fire-gilt, cameo, feathers,
pearls, wet-formed leather.

Brooch (Right) by Hiroko Sato Pijanowski. Silver, copper, feathers,
yarn and shells, Mokume, coiled and
fabricated.

APPENDIX

GLOSSARY

Abrasives. Natural or synthetic material in powder, grit, or solid form that is bonded to paper or cloth and used to clean metal surfaces mechanically.

Alloy. A metal composed of two or more metals or in combination with a chemical, as in bronze, brass, and solders.

Annealing. The heat treatment of metals to return them to their most malleable or softened condition for cold working.

Anode. The positive pole of an electrolytic cell, used specifically here in the electroplating process.

Asbestos. A natural fibrous material that is not affected by heat, used as a protective covering or support while handling hot metals or while soldering.

Asphaltum. A mixture of asphalt and turpentine used as a block-out solution. It is painted on metal surfaces to act as a resist against acids.

Brazing. A form of soldering or welding using spelter, used on metals other than precious.

Bright Dip. The use of an acid solution to create a bright, clean surface on metals.

Brittleness. A condition of metals that does not allow for bending without breaking or cracking.

Burin. An engraving tool also called a graver or scorper.

Bur. A specific drill point used to create a seat for setting a stone.

Burnishing. A metal polishing process using a burnisher. The burnisher is also used to set stones.

Burr. A sharp or rough edge on the metal as a result of cutting either with a saw or drill.

Bus Bar. The bar support and metal contact that is suspended over an electroplating tank holding the anodes and the cathode.

Cabochon. A round or dome-shaped stone, usually flat on the back. It is not faceted but polished smooth.

Capillary Action. The physical response of a liquid to a solid. An example is the tendency of flux to flow along a seam or for the solder to follow that seam when lead by heat.

Casting. The moving of molten metal into a mold by gravity or forces such as steam or centrifuge.

Cathode. The negative pole of an electrolytic cell, used specifically here in the electroplating process. It is the object on which the metal ions are deposited.

Centrifugal Casting. A process by which molten metal is thrust into a mold using centrifugal force.

Chasing. A decorative finishing process done on the face or front of a metal form using various punches and a hammer.

Cope. In sand casting, the upper section of a two-part mold.

Core. Here used to indicate a packed section of sand used in metal casting to create a hollow in the completed casting. In sculpture, the core can be made of other materials.

Cotter Pin. A "U" shaped steel pin that can be used as a jig during soldering.

Covering Agent. A resist material such as varnish, lacquer, or asphaltum that is used to protect metal surfaces from acids.

Damascene. The inlaying of one metal into another as a form of decoration.

Dapping Block. A steel block used in conjunction with dapping punches. It has graduated sizes of circular depressions and is used for doming.

De-greasing. The cleaning with acids of a metal surface prior to the photoetching and electroplating processes.

Die. A form of hard material used to back sheet metal in creating metal forms, as in punch and die.

Drag. In sand casting, the lower section of a two-part mold.

Drawplate. A flat steel plate with graduated holes in various profiles through which wire is pulled to reduce its size or change its profile. Also used in forming small tubing.

Drawing in. The forging process that makes a sheet of metal narrower and, at the same time, thicker without lengthening it. Similar to upsetting.

Ductility. The quality of metal that allows it to be worked into thicknesses for either sheet or wire.

Electroplate. The electrolytic deposition of metal ions onto a receptive surface; electroforming, the process of creating a new form using the electroplating process.

Engraving. The process of cutting into the metal surface with a burin to form a decorative relief surface.

Facet. One of the small, polished planes on the surface of a cut gemstone.

Filigree. A very fine wire used structurally as a decorative technique. It is soldered, formed with, or without, a thin background metal form.

Fillet. A very small puddle of solder at the base of an angle solder joint which tends to increase the joint's strength.

Firescale. An oxide forming on the surface of copper-bearing alloys that contributes to jewelry discoloration caused by prolonged and excessive heating. It must be removed with acids or polishing for a professional finish on jewelry.

Flux. A chemical in liquid, paste, or dry form used during the soldering or casting processes to assist in the flow of metal and hinder the formation of oxides.

Forging. A metal forming process using hammers and anvils or steel surfaces for support. Done on either hot or cold metals; cold metals must be annealed to maintain malleability.

Fusing. The merging or joining together of metals with the use of heat. Granulation is a fusing process.

Gate. Part of the spruing system that allows molten metal to pass freely into the mold cavity during the casting process.

Granulation. A decorative process using precious metals where small balls or flat snippets of metal are joined to a metal surface without the aid of solder.

Grinding. Here used in reference to the forming or reshaping of tools against an abrasive surface held and powered by a motor.

Heading. Forming of a rivit head by upsetting.

Inlay. The process of setting by forcing or laying-in of one metal into another; other materials such as wood, plastics, shell, lacquer, and niello can be inlayed.

Karat. The unit of measure indicating the pure gold content in its alloy. Twenty-four karat is pure; 18k has 18 parts pure gold and the remainder is another metal.

Liver of Sulfur. Potassium sulfide, used in a water solution to oxidize a metal's surface, particularly those with copper content.

Lost Wax Casting. The cere perdue or waste wax process where the model is made of wax, invested in a plaster mold, and then melted out in preparation for steam or centrifugal casting.

Mandrel. A solid or hollow metal rod, often tapered and with varying profiles; also, the base form on which electroplating can take place.

Matrix. In electroplating, the form or mandrel on which the ions are deposited.

Mokume. A traditional Japanese lamination technique, meaning "wood grain body" and using some repoussé processes.

Niello. A decorative process where sulfides of silver, copper and lead are fused into select depressions on a metal base producing a black metallic area.

Oxidizing Flame. A torch flame where there is an excess of oxygen over fuel, as opposed to a reducing flame.

Paillon. A snippet of solder or metal.

Parting Line. Where the cope and drag separate in the sand-casting process.

Parting Powder. A fine powder, usually French chalk or graphite, which is dusted on the face of the mold to assist the separation of the mold after casting.

Pickle. An acid solution used to clean metal surfaces.

Piercing. The drilling or punching of small metal holes in metal for functional or decorative purposes.

Pitch. A compound of natural pitch, plaster of paris, and tallow used to back and hold metal forms in the repoussé and chasing processes.

Planishing. The smoothing of a metal surface using an almost flatheaded hammer with the work supported on an equally hard and conforming surface.

Plating. The deposition of metal ions onto a receptive surface thus creating a thin layer of the plating metal.

Porosity. Very small, scattered holes appearing throughout the metal surface on casting. It is caused by incomplete releasing of gases during the casting or cooling process.

Punch. The movable part of a punch and die set, used to force the metal into a form.

Raising. To create a dimensional form from a flat metal sheet.

Ramming. To force and pack sand solidly into a mold.

Reducing Flame. A flame where there is less oxygen than fuel used, as opposed to an oxidizing flame.

Repoussé. A decorative process usually done from the back or reverse face of the metal while supported in a pitch compuund. Often chasing, done on the top or face of the metal and with more refined tools, follows.

Riddle. A sieve, used in sand casting to evenly sift sand onto the pattern.

Rifflers. Small, eccentrically shaped files.

Scorpers. Used to cut metal away, as with the chisels used for engraving.

Sinking. The raising of a form by administering blows to the concave metal surface which is supported on a sandbag, wood, masonite, or lead blocks.

Smelting. A process that separates metals from each other or metal from non-metals.

Soldering. The joining of metals with another lower flow temperature metal which is an alloy.

Spelter. Solders with low melting points, often copper-zinc alloys.

Sprue. Part of the casting system, a hollow which allows molten metal to flow from the sprue basin to the hollow form in the mold.

Stamping. The making of a shape by using a punch which cuts into the metal sheet. Also the cutting out of multiple blanks.

Stretching. The shaping of a thick metal disc or bar by hammering, thus thinning and raising the disc or tapering and lengthening the bar.

Tang. The end of a file or graver that is inserted into a handle.

Temper. Produced in metals through working or heating. Annealing tempers metal by heat; a hard temper is produced by working metals cold; spring temper works the metal harder than in cold working; and point tempering is the hardening of the working end of a steel tool.

Upsetting. The forging process that works metal at a right-angle to its axis. Rivit heads are upset when formed as is the edge of any metal shape which is thickened by hammering on that edge.

BIBLIOGRAPHY

Allen, B.M., *Soldering Handbook*. New York, Drake Publishers, 1970.

Ball, Fred. *Experimental Techniques in Enameling*. New York, Van Nostrand Reinhold Co., 1972.

Black, J. Anderson. *The Story of Jewelry*. New York, William Morrow & Co. Inc., 1974.

Bovin, Murray. *Silversmithing and Art Metal for Schools, Tradesmen, Craftsmen*. Forest Hills, New York, 1963.

Choate, Sharr. *Creative Gold and Silversmithing: Jewelry, Decorative Metalcraft*. New York, Crown Publishers, 1970.

Fishlock, David. *Metal Coloring*. New York, International Publications Service, 1962.

Franke, Lois. *Handwrought Jewelry*. Bloomington, Ill. McKnight Publishing Co., 1962.

Gentille, Thomas. *Step-by-Step Jewelry: A Complete Introduction To the Craft of Jewelry*. New York, Golden Press, 1968.

Hollander, Harry. *Plastics for Jewelry*. New York, Watson-Guptill Publications, 1974.

Maryon, Herbert. *Metalwork and Enameling*. New York, Dover Publications, 1971.

Morton, Philip. *Contemporary Jewelry: A Studio Handbook*. New York, Holt, Rinehart and Winston, 1970.

Ritchie, Carson. *Bone and Horn Carving; A Pictorial History*. Cranbury, New Jersey, A.S. Barnes and Co., 1974.

———. *Scrimshaw*. New York, Sterling Publishing Co., 1972.

Sperisen, Francis. *The Art of the Lapidary*. Milwaukee, Bruce Publishing Co., 1950.

Untracht, Oppi. *Metal Techniques for Craftsmen*. Garden City, New York, Doubleday and Co., 1968.

Von Neumann, Robert. *The Design and Creation of Jewelry*. Radnor, Pennsylvania, Chilton Book Co., 1972.

Wilcox, Donald. *Body Jewelry: International Perspectives*. Chicago, Henry Regnery Co., 1973.

———. *Modern Leather Design*. New York, Watson-Guptill Publications, 1969.

Note: A very extensive bibliography may be found in *Contemporary Crafts Market Place*, pp. 355–473, including periodicals. New York and London, R.R. Bowker Co., 1975–76 edition.

TABLE 1. METAL GAUGES, THEIR FORMS AND USES

GAUGE	USES
12	Very heavy rings and forged bracelets
14	Heavy rings and bracelets
16	Average rings
18	Lightweight pierced designs
18	
20	
22	Brooches, earrings, beads, buttons, and bezels for settings, etc.
24	
26	

Metal sheet is available in standard gauges and varying widths. When ordering it is best to designate the sheet size in multiples of 3″. For example, 12″ x 6″, 6″ x 6″, or 6″ x 3″.

ROUND B&S Gauge	SQUARE B&S Gauge	HALF-ROUND B&S Gauge	RECTANGULAR B&S Gauge
9	8	5/16″ base	4 x 16
12	12	6	6 x 18
16	14	10	8 x 22
18	18	15	8 x 26
20			14 x 30
24			14 x 32

When ordering round, square, or half-round wire give two dimensions: gauge and length. When ordering rectangular, bezel, and cloisonné wire give three dimensions: gauge, width, and length.

TABLE 2. SAW BLADE SIZES AND DRILLS

Blade No.	Thickness	Depth	Drill
8/0	.006	.013	80
7/0	.007	.014	80
6/0	.007	.014	79
5/0	.008	.015	78
4/0	.008	.017	77
3/0	.010	.019	76
2/0	.010	.020	75
0	.011	.023	73
1	.012	.025	71
2	.014	.027	70
3	.014	.029	68
4	.015	.031	67
5	.016	.034	65
6	.019	.041	58
8	.020	.048	55
10	.020	.058	51
12	.023	.064	51
14	.024	.068	50

TABLE 3. ANNEALING

Metal	Temperature F.°	Quench	Special Notes
Aluminum	640 - 670	no	Anneal only when necessary
Britannia metal	none needed		
Copper	700 - 1200	yes	
Gilding metal	800 - 1450	no	
Muntz metal	800 - 1100	no	
Red brass	800 - 1350	no	Work hardens, anneal often
Forging brass	800 - 1100	no	
Architectural bronze	800 - 1100	no	
Phosphor bronze	900 - 1250	no	
Nickel	1500 - 1700	either	
Nickel silver	1100 - 1500	no	
Monel metal	1500 - 1700	yes	Annealing a must, but not too often
Pure gold	none needed		
Yellow, green white gold	1200 - 1300	either	Use care or the form will collapse
Red gold	1200 - 1300	yes	Quenching a must or it will harden
Pure silver	572	either	
Sterling silver	1200	yes	

TABLE 4. MATRIX MATERIALS USED IN ELECTROFORMING							
	PERMANENT			EITHER		EXPENDABLE	
Material	Brass	Wood	Glass	Aluminum (1)	Plastics	Low Melting Alloys (2)	Wax (3)
Machinability	easy	easy	very difficult	easy	easy	cast	cast
Attainable Finish	good	good	good	good	varies	fair	good
Damage Resistance	fair	poor	poor	poor	poor	poor	very poor
Cost	low	low	high	high	high	low	low
Parting	easy	easy	easy	varies	easy	easy slow (4)	easy
Tolerances	close	not close	close	close	fairly close	fairly close	not close

1. Aluminum alloys are soluble in strong, hot, sodium hydroxide solutions.
2. Zinc alloys are dissolved out in hydrochloric acid solutions; others are melted and shaken out.
3. Waxes are melted out and the residue dissolved by an organic solvent.
4. Thermal plastics only. Soften by heating, then withdraw the bulk before cleaning with appropriate solvents.

TABLE 6. TAPS, TAP DRILLS, AND WIRE SIZES						
			Size of Tap Drill		Nearest Wire Size for Matching Screw Brown & Sharpe	
Size of Tap NC	Outside Diameter Inches	Root Diameter Inches	Number	Decimal Equivalent Inches	Gauge	Decimal Equivalent Inches
1-64	0.0730	0.0527	53	0.0595	12	.0808
2-56	0.0860	0.0628	50	0.0700	11	.0907
3-48	0.0990	0.0719	47	0.0785	10	.1019
4-40	0.1120	0.0795	43	0.0890	9	.1144
5-40	0.1250	0.0925	38	0.1015	8	.1285
6-32	0.1380	0.0974	36	0.1065	7	.1443
8-32	0.1640	0.1234	29	0.1360	5	.1819
10-24	0.1900	0.1359	25	0.1495	4	.2043
12-24	0.2160	0.1619	16	0.1770	3	.2294

TABLE 5. COLORING METALS

CHEMICAL	AMOUNT	COLOR	USED ON	COMMENTS
Potassium Sulfide Water	lump the size of a pea 4 oz.	Charcoal gray	Silver, copper, bronze	Dip in either a hot or cold solution. Dry chemical must be stored in an air-tight container to avoid de-terioration.
Potassium Sulfide Ammonium Chloride Water	lump the size of a pea drop or two 4 oz.	Blue-black	Silver, copper, bronze	Dip in either a hot or cold solution.
Potassium Sulfide Water	lump the size of a pea 4 oz.	Black	Karat golds, alloys with copper	Use in a hot solution. The metal is hot when dipped.
Barium Sulfide Water	10 grams 5 oz.	Blue-black	Silver, copper, brass	Dip in a hot solution.
Barium Sulfide Water	5 grams 5 oz.	Gold tone	Silver	Dip in a cold solution.
Platinum Chloride Alcohol		Light gray	Silver, copper	Use a hot solution. Dip or paint with a brush.
Hydrochloric Acid Iodine Boiling water	3 parts 1 part 3 parts	Green	Silver, copper	Add iodine to boiling water, then add acid — in a Pyrex or porcelain container. Dip in a hot solution.
Ammonium Sulfide Water	1 gram 7 oz.	Gold	Silver	Dip in a cold solution.
Ammonium Sulfide Water	1 gram	Dead black	Silver, copper, brass	Dip in a hot solution.
Copper Sulfate Water	1 part 2 parts	Brown Blue-black	Copper Brass	Dip in a hot solution.
Copper Nitrate Water	1½ grams 6 oz.	Sage green	Copper alloys	Use in a hot solution. Applied with a brush.
Ammonium Chloride Water	1 part 1 part	Olive green	Copper alloys	Use in a hot solution. Applied with a brush.
Copper Sulfate Zinc Chloride Water	1 part 1 part 1 part	Dark green	Copper alloys	Apply with a brush. Paste — allowed to dry before washing off.
Ammonium Sulfate Water	1 part 1 part	Black	Bronze	Apply with a brush on warm metal.
Copper Carbonate Caustic soda Water	2 parts 1 part 10 parts	Yellow to Bright red	Brass	Dip in either a hot or cold solution.
Lead Acetate Sodium Thiosulphate Acetic Acid Water	2 - 4 oz. 8 oz. 4 oz. 1 gallon	Blue	Brass, carbon steel	Work at 180°F. Must be waxed or lacquered for permanence.
Iodine		Blue to black	Gold	An Antiquing. Dab with a swab or brush.

NOTE: The amount of time an article is left in a color bath is an individual choice. Continued dipping will sometimes result in colors different from those indicated on the chart. Do not leave your work unattended during the coloring bath. Excessive coloring done too quickly will flake off.

TABLE 7. MOHS SCALE

Mohs Scale was developed as a system to identify the relative hardnesses of minerals. The following list includes some of the more popular and better known gem minerals.

1	Graphite, Talc
2	Alabaster (onyx), Gypsum (plaster)
2-2½	Amber
2½-3	Ivory
3	Calcite, Limestone, Mexican Onyx, Pearl
3½-4	Malachite
4	Fluorite
4-5	Azurite
5	Apatite, Obsidian (Apache Tears)
5-5½	Thomsonite
5½-6	Lapis Luzuli, Brazilianite, Hematite
6	Feldspars including Amazonite and Moonstone, Anatase, Hematite, Opal, Sodalite, Turquoise
6-6½	*Fabulite, Kunzite, Nephrite, *Titania
6-7	Epidote, Jadeite
6½-7	Chrysocolla, Peridot
6½-7½	Cordierite, Garnet, Zircon
7	Quartz including Amethyst, Aventurine, Cairngorm, Citrine, Crystal, and Rutilated Quartz, Agate, Bloodstone, Carnelian, Danburite, Tiger Eye
7½	Almandine, Andalusite, Fibrolite, Tourmaline, Zircon
8	Beryl including Aquamarine, Emerald, Morganite & Golden Beryl, *Chatham Emerald, Spinel, Topaz
8½	Alexandrite, Cat's Eye, Chrysoberyl
9	Corundum including Rubies, Sapphires, Synthetics in all colors
10	Diamond

*Synthetics

TABLE 8. WEIGHTS

TROY WEIGHT

Used in weighing the precious metals.

24	grains = 1 pennyweight (dwt.)
20	dwt. = 1 ounce troy
12	ounces = 1 pound troy
5,760	grains = 1 pound troy

AVOIRDUPOIS WEIGHT

Used in weighing base metals.

16	drams (or drachms) = 1 ounce Avoir.
16	ounces = 1 pound Avoir.
16	ounces = 7,000 grains
28	pounds = 1 quarter
4	quarters = 1 hundredweight (cwt.)
20	hundredweight = 1 ton Avoir.

To convert ounces troy to ounces avoirdupois, multiply by 1.09714.
To convert ounces avoirdupois to ounces troy, multiply by 0.91146.

GRAM WEIGHT

1	gram = 15.43 grains troy
1.555	grams = 1 pennyweight (dwt.)
31.104	grams = 1 ounce troy
28.35	grams = 1 ounce Avoir.

CARAT WEIGHT

Used in weighing precious and semiprecious stones.
(The term Karat refers to the quality of purity in gold.)

1	carat = 3-1/16 grains troy
1	carat = .007 ounce Avoir.
1	carat = 1/5 gram

The carat is further divided into points for simple measurement:

1	carat = 100 points
1/2	carat = 50/100 points
1/4	carat = 25/100 points
1/8	carat = 12½/100 points

TABLE 9. COMPARATIVE WEIGHTS

1	ounce Avoir. = 0.912 ounce troy = 28.35 grams
16	ounces Avoir. = 14.6 ounces troy = 1 pound Avoir.
1	ounce troy = 480 = grains = 31.1 grams
1	ounce troy = 20 pennyweight = 1.1 ounces Avoir.
1	pennyweight (dwt.) = 24 grains = 1.555 grams
1	pound Avoir. = 453.6 grams = 7,000 grains = 16 ounces Avoir.
1	pound troy = 373.2 grams = 5,760 grains = 12 ounces troy
1	dram = 60 grains = 3.888 grams
1	gram = 15.43 grains = 0.032 ounce troy
1,000	grams (1 Kilogram) = 2.2 pounds = 35.26 ounces Avoir.
1	grain = 0.065 gram
100	grains = 6.5 grams

APOTHECARIES' WEIGHT

The grain, the ounce, and the pound of the apothecaries' weight system are
the same as for the troy weight system.

TABLE 10. DECIMAL EQUIVALENTS OF DRILL SIZES

Size	Decimal Equivalent	Size	Decimal Equivalent	Size	Decimal Equivalent	Size	Decimal Equivalent
1/2	0.500	G	0.261	23	0.154	1/16	0.0625
31/64	.4843	F	.257	24	.152	53	.0595
15/32	.4687	E−1/4	.250	25	.1495	54	.055
29/64	.4531	D	.246	26	.147	55	.052
7/16	.4375	C	.242	27	.144	3/64	.0468
27/64	.4218	B	.238	9/64	.1406	56	.0465
Z	.413	15/64	.2343	28	.1405	57	.043
13/32	.4062	A	.234	29	.136	58	.042
Y	.404	1	.228	30	.1285	59	.041
X	.397	2	.221	1/8	.125	60	.040
25/64	.3906	7/32	.2187	31	.120	61	.039
W	.386	3	.213	32	.116	62	.038
V	.377	4	.209	33	.113	63	.037
3/8	.375	5	.2055	34	.111	64	.036
U	.368	6	.204	35	.110	65	.035
23/64	.3593	13/64	.2031	7/64	.1093	66	.033
T	.358	7	.201	36	.1065	1/32	.0312
S	.348	8	.199	37	.104	67	.032
11/32	.3437	9	.196	38	.1015	68	.031
R	.339	10	.1935	39	.0995	69	.029
Q	.332	11	.191	40	.098	70	.028
21/64	.3281	12	.189	41	.096	71	.026
P	.323	3/16	.1875	3/32	.0937	72	.025
O	.316	13	.185	42	.0935	73	.024
5/16	.3125	14	.182	43	.089	74	.0225
N	.302	15	.180	44	.086	75	.021
19/64	.2968	16	.177	45	.082	76	.020
M	.295	17	.173	46	.081	77	.018
L	.290	11/64	.1718	47	.0785	1/64	.0156
9/32	.2812	18	.1695	5/64	.0781	78	.016
K	.281	19	.166	48	.076	79	.0145
J	.277	20	.161	49	.073	80	.0135
I	.272	21	.159	50	.070		
H	.266	22	.157	51	.067		
17/64	.2656	5/32	.1562	52	.0635		

TABLE 11. COMPARISON OF STANDARD WIRE GAUGES
Thickness in decimals of an inch

No. of gauge	Birmingham wire (B.w.g.), also known as Stubbs iron wire	American wire or Brown & Sharpe	American Steel & Wire Co. formerly Washburn & Moen	British Imperial Standard Wire (S.w.g.)	Standard Birmingham sheet and hoop (B.g.)	London or Old English	United States Standard	Gauge No.
00	0.380	0.364796	0.3310	0.348	0.4452	.38	.34375	00
0	0.340	0.324861	0.3065	0.324	0.3964	.34	.3125	0
1	0.300	0.289297	0.2830	0.300	0.3532	.3	.28125	1
2	0.284	0.257627	0.2625	0.276	0.3147	.284	.265625	2
3	0.259	0.229423	0.2437	0.252	0.2804	.259	.25	3
4	0.238	0.204307	0.2253	0.232	0.2500	.238	.234375	4
5	0.220	0.181940	0.2070	0.212	0.2225	.22	.21875	5
6	0.203	0.162023	0.1920	0.192	0.1931	.203	.203125	6
7	0.180	0.144285	0.1770	0.176	0.1764	.18	.1875	7
8	0.165	0.128490	0.1620	0.160	0.1570	.165	.171875	8
9	0.148	0.114423	0.1483	0.144	0.1398	.148	.15625	9
10	0.134	0.101897	0.1350	0.128	0.1250	.134	.140625	10
11	0.120	0.090742	0.1205	0.116	0.1113	.12	.125	11
12	0.109	0.080808	0.1055	0.104	0.0991	.109	.109375	12
13	0.095	0.071962	0.0915	0.092	0.0882	.095	.09375	13
14	0.083	0.064084	0.0800	0.080	0.0785	.083	.078125	14
15	0.072	0.057068	0.0720	0.072	0.0699	.072	.0703125	15
16	0.065	0.050821	0.0625	0.064	0.0625	.065	.0625	16
17	0.058	0.045257	0.0540	0.056	0.0556	.058	.05625	17
18	0.049	0.040303	0.0475	0.048	0.0495	.049	.05	18
19	0.042	0.035890	0.0410	0.040	0.0440	.040	.04375	19
20	0.035	0.031961	0.0348	0.036	0.0392	.035	.0375	20
21	0.032	0.028462	0.03175	0.032	0.0349	.0315	.034375	21
22	0.028	0.025346	0.0286	0.028	0.03125	.0295	.03125	22
23	0.025	0.022572	0.0258	0.024	0.02782	.027	.028125	23
24	0.022	0.020101	0.0230	0.022	0.02476	.025	.025	24
25	0.020	0.017900	0.0204	0.020	0.02204	.023	.021875	25
26	0.018	0.015941	0.0181	0.018	0.01961	.0205	.01875	26
27	0.016	0.014195	0.0173	0.0164	0.01745	.0187	.0171875	27
28	0.014	0.012641	0.0162	0.0148	0.015625	.0165	.015625	28
29	0.013	0.011257	0.0150	0.0136	0.0139	.0155	.0140625	29
30	0.012	0.010025	0.0140	0.0124	0.0123	.01372	.0125	30
31	0.010	0.008928	0.0132	0.0116	0.0110	.0122	.0109375	31
32	0.009	0.007950	0.0128	0.0108	0.0098	.0112	.01015625	32
33	0.008	0.007080	0.0118	0.0100	0.0087	.0102	.009375	33
34	0.007	0.006305	0.0104	0.0092	0.0077	.0095	.00859375	34
35	0.005	0.005615	0.0095	0.0084	0.0069	.009	.0078125	35
36	0.004	0.005000	0.0090	0.0076	0.0061	.0075	.00703125	36
37	—	0.004453	0.0085	0.0068	0.0054	.0065	.006640625	37
38	—	0.003965	0.0080	0.0060	0.0048	.0057	.00625	38
39	—	0.003531	0.0075	0.0052		.005		39
40	—	0.003144	0.0070	0.0048		.0045		40

TABLE 12. FLUID MEASURES

1   ounce = 29.57 cubic centimeters = 1.8 cubic inches
1   dram = 1/8 ounce (0.125 ounce) (fluid)
1   gill = 4 ounces (fluid)
1   pint = 16 ounces (fluid)
1   quart = 2 pints = 1/4 gallon = 57¾ cubic inches
1   gallon = 4 quarts = 128 ounces (fluid) = 3.78 liters and
        231 cubic inches = 0.134 cubic foot
1   cubic centimeter (cc.) = 16.23 minims
1   liter = 1,000 cc. (a little more than 1 quart U.S.) = 0.264 U.S. gallon
1   cubic foot = 7.481 U.S. gallons = 1,728 cubic inches
1   Imperial gallon = 1.2 U.S. gallons = 4.54 liters = 277.27 cubic inches

TABLE 13. MEASURES OF LENGTH

1   inch (1″) = 2.54 centimeters = 25.4 millimeters
1   foot (1′) = 0.305 meter = 30.48 centimeters = 304.8 millimeters
1   meter = 39.37 inches
1   centimeter = 10 millimeters
10   centimeters = 1 decimeter = 100 millimeters
100   centimeters = 1 meter = 10 decimeters

TABLE 14. RING SIZES

The diameter of a ring is measured at the inside diameter at the center of the band width.

0	=	0.458″ dia.
¼	=	.466
½	=	.474
¾	=	.482
1	=	.490
1½	=	.506
2	=	.522
2½	=	.538
3	=	.554
3½	=	.570
4	=	.586
4½	=	.602
5	=	.618
5½	=	.634
6	=	.650
6½	=	0.666
7	=	.682
7½	=	.698
8	=	.714
8½	=	.730
9	=	.746
9½	=	.762
10	=	.778
10½	=	.794
11	=	.810
11½	=	.826
12	=	.842
12½	=	.858
13	=	.874
13½	=	.890

TABLE 15. TEMPERATURE CONVERSIONS

To convert degrees Fahrenheit (°F) to degrees centigrade (°C), first subtract 32, then take 5/9 of the remainder. To convert degrees centigrade to degrees Fahrenheit, first multiply by 9/5, then add 32.

or

To convert degrees centigrade to degrees Fahrenheit, first multiply by 1.8, then add 32. To convert degrees Fahrenheit to degrees centigrade, first subtract 32, then divide by 1.8.

or

To convert degrees centigrade to degrees Fahrenheit, first multiply the centigrade figure by 9, then divide the obtained figure by 5 and add 32. To convert degrees Fahrenheit to degrees centigrade, first subtract 32 and multiply by 5, then divide the obtained figure by 9.
Each 1°C = 1.8°F. The number 32 represents the difference between the nominal starting points 0 and 32.

TABLE 16. MELTING POINTS AND SPECIFIC GRAVITY OF PRINCIPAL NONFERROUS METALS

Metal	Melting Point Fahrenheit	Melting Point Centigrade	Specific Gravity
Platinum	3224	1773	21.45
Nickel	2654	1452	8.85
Copper	1981	1083	8.93
Gold	1945	1063	19.36
Silver	1761	962	10.56
Sterling silver	1640	893	10.40
Zinc	787	419	7.14
Lead	621	327	11.37
Tin	450	232	7.29

TABLE 17. CONVERSION FACTORS

To Convert:	Multiply by	From / To	To / From	Multiply by
LENGTH	0.03937	Inches	Millimeters	25.4
	0.3937	Inches	Centimeters	2.54
	39.37	Inches	Meters	0.0254
	3.2808	Feet	Meters	0.3048
	1.0936	Yards	Meters	0.9144
	0.62137	Statute Miles	Kilometers	1.6093
AREA	0.155	Square Inches	Square Centimeters	6.4516
	10.764	Square Feet	Square Meters	0.0929
	1.196	Square Yards	Square Meters	0.83613
	0.0015625	Square Miles	Acres	640.
	2.471	Acres	Hectares	0.40469
VOLUME	0.061023	Cubic Inches	Cubic Centimeters	16.387
		Cubic Feet	Cubic Inches	1728.
	27.	Cubic Feet	Cubic Yards	0.037037
	35.315	Cubic Feet	Cubic Meters	0.028317
	0.03531	Cubic Feet	Liters	28.32
	0.13368	Cubic Feet	U.S. Gallons, Liq.	7.4805
	1.3079	Cubic Yards	Cubic Meters	0.76456
	0.2642	U.S. Gallons, Liquid	Liters	3.785
	1.201	U.S. Gallons, Liquid	Imperial Gallons	0.8327
	0.12	U.S. Gallons, Liquid	Lb. of Water, 62°F.	8.336
	0.554	Ounces (Fluid)	Cubic Inches	1.805
WEIGHT	0.035274	Ounces, Avoirdupois	Grams	28.350
BULK	0.0022046	Pounds, Avoirdupois	Grams	453.59
DENSITY	2.2046	Pounds, Avoirdupois	Kilograms	0.45359
	2000.	Pounds, Avoirdupois	Short Tons	0.0005
	2240.	Pounds, Avoirdupois	Long Tons	0.000446
	1000.	Kilograms	Metric Tons	0.001
	62.425	Pounds per Cubic Foot	Grams per Cubic Centimeter	0.016019
	17.07	Pounds per Cubic Foot	Pounds per 9" Equivalent	0.05859
	3.6575	Pounds per 9" Equivalent	Grams per Cubic Centimeter	0.27341
	0.578	Ounces per Cubic Inch	Grams per Cubic Centimeter	1.73

INDEX